LOOKING BACK
TO SEE AHEAD

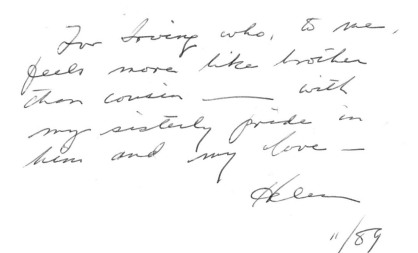

For Irving who, to me,
feels more like brother
than cousin ——— with
my sisterly pride in
him and my love —
        Helen

11/89

Helen Harris Perlman

LOOKING BACK
TO SEE AHEAD

The University of Chicago Press
Chicago and London

Helen Harris Perlman is the Samuel Deutsch Distinguished Service Professor
Emeritus in the School of Social Service Administration at the University of
Chicago. Her many published works include *Social Casework: A Problem-Solving
Process; Persona: Social Role and Personality*; and *Relationship: The Heart of
Helping People*; and, as editor, *Helping: Charlotte Towle on Social Work and
Social Casework.*

The University of Chicago Press, Chicago 60637
The University of Chicago Press, Ltd., London

© 1989 by The University of Chicago
All rights reserved. Published 1989
Printed in the United States of America

98 97 96 95 94 93 92 91 90 89   5 4 3 2 1

Library of Congress Cataloging-in-Publication Data

Perlman, Helen Harris.
    Looking back to see ahead / Helen Harris Perlman.
        p.   cm.
    Bibliography: p.
    ISBN 0-226-66037-0 (alk. paper). — ISBN 0-226-66038-9 (pbk. :
alk. paper)
    1. Social service—United States.   2. Social case work—United
States.   3. Social work education—United States.   I. Title.
HV91.P47 1989
361.973—dc20   89-31900
                                                        CIP

∞The paper used in this publication meets the minimum requirements of the
American National Standard for Information Sciences—Permanence of Paper for
Printed Library Materials, ANSI Z39.48-1984

To Jonathan, Fran, and Aaron,
with my abiding love

CONTENTS

When I want to understand what is happening today
or try to decide what will happen tomorrow, I look back.

—Oliver Wendell Holmes, Jr.

1

INTRODUCTION TO
WHAT'S AHEAD

A mild trepidation assails me as I choose the title for this book: Looking Back to See Ahead. It's the "looking back" that's threatening to me.

You may recall, as I do now, that there are two ancient myths that warn us against looking back, one Hebraic, one Greek. The former tells of the fate of Lot's wife, the other of the wife of Orpheus. When the Lord allowed Lot and his family to flee those miserable twin cities of Sodom and Gomorrah he set up one condition: "Look not behind thee," He said. But Lot's wife "looked back from behind him, and she became a pillar of salt." (But *why*, for heaven's sake?) Then there was the nymph, Eurydice, the beloved wife of Orpheus. Eurydice died of a serpent bite and went to Hades. The broken-hearted husband pleaded with Pluto to release her, and that god agreed. He stipulated, however, that with his lyre Orpheus might lure her back to earth, but on condition that he not look back to see if she were following him. Unable to resist, Orpheus glanced back, and his Eurydice vanished forever. (Again—why?)

Since myths are said to persist because they embody some universal truth or experience in human living I have pondered on these two myths now and again, wondering what their meaning was. Unable to get a satisfactory answer from several scholars whose academic robes I've tugged at, I have had to resort to my own rationale.

If looking back represents a reluctance to leave the known for the unknown, if it expresses a fear of present prospects, if it is a temptation to escape the here-and-now reality and thus becomes a deterrent to looking ahead with courage, it is to be deplored. If, however, it is a way of gaining perspective, a means by which we may recognize and thus avoid earlier errors of judgment and action, or if, in reverse, it is a means by which to identify and preserve what is still to be developed further, if, in short, we look to the past as a way of seeing more clearly and penetratingly its meanings and uses for our immediate present and near-future, then it may serve as well. So my malaise is temporarily put to rest, and I look back in order to see ahead.

Let me reassure you that while in the final essay I do take a long look back, the rest of what is offered here focuses upon our profession's quite recent past. It is not a eulogy for the good old rather less than ideal. Nor is it an indulgence in nostalgia. (As Simone Signoret put it crisply not too long ago, "nostalgia ain't what it used to be.") Rather, my purpose has been to select out from among my more recent published writings those essays that are central and relevant for this day's social work (especially in its case-and-group-work forms). My choices, subjective though they may be, have been determined by considerations of several trends affecting social work practice today.

Among them is the entry into social service by large numbers of interested and energetic young women and men whose preparation for the infinite complexities of helping people to cope in personally satisfying and socially responsible ways has taken place within recently developed undergraduate programs in colleges and universities. Some of these programs have been accredited by the Council on Social Work Education; some are working toward such accreditation. But many new entrants into social work have had no more than a course or two, offered within social science departments. Most of these two groups go to work in the publicly supported family and child welfare programs across the country. Thus, most of them carry out their responsibilities under the most difficult working conditions and with some of the most hard to engage but at the same time most needful people in our society, in terms of opportunities, assets, and protections. There is no question but that this swelling cadre of human-welfare workers is needed. Neither is there a question but that they must be nourished and supported by some ongoing education, such supervision as combines teaching with overseeing, such stimuli to reading and learning as will keep them focused, purposive, and, yes, questioning and seeking, too.

Even among those who are products of long-developed graduate-school professional programs, there is need for this same kind of ongoing underpinning to help them maintain focus and direction and conviction too, to enable them to separate the more from the less important, to maintain balance and insights into the often assaultive complex of varied human problems they encounter daily, to retain clarity about what works, and why, and when and where. There is today a veritable deluge of theories and notions among the several helping professions, of "how to" books on problems that have been so highly publicized as to seem to require specialized knowledge; thus, the neophyte, or even the sophisticated, professional social worker may lose sight of social work's central, basic guiding ideas, goals, and action principles.

Further, many of the recent graduates of advanced professional training have been prematurely pushed or tempted into taking positions with supervisory or teaching responsibility when they themselves have scarcely achieved firm footing in their practice. They, too, need support now and then to find and hold their steady centers that serve as core to what they know, do, and teach.

These few but vital circumstances fired my decision to move forward on the suggestion that I put together a new book. One overarching criterion determined my choice of the ten papers, from among many others, that appear in the casework and teaching sections of this book. It was potential *usefulness:* usefulness to the student, the practitioner, the teacher (in the classroom or the field); usefulness to considerations of method, of values, of evaluating outcomes from action taken, of next steps ahead, of the connections between the individual case and the common social welfare, between the case instance and the knowledge and theory that infuse and guide its conduct.

The titles within the casework section may appear to be highly specialized, as, say, the piece on "the client as worker," or the critique of one study done on a single agency's work in an all but unheard-of place. But it is my belief (or is it hope?) that you will find within them those ongoing red threads that run through the fabric all caseworkers weave, that connect the individual problem, the person, the modes of problem-solving with theory and principles.

The same claims hold for the essays on teaching. Whether in student or staff supervision on the job or in the formal classroom, most of the same teaching and educational principles and guidelines hold fast. Again, in that section I add comments that I hope will justify my selection.

And what, you may rightfully ask, is the "usefulness" of the section called "After Hours"? At its simplest, it is just to release some tensions, as after hours are supposed to do, just to remind ourselves that all of us social workers are "only human" too. It offers a down-to-earth touch to a literature that often may seem abstract, intellectualized, somehow wanting in flesh-and-blood pulse.

Only this far will I go here. You may discover more—or less— "seeing ahead" than I have promised. Till we meet again, as you move forward. . . .

PART ONE

SOME OLD AND NEW PERSPECTIVES

2

CASEWORK: ITS USES
AND MISUSES

Foreword 1989

Among the six articles on aspects of casework theory and practice that I had finally decided were worth some further consideration I debated which should come first. Common sense would suggest that the opening of a book should attempt to so engage the
potential reader's interest that, having eyed the first paragraph
warily, he would be drawn forward. But instead, burdened as I feel
with matters of unfinished business, I present the recurrent question
about the usefulness of social work's major methodology. The book
in which it appeared is now regrettably out of print. "Regrettably,"
in my opinion, because its seven chapters along with its explanatory
editorial comments are as instructive and impelling today as they
were at the time of its publication.[1]

Rereading my essay has, however, made me a bit uneasy. I do
wish Ralph Waldo Emerson would go away with his dictum,
"with consistency a great soul has simply nothing to do." True,
he was referring to a "foolish" consistency, to which I will not

1. With *The Multi-problem Dilemma* now out of print, a more recent publica-
tion, wider in scope, may serve as a useful source for the critical examination of
further experiments. It is *Evaluation of Social Intervention*, by Edward J. Mullen,
James R. Dumpson and Associates (San Francisco: Jossey-Bass, 1972). Within
that volume of special relevance to casework: "Is Social Work on the Wrong
Track?" by Edward J. Mullen and James R. Dumpson; "Thirteen Evaluative
Studies," by Ludwig L. Geismar (a "substantive message to the profession");
"Practice on Microcosm Level," by Carol H. Meyer (a caseworker's frank evaluation of assumptions, studies, and their implications for both practice and professional education); and my "Once More with Feeling," a title that frankly reveals
my frustration at the intransigence of the problems or perhaps at our all-
too-human resistance to change.

For examples of my efforts to defend social casework from its internecine attacks see nos. 50, 56, and 60 in the bibliography.

plead guilty, but will instead argue that a recurrent or stubbornly recalcitrant problem demands one's consistent concern and reconsideration. However, the ways and means by which the problem may be resolved, or at least ameliorated, ought not be rigidly reapplied. Rather these must be subject to exploration, experiment, turned upside down and inside out. So I go forward. . . .

Beginning in the early sixties, for reasons that cannot have space here, there was a veritable explosion of demonstrations and experiments in working with chronically dependent, so-called "multiproblem" families, and along with this a clamor of doubts and questions about the usefulness or effectiveness of "casework." Those questions came from within the ranks of social work as well as from the watchers and caretakers of the public and private welfare agencies' purses and purposes. "If caseloads were cut to reasonable size," "if there were less paper work," "if methodologies were more congruent with the culture of poverty"—these and other possible solutions plagued us all. As a result a number of experimental practice projects were launched, to be tested and evaluated by research. The Chemung County experiment and subsequent study was a salient one among them.

Its findings: the experimental group of long-dependent public assistance families with multiple problems who were "given" "intensive casework" by two professionally prepared caseworkers with lowered caseloads made no significant changes or gains compared with the matched control group dealt with by business-as-usual regular staff caseworkers. As the *Washington Post* had commented upon an earlier, widely publicized study, *Girls at Vocational High,* the Chemung experiment had social work "on the ropes."[2]

Now a group of designated "experts" were assembled for a three-day critical and soul-searching seminar on the what and why of the failure of expectations of the experiment. We were all aware, of course, that just as one swallow doesn't make a summer neither do two caseworkers make a case, pro or con, for the effectiveness of casework. What gnawed at us was the fact that the Chemung study clearly corroborated what a number of other studies (some poorly designed, but others, like Chemung, well structured technically) had revealed. (One seminar member com-

2. Henry J. Meyer, Edgar P. Borgatta, and Wyatt C. Jones, *Girls at Vocational High: An Experiment in Social Work Intervention* (New York: Russell Sage Foundation, 1965). For an astute essay-review of that study see Mary Macdonald, *Social Service Review,* vol. 40, no. 2 (1966): 320–23.

mented wryly that the seminar should have preceded rather than followed the experiment.)

From among the seminar group seven of us were designated to write position papers relevant to the planning and outcomes of the study. I was designated to do the critique of the casework. (The contributions of other group members, notably those of my fellow casework teachers, Carol Meyer, of Columbia, and Alfred Kadushin, of the University of Wisconsin, both underpinned and added substance to my paper.)

In these past few years as I have lectured and led seminars at various universities and agencies about the country I have encountered a new generation of students who are now or are would-be social caseworkers, along with many newly appointed teachers, some of them plucked out of practice with scarcely time to breathe, much less to scrutinize practice problems other than their own. Many of these students and teachers are in undergraduate courses on social work in programs leading to a bachelor's degree. Because it is from that educational level that the majority of caseworkers in public family-and-child-welfare agencies are drawn, I have become increasingly concerned that a clear, realistic understanding of the limitations and potentials and relevance of casework be reiterated. This is why I have placed the article that follows first—on the assumption (perhaps fallacious?) that it offers such substance. More, the critique suggests a kind of core content, which remains a continued necessity in education for social work.

A warning: one reviewer called the article "a tightly reasoned" piece. If that is so it means that he who runs can only skim it. It takes close reading, partly because it condenses many considerations into too little space. It should be taken on when you feel fresh and frisky—ready to grapple with an octopus.

"That which I should have done I did not do . . . " This is the title of the well-known funerary painting by the artist Ivan Albright, and it is the title more than the picture that haunts one. It haunts me as I examine and ponder on the Chemung study, sturdy and lively as it surely is. Over and over

Published under the title "Casework and the Case of Chemung County," in *The Multi-problem Dilemma*, ed. Gordon E. Brown (Metuchen, N.J.: Scarecrow Press, 1968), pp. 47–71. Reprinted with permission. The present version, retitled, is slightly abridged.

again its findings say to anyone who is concerned with them, researchers and caseworkers both, "that which I should have done I did not do."

The focus in what follows is upon casework. One can point a moral to researchers, to be sure, to the effect that impeccably conceived and designed though a study may be, it is essential that the researcher know the particular nature of the materials and processes he is studying or, questioning that knowledge, that he be in close and continuous consultation with someone who has it. Otherwise his expectations and perceptions may be incorrect or vague. "Casework," what it was supposed to consist of, what it was supposed to be for, was, it appears, taken by the Chemung research team as an unvarying process, guaranteed to give satisfaction regardless of the specific nature of the client, the problems, the agency's rules and resources, and the guiding conceptions of the caseworkers themselves. The caseworkers had earned their professional degrees and had had some successful experience as practitioners. This the researchers took as their warranty that what was to be done by these social workers was characteristic of what would be done by any representatives of social casework. Perhaps they were right. This is a disquieting thought. This is why I propose to focus on what a researcher with some casework knowledge in his background "should have done" and what a caseworker consultant to the project "should have done"—indeed, what every one of us, whether casework practitioners, or supervisors, or teachers in schools of social work should give thought to if we are to avoid undertaking those ambiguously or unrealistically defined efforts which can only end in frustration and in a pervasive sense that casework has failed again.

The question for social work is not "Was the casework on the Chemung County families good casework?" The basic question, rather, is "What would 'good' casework be?" The roughed-out answers to this should have preceded the first knock on a client's door. That the question was neither asked nor answered is the fault, I submit, of those of us who represent the practice of casework. I would even go so far as to say that if the findings of the Chemung study had been the opposite of what they were, if they had shown significant progress for the families who had, as we say, "had professional casework service," then we caseworkers should have asked, "For heaven's sake, how so? Exactly how was this made possible? Exactly what occurred between caseworker, client, and community?"

There is no cynicism in these questions. There is only the honest recognition of the hazards and pitfalls inherent in an undertaking of this sort and of the numerous factors that would have had to be considered and, insofar as possible, controlled, to make for a successful outcome. Upon the recognition and management of these, the use of casework as a helping means depends.

One begins with the necessity to try again to say—what "casework" is. It is easier to say what it is not, what it has often erroneously been assumed to be. It is not a bundle of services that can be "given" or "done" to those who "need it," though it is often spoken of in just such terms. It is, rather, a *process* which depends for its effective use upon a number of qualifying conditions and factors. (And now the reader will need patience to bear with yet one more effort to define and delineate "casework.")

Casework is one process by which social work aims to promote gratifying and constructive adaptations between individuals and their social environments. It is characterized by its focus
   a. on individual units (persons or families),
   b. who suffer or display problems in coping with any aspect of social interaction or functioning, and
   c. whose problems are assumed to be related to one or more of the following lacks: of motivation to cope, of capacity to cope, of opportunity to cope.

Thus its interventive efforts aim to restore, reenforce, rechannel, or reform
   a. the motivations of the individual (or family)
   b. the coping capacities of the individual (or family)
   c. the problematic behaviors of the individual (or family)
   d. the organized provisions or other resources of the community that bear on the individual (family) and his problem.

The choice and decisions as to the what, when and how of these interventions are determined by a number of factors in interaction, specifically
   a. the agency's function and the available resources in relation to the problems to be tackled
   b. the forces at work within the potential clients and their social situation that create or contribute to the problems, along with those forces that can be enlisted towards their solution
   c. the client's motivation and capacity in relation to the problem-to-be-worked
   d. a prediction (rough and subject to change) of feasible goals and possible outcomes based upon the assessment of the above-named sets of factors.

Imperfect as this delineation may be, it makes several things explicit. One is that the process called "casework" will be shaped, expanded, contracted, diluted, intensified, made complex or simple by the powers and conditions inherent in the combination of person-problem-place (that is, agency and field of action). It makes explicit that the aim and goal of casework must be relevant to the realistic appraisal of the materials to be worked—which is to say the *particular persons to be helped,* their *particular complex of problems,* in the *particular social circumstances and opportunities* available or lacking. It suggests that some *appraisal* of these interacting factors must be made in order to state *realistic expectable outcomes* and, then, *what the input must be* to achieve it.

Whether one accepts this definition or finds it faulty and prefers another, the fact is that there must be between caseworker and researcher, between caseworker and agency administration, between caseworker-student and casework teacher, some agreed upon understandings of what this enabling process is for, what the materials are with which it works, and what criteria and conditions modify its usage and its goals. These agreed upon understandings are nowhere visible in the Chemung undertaking. Unhappily, this is not unusual.

Now a second area of vagueness presents itself. It is the concept of the "multi-problem family." It is a designation, not a concept at all. It may be a good short-hand term for ordinary day-to-day talk between social workers. But it has no specificity, nor has it diagnostic or classifying value. On the face of it, it says that a family has many problems. But even a most naive observer knows that problems have chain-reactions and a problem of money-deficit is likely to affect matters of health care, and these deficits are likely to rouse a sense of stress which, in turn—et cetera and so on. The term "multi-problem" as it is used today often embraces such diverse categories as "lower class," "chronically poor," "socially disorganized," "noncommunicative," "hard-to-reach," "hard-core." What do we mean? The researcher *and* the caseworker must ask and answer this question.

If we are to plan intervention with a group of "multi-problem" families we must identify clearly the kinds of problems that characterize them and which make it valid to consider them a homogeneous group. Then, having identified the problems that are characteristic of such families, the next step would need to be the selection of "target problems" and of priorities. Target problems would be those to which the caseworker's attention would be regularly and systematically focused. Priorities would differentiate which among the many problems seemed most crucial (or perhaps most readily accessible), and thus should get first attention. Only with this kind of analysis, necessarily crude at the outset, could one plan intervention and make some estimate of realistically possible outcomes.

A like ambiguity exists in that designation of treatment called "family-centered." What did the Chemung research-team and caseworkers take this to mean? Reading across casework writings on the subject of family treatment one is aware of these several meanings:

1. The caseworker's overall concern is for the welfare of the whole family.
2. The family rather than one single individual is the unit with which interviews are held, decisions are made, plans are worked out.
3. The family is the unit of concern but one key member is the selected (self- or worker-selected) problem solver.
4. The family is the unit of concern, and interviews may be held with one member or all or several.

There is considerable difference among these meanings when they become translated into action. The family as a working unit requires of the caseworker skills in group and relationship management that are only now emerging and are being taught in very few places. Further, the notion of "family-centered casework" seems to be bulwarked by another notion—which is that what is good for the family is good for all the individuals in it. This is a questionable assumption; more important, it makes research on family improvement a tricky project.

Whether he knows it or not, the caseworker who undertakes a "family-centered" approach, no matter at what level, is undertaking a "multi-problem" situation. This is because each family member approaches the same problem (lack of money, mother's emotional disturbance or whatever) in personal terms; in terms of what it does to him, individually, as well as what it does to the family group. This, plus the swift-running chain-reaction of problems, makes it absolutely essential that the caseworker (and those who guide or study his efforts) should select the particular ones of the multiple problems in the multi-problem, multi-member family that need or deserve concentrated and/or foremost attention at any given time.

One of the common reasons for a person's inability to cope with his problem(s) on his own is that he feels overwhelmed by its immensity or complexity. So he must do one of several things, in accordance with the laws of human behavior under stress: he retreats from it into apathy or sickness or denial; he tries to tackle it, but because he feels overwhelmed he tends to do so in ways that are more disorganizing than problem-solving. Multiple problems flood their carriers with a sense of helplessness and excite in them either feelings of defeat and hopelessness or anxiety so high that it leads to poorly planned, poorly aimed, disintegrated activities. This, in crude form, is the basic explanation for the futile behaviors and poor adaptation that are so frequently seen in those families who live under chronic stress.

What is perhaps not given adequate recognition is that caseworkers also operate according to laws of human behavior under stress. Caseworkers also may find themselves flooded and overwhelmed by the burgeoning of problems that pop out from all directions as soon as they give an attentive eye and ear to a family situation or a gentle probe to a "presenting" problem. Caseworkers too, then, may be caught up in a number of defensive maneuvers in the effort to reinstate their balance: they may retreat from the overwhelming situation by writing it off as "hopeless"; they may retreat into the protection of "professional magic" by going through certain rituals of words and actions—and perhaps the more psychiatric the magic the more potent it promises to be; or—and this is probably the most frequent—they may hold their ground and take on everything that comes at them, indiscriminately, in a scattered and disorganized way. All ten fingers plugging holes in the dike, so to speak, and leaks springing up all about.

There are certain organizing and integrating ideas that have for some time been articulated in casework writing but have not been sufficiently put to practice. One is that a caseworker may see many problems at once but he cannot, nor can his client, deal with them all at once. The more constricted and depleted the ego the greater is the necessity to deal with one small piece of problem-solving at a time. Problems that are experienced as too much and too many and too hard must be denied or escaped or detoured. They can only be faced as they are taken up in small part, so that the problem-carrier can bear to look at the part and examine its relation to himself and plan on what action he (or the caseworker, or both together) can take on it.

Supporting the idea of "partialization," stated above, is that of identifying and selecting the *"problem-to-be-worked"* from the galaxy of problems that beset a person or family. The idea of the problem-to-be-worked is simply that of lifting out at a given time of one problem or a part of it for work. The "given time" might be fifteen minutes in an interview, or a whole interview, or a series of interviews over a time phase. The problem-to-be-worked may be anything that presents a current obstacle to the client. It is usually not at all the "basic" problem—it is not necessarily the problem or the root cause of all the others. The fact is the "basic" problem is often too big to be tackled or too deep-rooted to be gotten at. So one must deal most often with derivative problems. Which ones? Which parts? The criteria for selection of the problem(s) to be concentrated on between client and caseworker are fairly common sense ones: what seems uppermost in the client's concern—what hurts him most or bothers him most of the time; what to him seems urgent and cannot wait; what seems accessible to ready management with the worker's help—this latter choice on the assumption that the client's sense of mastery and hope climbs on the rungs of small achievements. A small problem solved or laid to rest may constitute one of these rungs. The choice of problem-to-be-worked at any given time, then, is a choice based on client *capacity,* his *motivation*—his sense of urgency and discomfort—*combined with* (and often needing to be influenced by) the caseworker's realistic assessment of priorities and *possibilities for success.*

What does all this—the multiple-problem, family-centered, problem-focus—discussion have to do with the Chemung study?

It is not possible to know from reading the study what definitions and agreements were arrived at between researchers, caseworkers, or anyone else as to what characterized the target population—what was held to be "multi-problem" or "family-centered." Nor does one learn from the data what target problem(s) the several professional caseworkers took as their focus or placed in their center of attention in the carefully limited caseloads they were assigned. But, based on past experiments, one can speculate on these likelihoods: the limited number of cases and the frequency of contact with their clients made these caseworkers far more aware of the number and complexities of the problem in their families than would be the case for the usual public assistance worker who would visit infrequently, and whose clear charge was to focus upon financial need and eligibility. Scratch the surface of any family and you will find problems—they are inherent in human beings' living together. When "the problem" is defined by both caseworker and client as money-need and money is provided adequately and regularly, other problems fade into the background. When the problem is defined as "multiple," the caseworker may become involved on all fronts at once. This greater awareness and its inevitably attendant anxiety are probably heightened for the professionally prepared caseworker who, as a result of training in diagnostic thinking, may not only recognize more problems, but may attribute greater significance to them than a less clinically attuned worker would.

This is not to say that the diagnostically sensitive caseworker is always correct in his appraisal, and certainly it is not to say that his insights are always relevant. Often they are not. This is a problem, it must honestly be said, that casework courses in many schools of social work have not yet mastered: that their focus on elaborations of diagnosis outstrips and outweighs their focus upon its utility in treatment. The result may be that the trained worker is paralyzed by seeing too much! Diagnostically correct or incorrect though he may be, the trained caseworker will tend to see more problems and at more levels than the untrained worker. This very sensitized perception may swamp him unless he has some firm footing provided by predetermined understanding about *focus* and *expectations*. While the regular public assistance caseworker is, indeed, regularly "swamped," it is by work volume and procedural detail too great to be encompassed in the limits of work time. But he has the advantage—at least he did in the Chemung experiment—of a clearly delimited purpose and service: the provision of basic economic and physical needs.

The trained worker, on the other hand, charged with the ambiguous task of meeting all the problems he discerns in a caseload of multi-problem families may find himself in a situation where he sees and knows too much about too many things over which he has too little control, or for which no reparative resources as yet exist. Moreover he finds himself under some expectation that what he will do will in some way be more elegant than run-of-the-mill—but when this expectation is vague and undefined it can only add to the already distracting set-up he enters. That which he and the experimental design and the supervisory personnel should have done they may not have done: to define the target population; to delineate the problems in the center of concern and priority; to match those problems against variable agency and community resources; to clarify feasible goals. "Feasible goals," incidentally, are always subject to stretch in the happy event that things go better than anticipated. It is the recurrent illusory goal of radical change or permanent cure that over and over again lets down caseworkers and researchers alike.

Agreements on population-to-be-served, on problem-focus and on task boundaries need to take place before the encounter between caseworker-client. Now there arise a number of other considerations. Many recent studies have supported what experienced social workers have long known: that those people who are thought to be most needful of social services—the chronically deprived population—are least likely to see the social work agency and its representative as a source of any help other than financial. There are many reasons for this that cannot have space here but the fact is that "social worker" and "relief worker" are synonymous for many people and certainly for most working-class and lower-class people. That a social worker has other services to offer—guidance, counsel, influence upon other persons and circumstances involved in a person's problem, linkages to other agents and agencies in the community—this conception has not yet become part of the general understanding of the function of a social worker. Particularly for persons who have been on relief, the perception of social worker is a constricted one. Worse, it is often shot through with feelings of distrust and antagonism, a displacement upon this representative of the Establishment of all the hostile feelings towards people in power who have been niggardly and depriving or who are assumed to be the "ins" while the recipient feels himself to be one of the "outs."

It follows, then, that an agency's client who has been for some time in the role of recipient and who, by definition, is one of those unable to meet norms of adequate social functioning, will view himself vis-à-vis his caseworker in certain predetermined ways. And thus his responsive behavior will be shaped and colored by the expectations he brings to the transaction.

In the light of those considerations one looks again at the Chemung experiment. What preparation, one wonders, was given the clients for their being transferred to intensive service? What was learned of their desires and expectations? Did they consider it a privilege or a punishment? What was their reaction to being visited and talked to so frequently? Was it considered a pleasure to see the worker weekly or was it felt to be an imposition of nosey paternalism?

These must have been the unasked questions in the minds of the experimental clients. One is reminded of a like situation in "The Girls at Vocational High" where, as in the Chemung experiment, those persons given intensive case-work showed small and statistically insignificant improvement over those in the untreated control group. That study records that the caseworkers found the girls "uncertain and confused about the basis of their selection and expressed the fear that they were thought 'crazy' or otherwise invidiously identified." It could be expected, then, that they would be wary of involvement with their assigned caseworker. Or it could be anticipated that even if, warmed by the caseworker's concern and helpfulness, they "gave out" feelingly, they might in after-thought pull back again into their old established pattern of mistrust, which had been enlivened now by this unusual and mysterious offer of helpfulness.

The Chemung study does not reveal whether or how the experimental clients were inducted into their new role of "change targets." We do not know what their reactions were, nor their expectations. Based on repeated experience one could almost surely predict that unless this role and goal change was openly discussed, worked over, and then freely chosen by the clients involved, the trained caseworker would be working with clients who were mystified at best by this sudden on-rush of agency attention, or who, under the surface, were resistant or suspicious of it.

Allied with the client's expectations of an agency and its representatives is the client's motivation for change. Motivation is a many-layered thing. Those conscious or close-to-the surface feelings and ideas about what one needs and wants and about how much it is worth stretching for are what is referred to here. Can we simply assume that the client who takes money assistance wants or feels the need for the other forms of aid and service that an agency decides he needs and ought to want? Like all the rest of us, the person with "multi-problems" is both driven and strait-jacketed by a complex of motivations. In differing degrees these combine realistic hope and far-fetched wish, aspiration and resignation, wanting yet fearing.

So, as the old casework saw adjures us, one must start where the client is—which is to say one must start with drawing out, coaxing out what his idea is of what he needs, what his idea is of what's wrong, what his ideas and feelings are about what the consequences for him and his family will be if some different things aren't made to happen. Then one must draw out and work over—sometimes over and over again—what his ideas are about the kind of help he can actually get, and their relation to reality, and what problems are involved for him in changing his usual ways of operation—and so on. The point is that one cannot set forth to "do intensive casework" or proffer service for multiple problems with the jaunty confidence of a salesman carrying a case full of bright gadgets for all household needs. Even such simple things as putting a room in order or keeping a clinic appointment or getting up in time to go to school—even these simple acts may take considerable effort and conscious reorganization of one's habitual behavior and they will require some inner push to do them. This is why the caseworker must first and always attune himself to what his client is driving toward, and this is especially the case when the agency and not the client decides a change is in order.

Whether or not the workers in the Chemung County experiment were grounded in this casework conviction and its implications for action we do not know. Whether they operated on their own steam or attempted to work up the client's motivational steam is not on record. Since one tends to record what one considers important, it seems probable that this attention to the increase and rechanneling of the client's motivation was not paramount. Technically skilled and resourceful as a caseworker may be, he will have little influence over one whose wants and ideas run on another track and in another direction.

In the past few years—actually after the Chemung study was designed and embarked upon, one must note—there has been a flood of light cast upon the "culture" of the poor, of the educationally as well as economically disadvantaged. Certain kinds of behavior, of cognitive modes, of attitudes, of self-other concepts and relationships tend, it is held, to characterize the majority of persons who make up the membership of the so-called multiproblem families. Certainly every individual in this class-culture will not conform to this characteristic pattern, any more than any middle-class individual is a walking incarnation of his class characteristics. With this warning against the substitution of stereotype for individualization, it is necessary to examine the findings of the numerous studies that bear on the ways chronically disadvantaged persons feel and act.

The characteristics of the "culture of poverty" or of the men, women and children who are the victim-creators of that culture cannot serve caseworkers as pejorative labels for disposal purposes. Rather, they must serve as diagnostic guides to the means and modes of intervention. If it is true, for example, that the long-poor tend to be more present- than future-oriented, then today's problem, it must be anticipated, will have to be in the center of the worker's and client's attention. If there is little capacity among this group to postpone gratification and a strong tendency to be impulse-ridden, then rewards for efforts made and the meeting of pressing needs must come at once and be frequent. If this group tends to be concrete-minded, unused and therefore unable to deal with abstract notions, if they most truly know what their sensory organs tell them is there, then casework communications must be plain and simple and the aids offered must be those that can be seen, felt, and tangible. If there is little experience in this group of the luxury of introspection and of the benefits of lifting feeling to the mind for its consideration, then the caseworker must know that talking will be of small use and that action (on the client's part and on that of the worker) must be counted on to change feelings rather than the other way around.

The fact is that casework's body of principles of conduct and influence has largely stemmed from a predominantly middle-class psychology and a middle-class value system. This is not a pejorative statement. It is a fact that has implications for action. A whole series of "if-then" propositions governs what and how the caseworker should act. The "if" says, "if this person adheres to a certain value system he will tend to think-act-feel in certain ways; then," we say, "one anticipates and says and acts in certain congruent ways to influence him." What newly emergent findings on the culture of the poor suggest is the necessity for a revised set of "if-then" propositions. Such revisions are currently taking place in the experimental practices of caseworkers who are involved in special projects with lower-class and socially disorganized families.

But, as has been noted, these intervention guidelines inherent in a grasp of the psychological make-up and value stance of the long-time economically and socially impoverished have for the most part been developed since the launching of the Chemung study. It is even possible that, guided by their schooling in principles and values of middle class expectations, the trained caseworkers found (or created) a wider communication gap between themselves and their clients than those other caseworkers who worked by impulse and habit.

While this is possible, it is not necessarily probable. Even though new and useful principles of working within the culture of poverty were not widely disseminated and would not, therefore, have been part of the knowledge carried by the trained caseworkers at Chemung, and even though there is to be found in social work as in all professions a considerable time-lag between the articulation of new theory and its translation into practice, there is to be found in all professional training for casework certain useful and influential principles of good human relationships. It could be assumed, then, that at the least the several trained caseworkers in Chemung followed the principles of receptivity to the client, of acceptance of him as a person worthy of respect and concern, of relating with sympathy and warmth to his expression of his feelings, of providing what opportunities and resources were necessary and available to him. These underpinnings to peoples' feelings of being supported, heard out, understood, felt with, and materially aided must not be underestimated.

But an insistent question remains and it bears on the whole relation of casework to situations where social, economic, physical, and psychological needs are manifold, basic, and essentially unmet. It is the question of the uses of casework in public assistance agencies when such agencies are themselves hampered by conditions of inadequate funds and lack of social resources. Under such circumstances, can casework work? Since it is only a process by which to promote and enhance people's social functioning, and not a panacea, nor a laying on of healing hands, nor a giving out of ready-made aids, must there not be present certain conditions of psychological and social resource in order for this process to work out successfully? Or, to turn the question about, are there psychological and social conditions that make casework all but futile? The Chemung findings, that those families who were involved in the casework process made no more discernible progress than those who were not, force one to look at these questions.

The conditions of client motivation, of mutual agreements and understandings, of clear communication, of focus and partialization; the conditions of the caseworker's capacity to assess, to modify treatment in accordance with his assessments, to remain concerned and supportive and compassionate, to rouse hope or even anxiousness when necessary—all these have been touched on. All these conditions may be present—and still there might be no measurable or "statistically significant" change for the better in the "multiple-problem" family. The probability is, then, that in order for casework to be effective as a "mover and shaker" certain further conditions must be present and viable. These, it seems to me, have been given insufficient attention. I move to discuss these conditions and the questions they raise with some tentativeness. I am not sure that I know what is "true"; I am sure only that they deserve careful consideration.

Present day ego psychology may serve as a partial reference frame here. One of its foremost theoreticians proposes that human beings are driven by two major kinds of needs: one, to fill in "deficit needs," that is, to gratify basic biological and psycho-social wants; and second, to meet "developmental needs," that is, to gratify strivings for growth, development, competence, self-actualization. "Deficit needs" include such physical wants as hunger and sex and needs for love and affection, for a dependable "floor" of economic and social security, and, beyond this, for a sense of having some recognizable place and function in a social system (within the small family group and beyond). It suggests that only when these deficit needs are met is the individual free to turn his energies to striving to be and to have more or better than he is and has. Only then is he free to take the risks involved in changed ways of behaving, only then is he free to give out from himself to other persons, interests, objects. In short, a person's ability to reach out, to strive, adapt or reshape behavior and attitudes; his capacity to put himself into new tasks, these strivings depend upon his having enough security of an economic, physical, affectional, and social sort so that he feels himself to be relatively on solid ground and in balance.

Reverse the picture. If income, earned or otherwise, is chronically inadequate to meet basic needs; if tensions arise within the person because of his chronic frustration and thus inevitably affect his capacity to relate with loving to other people; if, added to this repeated experience of feeling want and being found wanting, there is social denigration and constriction; if there is closure of social opportunity and social recognition, then a person is caught in a multi-problem trap. His life energies will be eaten up by rage or depression or by his continuing slogging to manage or make-do at a minimal level, with no energy surplus for new approaches to his problem.

The multi-problem clients of Chemung County, both in the experimental and control groups, were families suffering many deficit needs. Relief grants by objective standards were chronically inadequate. Agency policy, despite the "specialness" accorded the experimental group, held iron-fast on money matters. What the nature of the problem-complex was for the experimental families is not explicit but one can assume on the basis of typicalness that most of the women were without husbands or with husbands who did not work, and thus most children were without fathers or with fathers whose role was a denigrated one. One can assume that housing was poor, furnishing minimal, if not totally inadequate. Problems of health are characteristic of low-budget, low-morale families, and it is hard to know whether sickness is the cause or consequence of the other problems. The picture is too familiar to need further description.

Now the caseworker comes in. If the need lies in money for food, housing, clothing—and if the caseworker can furnish or increase the money income—then he can meet one basic deficit need. If, however, there are no further money resources to be had or allowed, then the caseworker, by his sympathy and appreciative understanding of his client's rage, depression or whatever, can only help him to bear the deficit. Kindly ministrations cannot take the place of what money must buy.

If this immutable deficit need is compounded by ill health or physical disability in one or more family members and if the caseworker can point to and provide acceptable medical care and can help the client use it, then he starts some change going. But there must be available medical resources. Moreover physical malfunctioning (like many kinds of social and psychological malfunctioning) may take its inexorable course despite medical skills. So while the effort has been made no actual change may occur.

If inadequate income and inadequate physical capacity are combined with family discord, whether between husband and wife, parents and children, or in both systems at once, then the caseworker may offer the opportunity to talk-over, think-over, feel-over these problems so that family life may meet its major function: to fulfill the basic affectional and security needs of its members. One of the deficit needs that frequent contact with the trained caseworker helps to meet, it is safe to say, is this one of affectional support. Working always to spark and sustain a relationship with the client that is concerned and compassionate, the caseworker often provides some substitute experience of being liked or cared for, respected, "believed in" to persons whose hunger for acceptance is rarely met in their everyday contacts. But the casework relationship cannot be a permanent substitute for that which must be found and sustained in the client's own family and friend group.

The difficulty is that talking-over, thinking-over, feeling-over one's problems of interpersonal relationships requires some freedom from other stresses. The examination of one's own behavior, the introspective exploration of the self as "actor" and "feeler" and "thinker" is a luxury usually only available to those who are free to take their eyes off the manifest dangers from the outside. It requires some cooperation from the "others" involved in the problem. It requires some considerable capacity to express things in words, to trust in the efficacy of talk, to have experienced thinking as a delay of impulsive action. All these capacities are not often found in the culture and habitual conduct of multi-problem, "hard to reach" families. So these deficits, when they exist, may not readily be filled in. Changes in attitudes and feelings about self-other relationships are, moreover, subtle to identify unless obvious behavioral change accompanies them.

The third type of basic need is that of having some secure place in a social system and some recognized and accredited function there. It is, in brief, the need for a respectable social role which one can carry with a relative sense of adequacy. In any society, to be an "in" one must be able to carry certain tasks in certain ways expected of one's age and status: a husband is expected to be a breadwinner, a woman with children is expected to be a wife, a mother is expected to meet the nurture-needs of her children, both physical and affectional, an adolescent is expected to be a student on his way to school-completion—and so on. The needs that are met by these activities are those of social recognition of their desirability and their value, and the combined rewards of social approval and self-esteem that accrue to their being well done.

One of the major deterrents to adequate social functioning is the *actual lack of means* by which to carry a function. This "lack of means" may lie in the client himself—in his mental, physical, or emotional handicaps. But it may also lie in the life conditions of the person. If a job is not to be had, a man cannot be a breadwinner. If day-care for children is not to be had, a mother cannot work. If soap and mops and dresser drawers and dishes are not to be had, a woman cannot be a good housekeeper. If home-maker service is not to be had, a sick mother may not be able to cope with home and children. If dental care is not to be had, if organized free recreation is not to be had, if decent housing is not to be had, if special classes for mentally or culturally retarded children are not to be had—then these deficits in social provisions will have their deficit-consequences in individual social functioning.

The caseworker traditionally has served to make and weave the lines of connections between individuals and organized social provisions. Traditionally he works both sides of the transaction— to facilitate the client's knowledge of the resource, and to influence him to use it, and to prepare the resource to receive the applicant in the light of his special needs. These arrangements and ongoing supports are one vital way by which caseworkers can fill in social deficit needs. But the resources must be present. A caseworker cannot manufacture them.

In short, the "multi-problem" family is usually a "multi-deficit" family. Usually the caseworker assigned to it encounters not one but a complex of deficit needs. Some of these may be filled in by the caseworker's efforts. Others cannot. Until physical, affectional, and social hungers have had some fulfillment (one will not say "been satisfied" for that would be unrealistic), until some underpinning security is felt as certain, people do not seem to be able to look or reach beyond the here and now. "More and better" in terms of material advantages and arrangements may be hoped for and striven for only when minimal needs are assured. Relationships with other people may be improved only when the energy used to lick one's own wounds and keep body and soul together can be released outward from the self. Beyond feeling the need of love and trying to get it is the capacity to "give out," to invest one's self whether in one's family or in a wider circle of friends and associates, or in work and its gratifications. Taking the responsibilities and gaining the rewards that participation in church or school or neighborhood groups affords rests on the will and energy to "put one's self out." The motivation for development, for self and family well-being is dependent on some surplus of free energy and is sustained by realistic confidence.

Herein, perhaps, lie the core questions in the Chemung experiment, in other experiments like it, or in all those plans for an all-out attack upon social problems that begin "If we had enough case-workers. . . ." The questions: Is "casework" being expected to substitute for lack of material and psycho-social resources? If casework is validly to be used as a process to enhance individual motivation and capacity for constructive change and to make available social opportunities useable by the client, are there certain minimal conditions that must serve as floor for such efforts? If those conditions are not provided or possible, should there be appropriately delimited expectations of the outcomes of the casework input? If casework is understood in its relationship to the dynamics of human need, motivation, and consequent behavior should it be tested for its efficacy in a situation where all odds are against its efficacy?

Perhaps the most efficient use of the trained caseworker is in those situations where the "bootstraps" are securely attached to boots, and the lifting up process seems plausible. Perhaps for those families with most multi-deficit needs (and one must remember these are not all the families on public assistance, only those judged most chronically problematic) there must be bootstrap provisions of all available material means, medical care, tender concern and ready availability of a helper, but that helper may not need to be professionally prepared for full caseworker responsibilities. Perhaps such families or individuals could be transferred to professionally prepared caseworkers when conditions seemed favorable for "intensive" work: when, for example, some crucial occurrence makes the family either more vulnerable to hurt or more accessible to help, or when some changes in levels or degrees of motivation or functioning result from the meeting of deficit needs. Perhaps social caseworkers should stubbornly affirm that certain social provisions must be present as the baseline from which casework can be expected to "work" and certainly if it is to be assessed. And perhaps social work as a profession should further examine the balance between the responsibilities it has taken upon itself (or allowed itself to be charged with) and the powers it has (or has not) to effectively carry them. Its skilled use of methods is one form of a profession's power, but only one. To be exercised it must have some control over the policies and conditions which support or serve to undermine that power.

A whole series of implications arise now, for professional education for social work. In many schools the implications have already been faced, agonized over, and are in the process of being explored and debated and translated into action principles, but perhaps not widely or consistently enough. Schools of social work are being asked—and demanding of themselves to know—what they are preparing their students to do as social workers, what relevance their curriculum has for social policy and politics in the large, for that newly visible bottom layer of our social structure, where social problems fester and reinfect each new generation. If one considers only the one process of influence, social casework, this much may be ventured: teachers of casework need to review and to revise or ramify their practice theory. Not only does the relation between casework and other social work methods need our careful thought but also the relation between all of these and present-day social conditions and resources.

The bottom-line question which the Chemung County study raises—certainly in the minds of the public—must be faced. It is this: is casework necessary and can it be disposed of (because it has been "proved" wanting)? My answer as a caseworker is, "No—casework is not necessary," and "Yes—it can be disposed of." It can be disposed of if one is ready to dispose of the idea that there are times and conditions when any person may be unable to cope with his problems of daily functioning. It is unnecessary if one holds that any person who cannot cope on his own should be left, along with his heirs, to take the consequences. It can be disposed of if one believes that individual aspiration and well-being are of minor concern in our society. It is unnecessary if one believes that all men are in fact created equal and that, therefore, they have equal capacities and opportunities.

But if one believes that any person at some time and place and condition may need help over some obstacle to his better and more satisfying functioning, if one believes that people differ one from the other and that, therefore, they may need help that is attuned to their particular capacities and their particular wishes in their particular situation, if one recognizes, on the basis of historical fact, that the growth of humanness and the development of human self-other relationships rest upon a rising floor of basic security from which, then, people reach out and stretch to use themselves more constructively—then casework as a process in social work is not dispensable. If we believe in individual worth and are troubled by individual hurt then we must maintain a socially supported mode of helping people to bear that human condition and of influencing them to better it.

Casework is one such mode. It is not *the* mode. It is not a substitute for basic deficit needs. It is not magic, placebo or panacea. And it ought not to be assessed as if it were or could be. It is dependent upon certain other conditions being present and viable. Just as an orthopedist could scarcely teach his patient to walk again without the sticks and braces and other rehabilitative devices and personnel that support not only the crippled limb but also the hope-level of the patient, so a caseworker needs for his clients the underpinnings of minimal economic adequacy and external evidence that there is reason for his hope. Without these one person may help another to "feel better," and perhaps thus to "do better," by compassion and the input here and there of some special service or aids. But these small and unregular gains which often make endurance possible may not make change possible or visible. And the research question is not "Does the casework make it possible for people to endure?" It asks "Does casework make it possible for people to change?" I daresay that our orthopedist friend who has been borrowed for analogue would decry a study that assessed his treatment in a hospital where there was nothing more for the patient than bed and board.

This is in no sense an argument to abandon the long and chronically poor or those families with so many deficits, so "multi-problem" as to be drained of energy or hope or incentive. Such people may have long and deep and fully explainable dependency needs. Let us meet them. They may have immutable mental or physical handicaps. Let us protect them. They may be permeated by hopelessness and apathy or by smoldering volcanic hostility. Let us labor to give them less reason for these. Whether such help is to be carried by professional caseworkers or by "subprofessionals" or "casework aides" is a matter for thought and experiment. But let us not assess the efficacy of casework in helping people to lift themselves by their bootstraps when they have no boots.

In sum, this paper has attempted several things. One is to point up to researchers and caseworkers both that if experiments in the change-effects of any method are to be tried there need to be definitions of the change-target, selection of the problems-to-be-worked, agreements as to expectable outcomes (based on real-istic assessment of the forces and factors of time-place-person-problems) and some delineation of the means by which these outcomes might be achieved. When "change targets" are real and live people who will bring their particular perceptions and prejudices and expectations and resistances to any new approach to them, then these human reactions and their effect upon the planned intervention will need always to be taken into account. More, they will need to be dealt with. Caseworkers are guilty of not making clear to themselves, to their clients, to the community, and thus to their research colleagues what the nature, and conditions and possibilities and limits of their operations are.

One looks back, then, at the Chemung County study with regrets for our sins of omission, for that which we should have done—caseworkers, teachers, supervisors and administrators, researchers—all of us. But if our complacency has been shaken, or even if we feel variously guilty or uneasy or angry at its findings it will have served an important purpose: to sharply alert us to our own as yet unsolved problems and to motivate us to tackle them yet again and with new vigor and clearer perspectives.

3

ON THE ART OF CARING

Today's major concern in child welfare is with the abuse, neglect, and abandonment of children. Many of us seem to believe that these are new evils, offshoots of the malignancies in our complicated society. But even a cursory glance across the history of childhood reveals that abuse, neglect, even murder of unloved or unwanted children, were widespread across the world and across the ages.

In ancient Greece, that golden place and time that we glorify as the birthplace of democracy and the temple of reason—in that society deformed or unwanted children were simply disposed of—into slavery, or left to die. The beautiful young—especially boys—were used sexually from early childhood. Leap across time and place, and one finds in nineteenth- and early twentieth-century England autobiographical accounts of sexual practices to which boy children had been introduced by nursemaids or other servants to whose care they had been entrusted. In England's and Scotland's nineteenth-century factories youngsters were often chained to machines they were to tend, for as long as ten hours a day. In Scandinavia young children were indentured as farm laborers. Brutal flogging of children, whether by parents or by sadistic school masters, was often piously supported by dicta about the need to break the child's will or to exorcise demons.[1] That there were and

Presented at the one hundred fiftieth anniversary celebration of the Brookwood Child Care Agency, Brooklyn, New York, on November 8, 1983. Published in *Child Welfare*, vol. 64, no. 1 (January–February 1985). Permission to reprint by the Child Welfare League of America. This version is somewhat abridged.
1. See Lloyd de Mause, ed., *History of Childhood* (New York: Harper & Row, 1974), and Philippe Aries, *Centuries of Childhood* (New York: Random House, 1965), along with the nineteenth-century novels of Charles Dickens *(Oliver Twist, Nicholas Nickleby, David Copperfield)*, as examples of attitudes and treatment of *un*cared-for youngsters.

are explanations for all this goes without saying. Explanations, however, do not lessen the pain of body and spirit.

In brief, the maltreatment of children, with which we are today concerned, is as old as human sin. But there is something remarkably new at which to take heart. It is twofold. One is the growth, in this twentieth century, of widespread recognition and understanding of the child as a selfhood and as a person-in-the-making. The consequence of this is the remarkable spread of public concern about the individual child's well-being. That public concern has been translated into legal protections for children. Beyond protection is the creation of all sorts of social, educational, and psychological opportunities by which the child's full development may be promoted.

And further still: Because it has come to be understood that both parents and children must often be drawn in and influenced to want such opportunities and to use them well, conviction and support have flourished for the study and development of the interpersonal methods by which motivations and behaviors may be influenced and rechanneled. We call those methods and skills the "*art* of caring."

The motivations that push and pull us into work with and for children are multiple, as are most human motivations. Dominant among them is our swift, spontaneous sensitivity to the needs and wants of children—because children seem most vulnerable to hurt, most malleable, most often victimized, and most innocent and appealing. We want to heal the hurt child; to rescue the child whose person and personality are about to be disfigured or destroyed by powerful adults; to provide the nourishment and security, physical and psychological, for a healthy development; to offer new and dependable opportunities with which the child can nourish his or her potentials for full self-actualization. We *care*—and we want to reach eagerly and wholeheartedly into the lives of the children who come to our attention. But caring is not enough.

It is not long before we discover some troubling and puzzling obstacles on the way to our goals. And it is particularly these obstacles that require of us not only that we care for and about children, but that we work at the development of an "art of caring." Let me cite only a few examples of our common obstacles.

There is the frequent and paradoxical phenomenon of abused children who perversely want to return to their abusing parents rather than live in a foster home or treatment center where they may experience security, safety, and solicitude. Why is this? Is there some blood bonding that exists between a child and his or her own parents? Or is it a relationship bonding that is entrenched in the early months of infancy, when body contact and fondling occur between even the immature mother and her doll-like infant? Or is it a preference for the known, no matter how hellish, over the fear-filled unknown? We still do not fully understand this.

Further, there is the disillusionment that we experience when we come up against the actuality that many children we deal with seem unable to respond to our outgoing love. They either have lost or have never developed the capacity to trust an adult, to take in the love and caring we hold out to them. They relate in only the most superficial, shallow ways. And this puzzles—even, at times, threatens—us. We tend to believe that a neglected, unloved child is like an empty vessel, awaiting only a pouring in of love, our tangible and emotional demonstration of caring. But the fact is that nature abhors not only a physical vacuum but also a psychological vacuum, and children who have been starved for affection and consideration have a shrunken stomach, so to speak, for the rich food of love; or have filled in their emptiness with defenses against unmet hungers. Like a food-starved person they may need, for a long time, to be stood by, steadily, reliably, and patiently fed with an eyedropper.

Another obstacle is perhaps one of the most common of all. We have learned that we must so deal with the child's parents that they may become our collaborators rather than our opponents. We must do so if we are to keep them from running interference between their children and us, and certainly if we hope to return their children to them at some time in the future. And yet—the persistent thorn in our flesh and in our conscience is that we really do not care for these parents (with exceptions here and there, of course). We do not even *like* them. And they do not like us. For many reasons they fear us, and sometimes even hate us. On the surface, it is because we have created a crisis for them—we have been the bearers of bad tidings that persons and forces in the community hold them to be deficient or harmful as parents. Below the surface is the long experience these parents have usually had of being outcasts from approved social groups; they have had frequent experiences of blame and punishment for their own parents, teachers, doctors, neighbors—in short, from persons who to them represent the Establishment. Those past experiences create expectations that are transferred onto us, however different our initial approach and attitude may be. Many persons act not in response to the reality we present but to past persons we remind them of. On our side is the clear evidence that they are victimizing helpless children with whom our empathy and identification are immediate and strong, and such parents become very difficult to like and relate to.

Just this far, and it becomes evident why caring *about* and *for* children is not enough. Nor is it enough to give our reaction to the parents a respectable professional name: "countertransference." We must face what has been faced in titling this symposium: that beyond our spontaneous "caring" we must learn and practice the *art* of caring, which is to say that we must learn and practice the skills by which we can put our intentions into effect.

According to Webster, one definition of an art is "exceptional skill in conducting any human activity." It is only in the latter half of this century that we have grasped that exceptional skill is involved in undertaking to give children substitute parental care and to prepare parents themselves for the tasks of parenting. It is only recently that there have been widespread glimpses and some penetrating insights into all the irrationalities, ambivalences, and inconsistencies that pervade human behavior—the gaps, for instance, between reasonable thought and impulsive behavior or feeling, between what a person needs and what he or she wants. So we face the fact that we must move from caring as a feeling only to developing caring into a teachable, learnable "high skill"—if we are to bring it to the level of art.

Every art that is more than some lucky spontaneous splash of self-expression is developed by a combination of certain common basic conditions. This holds, I believe, whether the art is one of creation or performance. Again, too briefly, I can only touch on those conditions.

First, there must be in the artist some innate or acquired but deeply incorporated bent or talent or gift of a special capacity that drives his or her interests or actions. (Of course, such a gift or capacity may be dwarfed or constricted by lack of opportunities for its expression and development; or, in reverse, it may be brought to full flower by its nurture and exercise.)

In the field of human relations, especially when the motive is to reshape or rechannel feelings, thoughts, and behaviors, the artist must start with the special gift of a sensitive capacity for empathy. That means the spontaneous ability to feel with other people, to temporarily step inside the skin of another. The German term Freud uses, *einfuhling*—"feeling into"—is much more expressive than our term "empathy" to conjure up the sense of being *at-one,* of being *with* another. It goes without saying that empathy is easiest when the other is felt to be like oneself in vital, emotionally charged ways. Empathy needs to be "worked at," however, when others' acts, feelings, or thoughts are unfamiliar, certainly when they seem unacceptable.

Whether empathy is inborn, or is the product of early and continual experiences of loving, reciprocal interchanges between parents and child from birth onward, no one really knows. What is reassuring, however, is that a few recent research experiments have indicated that the capacity for empathy can indeed be heightened in adult professionals by certain kinds of training.[2]

More reliably, and certainly more usual in professional training, is the continual pursuit of knowledge and search for understanding for the explanations and the reasons that underlie the attitudes and behaviors of persons who "turn us off." In that effort what comes in through the head may be transferred to the heart. That is not strange, because the person who is open to learning will find that not only do feelings affect our thoughts but knowledge and thoughts also affect our feelings. When, for example, we grasp the fact that persons may be the victims of their own unrecognized drives it becomes more possible to feel with and for them. When we realize that most of the parents we encounter had affectionally impoverished and punishing childhoods, it becomes possible to understand empathically why they remain needful children them-selves, despite their physical adulthood; and how it is that they have little to draw upon and that they can scarcely be expected to give what they have never had.

When we understand, too, that many parents are abysmally unaware of the effect of today on a child's tomorrow, when we recognize that in producing a "bad" child the parents have unwit-tingly created a Frankenstein's monster who eats life out of them— when we understand only some of these things we become able, at least, to say, in effect, "I can feel with you. But I can also feel with

2. Bearing on the question of whether empathy can be learned or developed: Pauline Lide, "An Experimental Study of Empathic Functioning," *Social Service Review,* vol. 41 (March 1967); and Ruth Matarazzo, "Research on the Teaching and Learning of Psychotherapeutic Skills," in *Handbook of Psychotherapy and Behavior Change,* Allen Bergin and S. I. Garfield, eds. (New York: John Wiley & Sons, 1971).

your wishing that things were a lot different for you, and maybe then for the child, too." This may be the beginning of the bonding that a working alliance grows from—the client's sense that "you are with me and for me." But the talent for empathy must be accompanied by other conditions.

The second condition for all high skill or art is that there must be—and I paraphrase an idea that was first put forward by John Dewey—an understanding and respect "for the materials" with which one works. He meant several things by his dictum. First, there must be interest in their special nature; then, careful attention to their potentials and also to their limitations; then, curiosity about and observation of their responsiveness to what is being done with and to them by the would-be artist.

In the graphic arts, for instance, the artist-painter (in contrast to the Sunday painter) examines carefully the nature of paints—the differences, say, between oils and acrylics and water-colors, between pencil and charcoal, between paper and canvas and plaster. The artist then makes an assessment, a diagnosis, if you will, of what this or that material and treatment are likely to yield. The artist-sculptor studies closely the special nature of marble, limestone, metals, woods, clay for what they require by way of instruments and for what can be expected of them in relation to the purpose he or she has in mind. The artist-musician must know deeply and precisely the nature, potentials, and qualities of the instrument he or she plays.

By extension, if we in social work are indeed to raise caring to an art, we need to attend closely, with interest and respect, to the materials with which we work—living human beings. Along with this we must be continuously attuned to and critical of the process we set in motion by our handling of these living materials.

The third condition upon which high art depends is that artists must rigorously govern themselves by a stern discipline.

Especially among the young there persists a kind of romanticism about art and artists. It is imagined that creativity is simply a rush or gush of self-expression, that artists spend their hours in garrets and cafes (or, these days, in lofts and pot-sessions) waiting for the spirit to move them, free from the onerous outside contraints of time or production expectations that have been set by other people. But any study of the lives of great artists reveals a very different picture. The dancer works at what is often a cruel discipline of submitting the body to continual and often torturing exercises. The hours of self-imposed practice by performing musicians are well known. Writers tell of their inexorable schedules—those many self-set hours every day when they sit in isolation behind the closed door, facing an accusing typewriter or an empty yellow pad, thinking, setting down, correcting, tearing up, and starting over.

The discipline of those of us who seek to enhance the lives of others is one of the most exacting forms of self-mastery. It starts with self-awareness so that our own needs and wants do not blind us to the nature of the materials with which we work. From self-awareness must follow self-control and self-criticism, a continual stepping back from the canvas, so to speak, to reachieve objectivity and perspective. It requires further a continually re-willed effort to understand—which means to get into or "under"—the often obdurate and difficult materials with which we work.

Beyond self-control is the necessity for self-management. It demands of us that in those transactions between us and those by whom we are "turned off," we behave in ways that are necessary for the ends we hope to achieve. To say, for example, "I can imagine how angry I must make you feel" rather than stiffening at the clients' hostility; to say, or act, "I am here to make things better for *you* not just for your children"—these words may stick in our craws at times.[3] And yet, the fact is twofold: it is the only way the nonvoluntary, resistive parent or the indignant foster mother or the exhausted child care worker can begin to feel allied with us; and, second, by those mysterious interconnections between action and thought and feeling in ourselves, any indication of positive responsiveness to what we say or do has its mellowing effect upon our own feelings.

I am reminded of the innate wisdom of Shakespeare, one of the world's greatest psychologists, as well as greatest writers. Almost four-hundred years before behavior modification was dreamed of he understood the effect of self-governed behavior upon our emotions (given, of course, the sought-for rewards). He had Hamlet trying to change his errant mother's behavior and hence her feelings: "*Assume* a virtue if you have it not," he counsels her. "For *use* may often change the stamp of nature" [emphasis added].

There is no more rigorous self-management and self-discipline than this. When it is rewarded, however, by some manifest and

3. Further detailing of modes of self-management as "art" may be found in the chapter "But Can You Love Everybody?" in *Relationship: The Heart of Helping People* (no. 6 in bibliography).

desirable change in the adult- or child-client's attitude or behavior, it becomes worth the effort.

"When it is rewarded"—that is the key.

All practitioners of every art need at least two kinds of reward, it seems to me, if they are to maintain their striving for high standards of performance and achievement. (There are other rewards, to be sure, but social workers rarely get them: money is one; public applause another; we forego these when we choose social work!) The two that seem to me most vital are those we share with all other artists.

In the performance of any art there must be a recurring sense that one is, by one's own talents and efforts, *making something to happen*—a sense that one is creating, refashioning, actualizing materials in a way that is desired and satisfying to the self in some way. Robert White first put forward this idea—that from infancy onward a person's sense of selfhood is sustained and expanded by the sense of being a "maker," a feeling of effectiveness, of competence.[4]

The signs by which our sense of effectiveness is realized are often small ones—the lighted-up faces of children when they catch sight of you, the verbal affirmation of adults who say (in their own way, of course) that they feel understood, that they believe you, that they feel better for having talked to you—these signs warm and rekindle us. And, of course, when manifest change occurs both in our clients' coping and their internal steadiness, we feel ourselves rewarded at having been of vital help to another human being, at having had some part in creating a benign rather than a vicious cycle.

The further reward that all artists need, if they are to maintain their striving, is social recognition. As social animals we continuously, if involuntarily, look for the image and reflection of ourselves in the eyes of our "significant others." We all need the heartening nourishment of knowing that those others think well of us—that what we do or what we have tried to do is worthy of respect, at the least, of admiration, at the best. That recognition need not be widespread or broadcast. Most of us in any field of endeavor live most intensely and meaningfully within the small worlds of our daily rounds. The people who are significant or meaningful to us are those we like or love, those we respect or admire or feel at one with, and those to whom we feel bonded by common emotional investments and a sense of partnership or colleagueship. In a professional endeavor they are our peers, our mentors, our models.

4. Robert F. White, "Motivation Reconsidered: The Concept of Competence," *Psychological Review*, vol. 66 (1959): 297–333.

1989 Afterword

Of course, the art of caring is essential in any form of social casework where our aim, always, is to help the human being so that, as Sir William Osler, that brilliant practitioner and teacher of modern medicine, put it, we "cure a few, improve the many, and comfort all."

For obvious reasons child welfare work is charged with stress—emergencies, crises, children at immediate risk—these and more become the "business-as-usual," no less demanding for all their expectability. So the need for us to turn to and join one another to give deserved support, recognition, approbation, affirmation of efforts made and actions taken is an ever-present one.

"Deserved" is not to say one has been "successful." It includes the recognition of honest intentions and thoughtful efforts that may have failed. (If the truth be told, as many uncontrollable and even unknown factors may enter into a "successful" outcome as enter into our failures, although it is only natural for any of us to tend to attribute our successes to our skills, and our failures to those other factors and forces that undermined our plans.) Thoughtful efforts and honest intentions and "best-laid schemes that gang aft a-gley" must be analyzed, criticized, corrected, but always with recognition and support of the person, if not the act. That holds as valid in relationships with colleagues and adjuncts as it holds in dealing with clients.

The whole business of intrastaff relationships up and down the line, the maintenance of an esprit de corps especially in demanding, crisis-charged organizations merits more attention than it has had. It is an extension of the "art of caring."

One further word as I look out to the larger world: What now of an *architecture* of caring for families and children?—of drafting a multistructured design to house and facilitate national goals and standards by which parents and their children can be secured, educated for personal and communal responsibilities, provided access to resources for physical and mental health care? What blueprints are being drafted? What floorboards being hewn? What undergirding foundation of public policy has been fashioned?

4

IN QUEST OF COPING

1989 FOREWORD

Several years after the publication of *Social Casework: A Problem-Solving Process,* I began to be urged by its readers to take its ideas forward, to develop the model's use in the on-going and ending phases of casework practice. Had I done so, one of its major thrusts would have been what is set forth in the article that follows.

After the long deep breath and mild post-partum depression that I suppose every author experiences when her/his brainchild is at last delivered and judged to be whole and sound, I began to look forward to a sequel. My motivation was heightened and spurred by the plethora of theories, supporting research and experiments that scholars and students of the conscious ego were publishing. In the wealth of their findings and propositions were to be found keys to aspects of enabling and therapeutic practice that had had rather skimpy notice in our period of immersion in psychoanalytic theory and its (sometimes questionable) application. They unlocked and opened doors and windows to considerations of the powers of knowing and understanding—cognition—in shaping behavior, and, further, the inextricable connections between acting-doing-making-to-happen and the human being's sense of self-actualization and self-esteem.

How, then, to help people—at whatever level of their capacity—to go from "feeling better" to "seeing better" to "doing better," how exercise their ego muscles, so to speak, how help them to know themselves as actors, not just as acted upon, as decision-makers and doers in the ongoing problem-solving that all living requires? This, I felt, was what we caseworkers needed to make central to our pursuit of practice knowledge. But it would require study and the time that study demands to read, to test against one's professional experience, to winnow, to connect and fit together. So study I did. Paradoxically, it was a pursuit that richly nourished but also consumed me.

And there were further diverting temptations. Compelling was the invitation to act as consultant to the St. Paul Family-Centered Project, of which Alice Overton, skilled, prescient, totally committed, was director. This was an experiment dealing with "multi-problem," often "hard-to-reach" families typically passive or "acting out" in their efforts at coping. For them action, out of impulse or desperation, preceded considered knowledge or thought. The result was more often than not self-destructive or futile. The challenge was to develop means by which to teach more effective coping; some of the means toward this, such as the partialization of the problem-to-be-worked or the focus upon engaging the client in what was at the center of *his* attention and feeling, were already in use, drawn from my book (no. 1 in the bibliography). So the project was for me in part a testing ground for further applicability.

Along with this, and not unrelated, was my continuous quest to identify and evaluate the impacts upon personality growth and behavior that were palpably present in people's everyday living, in their experiences of love and work, their interpersonal and person-to-task transactions. My book *Persona: Social Role and Personality* (no. 3 in bibliography) was one product of that exploration.

Thus my apologia, my rationalization, perhaps, for failing to cope with that second book on problem-solving. I had too many irons in the fire—or was it too many fingers in too many pies? I tried to console myself by cliches: "Well begun is half done"; "The end is inherent in the beginning" and so forth.

Suffice to say, when I was invited to present a paper on "coping" I happily took it on in some hope that it might serve as a précis of the book-to-be. Instead the article grew to distressing proportions—and you will be glad to know that in including it here I have cut it considerably. Here I focus upon one partial means involved in problem-solving: that of rehearsing a client for his out-of-the-interview work, his "home work" on one aspect of his problem. (The idea and use of rehearsal for some action was an old one for me in my practice, as I indicate in one of my earliest writings, no. 12 in my bibliography, but at last I had found and put together the theory that supported it!)

My hope is that despite its deletions the piece still maintains some unity, coherence and emphasis, and that it will explain and

illustrate such developments in the psychology of the conscious
ego which lend themselves to expanding our helping repertoire.

Coping is so common a term in
everyday speech that we use it loosely. Because it involves so many
everyday behaviors, it has been little observed, examined, or
analyzed as a process. Yet it is a process of central interest to anyone
in the helping professions, simply because it is at the point of
inability to cope that people reach out for, or are sent to get, help.

Inability to cope may be acute and transient or chronic and
entrenched; crisis situations are characteristic of the former; long-
extended maladaption is characteristic of the latter. The reasons for
the inability may be open and obvious, such as actual deficits of
resources or instruments in a person's environment. They may lie in
the person's own endowments—in deficits, disturbances, or distortions in the cognitive-affective system called the ego. They may inhere in the input-feedback transaction between the person and his
psychosocial realities. Whatever the locus of difficulty, whatever the
nature of the problem, the applicant for help says, in effect, "Help
me to cope." This is his implied intent, far more often, I daresay,
than "help me to change." If, indeed, clinical social work "is a
process used by certain human welfare agencies to help individuals
cope more effectively with their problems in social functioning,"
then the pursuit of the dynamics involved in coping is social work's
unavoidable task.

Coping is a person's effort to deal with some new problematic
situation or to deal in some new way with an old problem. Its
purpose is mastery or problem-solving at best; it seeks to reduce
tension and at least to ameliorate the problem. It is a process in
which we are engaged from birth onward at levels of the unconscious, the preconscious, and in full consciousness. As with most
behavior, combinations of strategies and mechanisms from among
the levels tend to be involved in varying degree. In the large,
unconscious coping strategies have been known as "mechanisms of
defense" (among which the defense called sublimation holds much
that is yet to be delineated and understood in relation to coping). At
the preconscious level are all those almost automatic modes of

Presented at the Fifth Annual Institute of the New Jersey Chapter of the National
Association of Social Workers, October 1974. Published in *Social Casework*, vol.
56, no. 4 (April 1975). Reprinted here (with minor modifications and abridgements)
by permission of Family Service America.

behavior by which people habitually keep their balance-in-movement; these are readily called into conscious awareness. Conscious coping occurs when the person is aware that he has encountered a problem that demands some differences in the way he deals with it and himself.

It is to conscious coping that this article is addressed: As used here, *coping* means a person's conscious volitional effort to deal with himself and his problem in their interdependence.

The faculties and strategies involved in the coping process are those of the ego.[1] It must be noted that despite the free and frequent use of this term and construct, the meaning of the *ego* has only begun to be explored and explained. What its powers are, how they operate, which functions are biologically determined and which learned are but a few of the questions currently being examined, limned, clinically observed and described, and, in a few instances, experimentally tested.

For many reasons the protective-defensive operations of the ego have been more clarified than its grappling-learning operations. Even among the former, the pathological uses of defense are better understood than their uses in the process of coping. In addition to ongoing rigorous biological-neurological and psychological researches into mental structures and processes, there is need for careful accounts by self-observing individuals of "how I solved" or "what is going on in me as I try to deal with" some problem, even if this accounting poses the constant dilemma of "the ego observing the ego." The faculties and strategies that constitute the ego have been named, listed, and grouped, but much yet remains unexplained. There is no choice but to limp forward with what knowledge-supports exist.

The main categories of ego functions are its clusters of cognitive, affective, motoric, executive, and intergrative operations. *Cognitive processes* have been in the recent spotlight, and such mental processes as imagination, recall, anticipation, control, and judgment in their relation to aspects of coping are under scrutiny. *Affective processes* seem better known in their problematic than in their constructive aspects—anger, anxiety, and guilt—and better understood for their powers than such affects as empathy, eagerness, and hope. *Action processes* present growing interest to researchers not only because external behaviors are observable

1. For some critical discussion of ego psychology, see Nathan Leitus, *The New Ego* (New York: Science House, 1971), especially pp. 3–37.

objectively but also because, for the subject, action makes thought and feeling "real."

This article is confined to conscious intentional coping because it is the main stuff with which we work. Conscious intentional coping is probably the major process in which we engage the client with whom we plan short-term treatment. It is clearly central to crisis-intervention. Even in long-term help, past the release of conflict-bound energies, past the necessary modifications of feeling and thought, there remain to be learned and practiced the strategies by which action-in-task and person-to-person relationships can be carried out more effectively.

Because this article is a preliminary exploration, I recall Freud's caveat in one of his lectures on ego psychology. "It will be difficult to escape what is universally known . . . it will rather be a question of new ways of looking at things and new ways of arranging them [rather] than of new discoveries."[2]

Let it be said at once that the use of the term *conscious volitional coping*—or its synonym, *volitional problem-solving*—does not mean that client and helper embark on a process of intellection, nor on some process of "pure reason" that moves in logical sequence from *a* to *b* to q.e.d. The frequent misconceptions about the nature of cognitive operations require a small detour here.

We have not fully taken measure of the obvious fact that those cognitive processes we call thought or thinking are charged with affective-emotional content. Thought is often heavily freighted with feeling; it is sometimes its product and sometimes its creator. We are the heirs of a Western philosophic tradition which, at least since Plato, has held rationality to be the mark of humanness. Toward that goal, it split thought from emotion. The former was held to be cool, cerebral, detached, ordered; the latter, visceral, involved, unruly. When Freud dared to open the Pandora's box of the passions and irrationalities in the human psyche, the cleavage between what human beings thought they thought and felt they felt seemed even more wide and unbridgeable than had been conceived of before.

Yet the means and the ends of Freud's therapy were to bring emotion and thought into workable harmony with one another, to bring powerful but unrecognized feelings into conscious awareness and to domesticate them, so to speak, by the gentling powers of

2. Sigmund Freud, "The Dissection of the Psychical Personality," *New Introductory Lectures on Psychoanalysis* (New York: W. W. Norton, 1965), p. 60.

relationship and by their exposure to thought, in its varied facets. His aim was congruence between the cognitive and affective content and workings of the mind in place of split or dissonance, because such congruence is the essential condition of personal balance-in-movement. "Where id was, there shall ego be" meant, so Freud's exegesists say, not that our powerful, irrational, and potentially creative drives would be expunged or cleansed out by therapy, but only that they would be subject to the ego's restructuring, directing, and mediating processes.

Long attached to the idea that emotions affect thought, we have tended to overlook the converse, known to each of us in his own experience: that thought may heavily affect feeling. If we perceive or think that someone we admire approves of us, we are likely to feel more comfortable, more worthy. If we learn or know that certain attitudes are usual and expectable in a given role or group, we are likely to feel more open toward them. If we believe or think that certain behaviors are heinous or forbidden, our feelings and our actions will be shaped and colored by those beliefs.

Thought consists both of content and process. Thought process consists of the ways by which content is taken in, stored, retrieved, assessed, reshuffled, organized, separated, or connected with other mental-emotional content. Thought content consists of facts, assumptions, ideas, images, notions, fantasies, memories, concepts, and beliefs. It is only necessary to begin to list the furnishings of the mind in order to become aware of how permeated each and all may be with emotion. Thoughts and feelings are in continuous interchange, the one affected by and affecting the other.

Some years ago, Heinz Hartmann wrote: "We do not share the malaise of our time . . . the fear that a surfeit of intelligence and knowledge will impoverish and denaturalize man's relationship to the world. We have no traffic with those who bemoan the mind as the 'adversary of the soul.' "[3]

In our long concern with the "psyche," we have tended to overlook its interconnections with the mind. We have learned, and learned well, to draw out, attend to, and explore feelings with sensitivity and compassion. By those processes we have provided many therapeutic experiences: the release of tension, the support of an emotional alliance, the defusing of fears and guilt, and so on. But we have given short shrift to the thought content and

3. Heinz Hartmann, *Ego Psychology and the Problem of Adaptation* (New York: International Universities Press, 1958), p. 65.

processes which might have been the cause, not only the consequence, of such affects. There has been an assumption that cognitive distortions or disturbances are the product of affective disturbance and that, therefore, feelings had first to be worked over in order to enable the person to think straight. Certainly this assumption is valid in many instances. But it is also true that ideas based on incorrect or insufficient information, beliefs derived, for example, from earlier experiences, are among the contents of cognition that may rouse or create emotional reactions of considerable intensity.[4]

Thus, a helper must continuously address himself to the cognitive accompaniments of feeling. ("How do you *see* this event?—or *understand*—or *explain* this feeling? What were your expectations? How do you see the difference between then and now? What seems to you to be good . . . possible . . . usual? Can you see any connection between what you said and how he acted?") These kinds of questions to the mind, so to speak, bring forth the interwoven connections of thought and feeling and open the opportunity for such corrective cognitive grasp that may result in our much-valued "corrective emotional experience."

Cognition and affect ego functions—thought and feeling—affect the executive function—action; turned about, action affects thought and feeling. Because coping is an active process, the uses of action in helping people are of major concern.

"Thought," said Jean Piaget, "proceeds from action."[5] In his observations of the development of babies, he saw that the genesis of thought resulted from the active manipulation and experience with objects. Freud described thinking as an experimental action. That this *interiorized action* (Piaget's term) may involve difficult and complicated work is known to anyone who has changed his mind, who has set himself to learning, or who has consciously reorganized his thinking or considered a series of alternative actions. Such interiorized action is almost always involved in a conscious decision to cope.

There is among ego psychologists a markedly growing belief in the potency of action and its effect upon the personality system in

4. For research and discussion on the cognitive antecedents of emotion, see Richard S. Lazarus, *Psychological Stress and the Coping Process* (New York: McGraw-Hill, 1966), pp. 254–57.

5. As quoted in Henry Maier, *Three Theories of Child Development: The Contributions of Erik H. Erikson, Jean Piaget, and Robert Sears and Their Application* (New York: Harper & Row, 1965).

both its developmental and dynamic aspects. In her studies of children's coping, Lois Barclay Murphy concludes that "I do" is the precondition to the sense that "I am."[6] That this observation is not limited to children can be attested to by any adult whose doing, whether upon a puzzle, or in a verbal exchange with others, or in some form of physical activity, yields evidence he has been "a cause," that he has made something to happen. If that happening is judged to be good, his thought and feeling about himself as doer, as maker, is good—and vice versa. Erik H. Erikson's postulates on identity formation as the product of active involvement in age-appropriate role tasks and Robert W. White's propositions about the person's sense of competence and confidence arising from experiences of the self as effective in action are in complete consonance with the idea that action is how people "realize" themselves, how they know and feel their subjective and objective realities.[7] Hartmann put it thus: "Action is also one of our most efficient instruments for the development of insight or knowledge."[8]

"I do, or make to happen—therefore I develop a sense of who and what I am . . . I am good or bad, effective or incompetent, as shown by what and how I do . . . I am subject to or able to influence the action of others, as shown by the reactions and outcomes of my behavior"—all these expressions of feelings, visceral experiences, conceptions, emotional charges, and interpretations all at once of the self and others, of subjective and objective realities—all are created by taking action.

The implications within these executive functions for clinical work become fairly obvious. To cope with a problem is to intentionally undertake some form of action upon it. Such action may be the modification of thought or feeling that occurs in the verbal inputs and feedbacks of an interview. Or it may go further— to the taking of one small step within the orbit of the problem

6. Lois Barclay Murphy, *The Widening World of Childhood* (New York: Basic Books, 1962). For her discussion of action and the development of the sense of self see chapters 14–17.

7. Erikson's concept of identity and the factors in its development were first presented in his *Childhood and Society* (New York: W. W. Norton, 1950) and have had expansion in most of his subsequent books. Robert W. White, in *Ego and Reality in Psychoanalytic Theory, Pschological Issues*, monograph 11 (New York: International Universities Press, 1963), presents persuasive arguments for the existence of an "effectance drive," a drive to be a "cause."

8. Heinz Hartmann, *Essays on Ego Psychology* (New York: International Universities Press, 1964), p. 39.

toward modification of one's own behavior, or another's, or of a condition. The test of the use of changed feeling or thinking is in action, in the person's being able to *do* differently. Even in intrapsychic problems, the test of being better or feeling better is that the client's active coping with self in relation to others or with his life circumstances is more effective or is less consuming of psychic energy. His actions, not simply his introspective examinations, inform him of the reality of his betterness. Feeling and thought affect action, and conversely, action affects feeling and thought.

In clinical social work practice, there has been a tendency to underestimate the therapy of action—the values in the exercise of the ego's executive functions. This tendency has been the result of some questionable assumptions. One is that if a person feels better it will inevitably follow that he will act better; another is that if he understands better he will do better. But it is simply not true that appropriate behavior necessarily follows upon diminution of stress nor even upon the achievement of penetrating insight. It is possible to understand one's self and yet not fully grasp the expectations and requirements of external realities—or even know what to do and how to do it except as one explores what seems called for in order to cope successfully. Therefore, helping a person to cope requires, beyond explorations and reorganizations of feeling and thought and the objective realities, that there be a working over of the what and the how and, often, the why of *actions* to be taken.

No implications inhere in the concept of coping in regard to the nature of a problem, its simplicity or complexity, or even the nature of the client's ego strengths or weaknesses. The problem to be coped with at any given time, whether within one interview or many, may be as limited in time and nature as a schizophrenic patient's decision to attend a group meeting or an adolescent's agreement to get out of bed and accompany the caseworker to school. It may be as amorphous and extensive as an adult's complaint of his generalized lack of self-confidence, trouble in making friends, or difficulty in holding a job. The governing principle is that the greater the felt stress, whether from internal or external sources, the greater the necessity to carve out from the whole problem *some piece of it* that can be coped with.[9] It should be some part that, while connected with the whole, offers the

9. Re: criteria for partialization, see Perlman, no. 1, pp. 148–49.

possibility of focus and seems to the client to be encompassable. Thus, anxiety may be bound; perception, thought, and feeling may be concentrated; and some small action step may be rewarding.

Partialization of a problem permits, indeed provides, the exploration of it in depth. Rather than exploration over a wide range with the possibility of diffusion, floating anxiety, or loss of centeredness, there is an exploration of feelings and ideas and inclinations in relation to this part of a problem and to the possible coping means and resources that bear upon it. There is always the open opportunity to connect between this part and its concomitant parts or to shift to other parts.

The person asking for, or pushed into, help must be viewed as one who is trying to cope. His very presence in the interview, even if it is a reluctant one, means that he has taken a step toward some new approach to his problem. Even if in the past he has coped poorly, whether largely by costly, constrictive, defensive measures or by hit-and-miss impulsive reactions, he has been trying to maintain his balance-in-movement as he has encountered problems. Successful or not, he is seen and accepted as one-who-is-trying-to-cope. He is seen, thus, as a past and present and immediate-future *actor* in relation to his problem, not just as its passive victim and recountor. It is in his role as actor in relation to his problem that we validly make our working contract with him.

Because people come to helpers at a point of failure in their coping—whether that failure is due to an overload of externally imposed stress and deficiency or to intrapsychic disorder—we are all more wise about what Franz Alexander called "the failures of the ego" than about its past or potential competences.

The query (articulated, or held in the worker's mind) has tended to be, "Tell me what's wrong, how you have failed or been failed, of your mistakes and miseries." The client/patient wants to tell of these, of course; he needs to and so we help him to do so. But we ought also to give attention to how he has tried to cope: "Tell me what you've tried; why you figure it has not worked; in what parts of your life (past or present) you have been able to manage and have felt on top of things." *We have rarely taken histories of coping.* Most histories are of deprivations and failures, of "what happened *to* me," rarely of "what *I made* to happen, badly or well."

At the very least, some focus upon the client in his coping efforts will yield some understanding of the constriction or range of his conscious feeling, thinking, and acting capacities. Beyond this is the affirmation, conveyed by the helper's attitudes and queries, that the client is accepted not only in his needfulness, but also as a person still at work on his problem. The contract, then, is: "I will try to provide the aids, psychological or material, by which you can resume or enhance your coping capacities."

This focus does not deny that he may show reluctance or resistance. It does not deny temporary fragility or immutable dwarfing and underdevelopment of his ego. Nor does it deny the fact that every human being copes, badly or well, blindly or awarely, frustrated or rewarded, from birth to death and that self-respect and self-love (from which respect and love for others grow) rise and are sustained by the sense of being able, even in small part, to cope with both interpersonal relationships and role tasks.

Along with this basic acceptance and respect for the client as a past and potential coper as well as a presently needful, distressed, or "copeless" person, the clinical social worker brings all his skills to the nourishment and exercise of the client's ego capacities for dealing with his present problem in small part or large. These methods can only be touched upon, although each deserves an article in itself. One coping exercise—the rehearsal for action—will be dealt with in some detail.

Ego nourishment has several sources. Probably the most potent is the relationship, with its steady reliable input of caring and concern and empathic alliance along with the actual or imputed power-to-help that is vested in the helper.[10] It lowers the need for defensiveness, reduces distress through sharing, and feeds into an expanded sense of self.

Further ego nurture may come from actual provision of necessary means by which to cope, or from the provision of essential information from which the understanding of the problem and its possible outcomes may ensue.

Simultaneous with such nurture is the exercise of the client's own ego functions—the drawing out and stimulation, by queries, comments, and suggestions, of the thinking-feeling-action functions that are involved in coping. The problem-solving model of clinical social work grew out of what were seen as the ego's inherent coping strategies. Among the helping methods that this model identified as being consonant with the ego's coping strategies were several that

10. Relationship has its mysteries; it is as yet not subject to measurement or even quality analysis and therefore it is disregarded in some treatment models. However, if no account is taken of some combination of love and power elements in any helping relationship it is difficult to explain why so many different kinds of therapy are experienced by the client/patient as effective.

may be found in subsequently developed clinical modes, particularly in short-term, crisis, and task-centered treatment models.

One such method is the early and clear identification between client and helper of the "problem-to-be-worked." Not the basic problem, nor the casual problem, nor the whole constellation of problems that may be offshoots of the nuclear one, but some one problem felt by the client as the most pressing at this time. Lazarus presents research that strongly supports the proposition that coping strategies can not be organized or directed unless "the agent of harm" (some problem seen or felt as hazardous) is named, identified, and located.[11]

The problem-to-be-worked may be a miniscule one, it may be transient, it may be suggested by the social worker (when, for instance, initial resistance may constitute the initial problem to be worked over before the client will move to identify the problem for which he needs help).[12] What is important is that affect should be invested in it.

A second helping strategy, mentioned earlier, tailored to the tendency for the ego's perceptive functions to narrow and rigidify under stress, is that of partialization.

Another strategy that "works" the ego functions relies on inputs by the helper that stimulate the client to try to see connections and relationships between what he feels and what he thinks and how he acts, between what he does and its consequences, between then and now, between his actions and the feedback he gets from those who are its targets, and so forth. Clearly, this strategy requires considerable activity on the part of the helper beyond attentive and responsive listening. It requires tentative and jointly exploratory questions and comments that call upon thinking—upon recalling, speculating, trying to make sense of, selecting, anticipating outcomes, and choosing among alternatives.

How extensive these exercises are and how consistently repeated, or how brief, will be determined by all the considerations of person-problem-place. What is important is that the client be kept

11. See Lazarus, *Psychological Stress and the Coping Process.*
12. Should the reader possibly be interested in "how the problem-solving got that way," I add this note. My most recent (1986) publication, which seeks to explain this "coping" model, is recommended chiefly because its foot and end notes present my most inclusive accrediting of those "to whom I owe." It appears in Turner's *Social Work Treatment* (no. 80 in the bibliography, pp. 245–65; page 266 was added without my knowledge).

at work on his problem, not just as one who tells about it, not just as one who deposits it trustfully in his helper, but as one who is held to be able to take part in its modification—as one who has the right but also the responsibility to take some action to affect it.

To take some action, to know what to do and how to do it, is perhaps the most vital experience for the person himself. To take externalized action, however, often requires considerable preparation. It is this aspect of helping to which special attention is given here, because it is a process that has had little attention in clinical literature and practice.

A rehearsal for action seems to be indicated when the client must take some unfamiliar steps or must deal in some different way with another person or some aspect of his problematic situation. It could be as small an action as a woman's telling her husband that she has applied for marriage counseling or as big, depending on the client's feelings, as how to deal with her husband's probable reaction. It is a corrective action we aim toward—action that has some better chance of successful outcome than previous trial-and-error efforts. The aim is to help the client operate not in habitual or impulsive ways but by some planned strategy, by some conscious self- or situation-management.

Corrective action does not happen just because the client has placed the problem before his helper and vented his feelings. Nor does it happen because he and his helper are agreed that certain action ought to be taken. It often requires a preplay in preparatory ways, an exercise of the capacities for perception, anticipation, imagination, judgment, self-observation, awareness of the other, choice, and other ego processes too. Perhaps the one generalization that can safely be made is that the greater the client's emotional disturbance, the smaller the action-task should be and the greater the necessity for rehearsal between client and helper within the emotional safety-island of the interview.

Rehearsal for action is a common prelude to competent ego functioning. When a "good coper" anticipates having to deal with a new or difficult situation, he goes about it thus: He tries to marshal the available facts, to put together a picture, a mental representation, of what the situation and encounter will be like. He imagines it, calling upon whatever actual knowledge of it or of situations like it he has known before. He tries to put himself into the shoes of the "other": to anticipate what it will be like or will feel like and what the other may say or do or expect of him. He fantasizes his own behavior in the imagined circumstances, his own feelings and how he will handle them, what he will say or do and how he will respond if. . . .

In that fantasy, he tries to select behavior that seems most likely to get him what he wants or to get him out of what he does not want. So he weighs and judges alternative actions by anticipating their probable outcomes. This process may take hours or days of rumination and indecision, especially when thought and feelings are in conflict. Times of heavy stress and tension can make anyone feel unable to handle the reality. At such times, perceptive capacities may be distorted or narrowed, anxiety signals may run loud and high, and the need for defenses may paralyze the person or catapult him into frantic but fruitless activity. Then, any one of us may turn to another—a friend, a relative, a professional helper—for guidance.

Beyond wisdom and caring, the helper must guide the client through some active problem-solving steps—sometimes in a one-time discussion and sometimes in several. His perceptions may need to be clarified and reclarified: The naming of the nature of the problem in its objective and its subjective aspects and in their interplay is essential, as is the release and consideration of complicating feelings. The nature of the difficulty in coping is another consideration, as are ideas for solution, the possible actions to be taken, resources needed, problems to be anticipated, and so on. In such discussions the ego's capacities are all at work.

The insistent question, "What to do, now, at once?" must be faced. The more acute the problem is or is felt to be, the greater the drive to take some action, to discharge accumulated tension by doing. It is a commonplace observation that when people see and feelingly realize their problem they tend to seek release from it in motor discharge, in doing something. Whatever form it takes, there must ensue a sense that something is being made to happen. The selection of a next step or of an immediate target of action lowers the overload, it makes focus possible, it may temporarily bind the anxiety and raise the hope of manageability.

In usual clinical practice, some small piece of joint or separate action is often agreed upon. The client will go to the school, talk to her mother, try to keep a list, and so forth. But the next interview too often reveals that somehow the plan was not carried through, or it came out all wrong; or, worse, there may be no next interview. Why? One possible reason is that the client, left on his own to take an action that is different or new, tends to fall back into the coping ways he has habitually used, which may be problem-creating in themselves. So the good helper—social worker or trusted friend and advisor—would do well to take him through an anticipatory, imagined experience.

What should *rehearsal for action* consist of? There should be an agreement between helper and client upon one small bit of homework for the client. It should have immediate relevance to the part of the problem presently the center of attention. The helper must introduce the consideration of how it might be done. If it has not been tried before, is it because the client has felt conflicted about it? Afraid? Unknowing? If it has been tried and has ended in failure, what is the client's opinion of the cause of failure? Is it the other person or situation that proved intractable? Does the client want or need the helper's intervention with that other?

The helper's input is not simply the injection of these queries but also the empathic response to the affects that accompany the replies. Along with this continuous responsiveness and support, the helper may offer tentative or direct suggestions about different possibilities, along with comments and questions to stimulate the client's seeing in his mind's eye how what he does may work (for or against him); how the other person may react; how this will affect him; what alternative ways are open to him; what the outcome may be for him, and so forth.

This preparation for homework may occur in a verbal interchange between helper and client. Or it may be done by role-play, with the caseworker taking the part of the other and the client practicing on him or, turned about, with the client acting out the meanness or imperviousness of the other and the helper demonstrating as simply and clearly as possible what a desirable and feasible strategy might be. The mode chosen may be a matter of personal capacity and style; not all clients are free to role-play, any more than all are able to put their amorphous feelings and thoughts into words.

What follows is a simple example, one of my own tryouts.[13]

Mrs. M is at a family agency complaining of her adolescent son's school truancy, inaccessibility, indifference, etc. She was sent by the school social work counselor. She had begun to be helped in the first

---

13. In my original publication I erroneously called this a simulation." It is, rather, the account of the interview as close to its actuality as notes recorded immediately thereafter could make it.

interview to put her finger on her problems with Mark, and to express both her anger and sense of defeat, to describe how she has tried to cope (scolding, threats about his future, etc.) and how futile it has been. Asked about Mark's father, who had separated himself from the household several years ago, she brushed him off as an influence on Mark. He pays child support regularly, and Mark sees him about once a week.

I had responded empathetically to Mrs. M's worry and frustrations with comments on how "natural," how "understandable" her reactions were. We agreed that Mark as well as Mrs. M would need to be talked with—possibly Mr. M, too—but that could wait for later.

I ask what she herself most wanted right now, and she quickly says she hopes we could "change Mark." I laugh and she joins me as I say we all wish we had magic wands to wave against problems. I suggest that she and I need to consider some things further before we try to reach Mark.

In our second interview I ask whether she has told Mark of her coming to the agency. No, not yet, but she will, as soon as she gets home, or as soon as she catches him. Then she launches into a diatribe on how he does not come home at mealtimes, and so forth. From her recurrent anger and helpless frustration, I can foresee that, well-meaning though she may be, her coping with the boy, if only to get him to the agency, will be virtually the same as it has been up to now. She will present the agency as a threat or as some reforming force. Her son, embattled, will refuse her outright or arrive at the agency locked in suspicion and resistance. So the first problem to be worked on is how to get one major actor in the problematic situation to be an applicant for help. How, then, is the worker to enable the mother, the co-actor, to deal with the task of telling the boy about applying for help? How help her to experience some modicum of success with this small but crucial step?

Rehearsal for what she will say and do is a safeguard; it is also a small ego exercise.

CW: Will Mark be angry? Or surprised? Or scared when you tell him, do you suppose?
Mrs. M: Probably, probably—sure! I wish he would be scared. Maybe then he'd act different. Mad, I guess he'll be mad.
CW: Well then, do you think he'll want to come here?
Mrs. M: I don't care if he wants to or not. He *has* to.
CW: Can you actually force him to?

Mrs. M: (*Looks thoughtful and dejected*) Can you people force him?

CW: Actually we can't. But let's suppose we could. How do you suppose it would feel to him?

Mrs. M: Like I said, he'd be sore.

CW: When you're sore, do you feel like talking to someone, trusting them?

Mrs. M: Probably not. No, you don't.

CW: Can you see why we want Mark to not be afraid of us or mad at us before he even gets here?

Mrs. M: M-mm yes. I guess so. . . .

CW: . . . or why it might be a good idea to try to work out some way that might make him feel you and we are for him, not against him?

Mrs. M: (*Brightly*) Should I say you have a good job for him?

CW: Is it true?

Mrs. M: No, but. . . .

CW: Let's think together about what you could say that would be one hundred percent true—because you don't want to fool him. . . .

Mrs. M: Right. I guess. . . .

CW: . . . and that wouldn't send the two of you into a fight again. Okay?

Mrs. M: (*Shrugs and and looks puzzled*)

CW: Let's suppose you're Mark. Can you get into his sneakers?

Mrs. M: (*Silently wiggles about uncomfortably, smiles slightly*)

CW: . . . and I'm you. What would you want to hear from me?

Mrs. M: Well, no hollering, that's for sure.

CW: That's for sure. And—?

Mrs. M: Well, maybe something like—(*long pause*) I am worried about him?

CW: That's good! So he'll feel you're not just mad at him but you're worried, too. You feel for him.

Mrs. M: Look, I do feel, I used to feel for him.

CW: You've put a lot of feeling into him.

Mrs. M: That's for sure! And, brother, what a pay-off!

CW: That's been rough on you. We'll want to talk a lot more about that. But now we've got to work on Mark's getting here.

Mrs. M: Okay. So I'll say I feel for him and for me too. So I came here for both of us, to see if both of us could—could act better.

CW: That's good! You're saying to him, "The trouble is maybe me as well as you."

Mrs. M: Maybe. . . .

CW: Maybe yes, maybe not. But *he* must think so.

Mrs. M: Oh, sure, he thinks I'm too strict, too mean, I'm a terrible mother, he thinks. . . .

CW: What would happen, do you suppose, if you said that to him?

Mrs. M: Said what?

CW: That you feel he thinks a lot of things are your fault.

Mrs. M: He'd probably say "right!"

CW: Could you take that?

Mrs. M: Listen, I've taken plenty already.

CW: You have, it's true. Could you go on from there to say, maybe, something like maybe both of you have faults? So you've been in a war together and you're trying to work out a little peace together?

Mrs. M: Well, I can say it. . . .

CW: Try it, on me.

Mrs. M: (*Does so, somewhat embarrassed, repeating worker's words*)

CW: Sounds pretty good! Does it feel honest-to-God to you? Could you try it on Mark?

Mrs. M: I guess so. Mark will probably fall dead, if he listens, I mean.

CW: If he's surprised, that's all to the good. It'll be a break in the old routine, right? If he brushes you off, and he might, come on back and we'll talk about it. We'll see what else we can think to do. Okay?

Mrs. M: Okay, I'll take a try at it.

What has happened here? First to the negatives. This rehearsal has taken a lot of interviewing time, far more than just shaking hands on something the client agrees to do. Some other areas in an interview may have to be left unexplored if one is to keep within realistic time limits. But this time is well spent in the longer run because it prepares against time lost or potential client loss subsequently in resistance or dropout. If a client comes back it is always possible to return to uncovered ground.

A second negative is that there is no certainty that a rehearsal for action may not fail. Who can foresee or control all the variables that impinge upon a person as she emerges from the best-conducted interview? But nothing has been lost and possible gains may have taken root.

The gains may be multiple. The client has been engaged not simply in telling about her problem but in actually working on it, in experiencing herself not only as a problem-carrier but also as a beginning coper. Furthermore, if the social worker permits the client to fail, anticipates that the best laid plans may not work, it becomes possible for the client to return with minimal malaise. At the very least, she can be given recognition for her effort. She can be and feel accredited for her intent, if not for its outcome. With this support, she may feel ready for a reappraisal and a different effort.

In this simple illustration, it is possible to see a number of ways by which the worker readied the client for action, that stimulated the client's own coping capacities. The caseworker placed the immediate problem-to-be-worked before the client: how to engage the significant other, and how to cope with what might be an immovable object in the way of problem solution. To this end, a number of small, partial coping tasks were put forward for the client to work-over: first, anticipation of the boy's expectable reaction; then, some judgment as to whether this reaction would yield desired results; then, because the client was still perceiving the situation through her hot anger and was perhaps secure in it because she had the caseworker on her side, the caseworker presented the reality that the boy could not be forced into help.

Then, the caseworker asked if the client could empathize, could feel into the other. Could she perceive more clearly why a different form of behavior on her part might be necessary? The client's perception shifted, albeit reluctantly, and the worker offered partnership in thinking of a new way. The client was asked to picture, identify with, and take the role of her antagonist. Could she, from his perspective, think and feel what he might respond to? Grudgingly the client shifted roles and thus discovered and produced a different strategy of approach. Some restructuring of her thinking was involved. The worker rewarded this effort with honest praise along with recognition of the mother's hurt at the hands of her son.

The worker held firmly to the task at hand, and the client, apparently supported by the worker's empathy and recognition, went forward to fantasize how she might do what she must do. Again, she got an emotional reward. As is expectable, the regressive steps the client made when the ground on which she has stood seemed to be shifting under her can be seen. "Maybe," she said. The worker asked her (perhaps too quickly) to take the role of her son again. She dug her heels in and could perceive only his unjustifiable meanness. Then, the worker put in, tentatively, a surprising suggestion, a new "thought": that the mother consider an alternative mode of approach. "What would happen if. . . ?" It involved some mental and emotional maneuvering on the mother's part to take it in and to become aware of both her feeling and thinking so as to bring them into line with the suggested action. To that end, the worker proposed that she take mental action on it, a rehearsal. She tried, uncomfortably, but well enough so that her effort merited praise. Perhaps doing it, hearing herself, objectified and modified her feeling; perhaps the caseworker's positive response gave her some hope or sense of potential competence; at any rate she was able and willing to take the risk of a small but different action in dealing with her son. The partnership that followed includes the possibility of failure for which joint rework was promised.

This example of rehearsal for action shows several things. First, a rehearsal for action is, in itself, coping work. It prepares a client for greater rather than lesser success in the small next steps he may have to take in his problem-solving effort. It consists of the exercise of some of the ego functions involved in dealing with the people and circumstances that are problematic. A by-product of such a coping exercise within an interview is that the person's ego capacities, their resilience and range (or their rigidity and impoverishment) are revealed for assessment in relation to treatment means and goals.

There are few problems or dilemmas that can be resolved by ready-made solutions or soul-quakes. Even the sudden illumination of insight or the freeing release of emotional catharsis leaves the person with the question of how to cope, now that he understands or feels better. Thus, most problem-solving goes forward, small piece by small piece, through the conscious, effort to try out new or modified ways of behaving, thinking, and feeling.

What has been exemplified here is one step toward what must be our continuous, critical, curious, and untiring explorations of the failures—and the wonders—of people's coping.

1989 AFTERWORD

In a recent essay review of a new book Frederick T. Melges, M.D., professor of psychiatry, Duke University, comments: "a future orientation is fundamental to coping . . . *Rehearsals* [emphasis mine] of future situations and emotional tuning to them is an important aspect of psychotherapy. Most patients come for psychotherapy because they are demoralized about their futures. Rather than address this problem by just digging into their pasts, we should learn to help them reshape their images and plans of the future."[14]

I remind us: the future begins a minute from now.

14. Quoted with permission from *Readings: A Journal of Reviews and Commentary in Mental Health*, vol. 3, no. 1 (March 1988), © American Orthopsychiatric Association, New York.

5

FREUD: AN APPRECIATION

1989 FOREWORD

As I reviewed the essay that follows I was struck by two quite disparate "contributions" to present-day social workers it proffers. One is its revelations of psychological aspects of life in its end phase; the other is a reminder to us social workers of some vital parts of our professional roots.

For reasons familiar to us all social work has never before in its history been so heavily involved in the provision of services and solace to the aged as it is today, and bids fair to be for years to come. The demands upon us for consistent compassion, for patience, for flexibility and ingenuity are persistent; the rewards often as small and fragile as are those with whom we work. Eager as we are to "change" and "cure" we must often settle for more realistic and limited goals, and the latter depend heavily upon our honest facing of the expectable, even inevitable losses and lapses that drain the old-old or the sick not-so-old. The sense of self-worth diminishes as sensory acuity fails, as cognition becomes clouded, as physical and mental capacities for self-direction and self-governance grow weak or unreliable; self-respect shreds away and with it self-love. That there are remarkable instances of the achievement of integrity no one denies but they are "remarkable" because they are few rather than common. So we who are still in full possession of vigor and health, physical and mental, must keep sensitized, tenderly attuned to those who know and feel chiefly their deficits.

In *Freud: Living and Dying* we are given a vivid if partial account of how a giant among us dealt with his old age, harrowed by constant pain, exiled from home and his familiars, hampered by losses of such elementary functions as chewing and swallowing food. And one stands in awe of his unflinching self-observation, his honesty, his anguished but sound rationality. What one sees further is the final act of self-determination, the final assertion of self-possession—his choice of the time and means of his ending.

So—of what use is it to read and know of this? Only, I suppose, to know and share, deeply in our veins and our hearts, yet once again, a universal human experience as it was suffered, borne, assayed, and dealt with by one of the greatest among us.

The second—and totally different—"use" I hope the essay may serve is that of reminding us of one of our profession's deep-running roots, indeed, of our own personal roots.

If I may paraphrase an essay of my own, written a full generation ago: the influence of Freud upon every one of us is all-pervasive, all but impossible to calculate ("Freud's Contribution to Social Welfare," nos. 29 and 5 in the bibliography). So permeated have we become with the seedlings that were blown or drifted out from that small study in Vienna that we can scarcely know in what ways we would have been different had Freud not lived. The ways we behave, the meanings we read into human motivations and behaviors and attitudes, our judgment of what is funny or sad, good or bad, healthy or sick, the total mental-emotional vocabulary of even those who do not know of Freud—all these and more derive from him.

It is not important to the appraisal of Freud's contributions that many of the ideas and assumptions that guide our professional practice and personal lives today have been developed, revised, creatively variegated by the men and women who followed upon Freud and by those who took radical difference from him. He was their fountainhead, their reservoir. Nor is it important to determine whether his discoveries were all "true" in any absolute sense—whether, for instance, a "death instinct" does exist, or whether the Oedipal conflict is indeed the core of present-day neurosis. Columbus was not less a discoverer because he mistakenly thought that a small Caribbean island was Cathay. He opened the way to the Americas, and fired the imaginations of others who were enabled to venture further or by different routes. In the same sense that Columbus was a discoverer of terrestrial space of which European man had only some vague idea so Freud may be said to have been the discoverer of inner space. He too may have taken an island to be a continent, and he was surely not the first to recognize that, within the bounds of the human body, the mind and spirit hold volcanic islands and dark seas. But he was the first to dare to explore those unknown realms, and to risk himself by setting down when he understood and believed. And thus he lighted up and reshaped man's conception of his inner world.

We social workers are among his progeny, whether we recognize it or not. All of us need now and then to remind ourselves "to whom we owe," whose were the giant shoulders we climbed upon in order to see what he saw and, sometimes, beyond. This is the point or "use" of the essay that follows.

He was a princely man—set apart by his towering intelligence, his dignity, his personal autonomy, and especially by his mastery of himself. He had no tolerance for cheap yielding to popular pressures or easy evasions of reality problems. Self-critical, self-analyzed, self-controlled, self-possessed, he was able to pour that self unstintingly into lifelong productive study and work and at the same time to give of himself—his grave and tender concern and his gracious attentions—to family, patients, students, and those intellectually and emotionally attached friends who turned to him repeatedly to be rekindled by the fire of his creativity.

When the time came after sixteen years of acute discomfort and agonizing pain, of being eaten alive by cancers in his mouth and jaw, he asked that he be released from life. His good and faithful physician helped him into his longed-for end. So he died like a prince, too, by his self-determined decree, dignified, grave, spared those demeaning, dehumanizing weeks when death takes its own exquisitely torturing time.

That was Freud. His devoted friend and physician was Max Schur, himself now dead before the publication of his book, *Freud: Living and Dying*. Adding to the already prolific literature of fact and myth about Freud (a proliferation which in itself attests to the admiration, ambivalence, and activated imagination he inspired in those who knew him or his works), this book holds special interest for several reasons.

Essay review of *Freud: Living and Dying*, by Max Schur, M.D. (New York: International Universities Press, 1972), in *Social Service Review*, vol. 47, no. 1 (March 1973): 109–13. ©1973 by the University of Chicago. All rights reserved.

It is bound together by the dark filaments of illness, death premonitions, losses of loved ones, and the life threats of two wars (with the Nazi menace threatening death of the mind-spirit, not just of the body) which threaded through Freud's life. Death is a fact of life. Everyone among us, as he comes to middle age, knows the repeated anxiety and anguish of sickness and death among those we have held close; and, with each separation, we die a little. So it is instructive—at the very least, interesting—to trace through how a giant among men felt and thought and behaved in the face of these common human circumstances, common to all of us, banal in their usualness, inevitable, yet for each of us charged with fears and *angst* and sometimes a sense of helplessness and utter loss. These days, even the young have become obsessed with death in some attachment to the idea that, if life must end in nonbeing, then life itself is "absurd" or meaningless. Believing this, they annihilate the hours and days of their vital being and becoming. In recent years, too, the question of how to help the dying person has become a major concern of all those professional helpers who deal with dying patients and their families. And lurking beneath the professional concern lies the ever present personal one: How shall I, myself, die? How shall I manage ending with some dignity and integrity, with some self-possessed relinquishment of myself? To all these conscious or unconscious interests and speculations on preparations for and dealing with the end of living, the contents of this book give pause and stimulation.

Some forty years before his death, Freud commented on the evasions to which the terminal patient is subject. "The art of deceiving patients is certainly not a very necessary one," Freud wrote. "I hope that when my time comes I shall find someone who will treat me with more respect and tell me when to be ready." In 1923 Freud's first cancerous growth was recognized. Surgery (of a most inept and brutal kind) followed. His own physician reported that Freud had asked him for help in "disappearing from the world with decency if he were doomed to die in suffering." Sensitive as he was to the trauma of a child's death to the parent, he was deeply concerned lest his death would precede that of his mother. But actual death was not to come for sixteen more years. In those years, Freud knew death intimately and in many forms. For his proliferating cancerous growths he had more than thirty operations. They were often followed by complete physical exhaustion; they were always followed by agonizing pain. He lost a daughter and a deeply beloved grandchild; he was involved empathically in death losses among his friends; and, in the 1930s, all about him, under the rise of Naziism, he saw evidence of the collapse of the civilization he valued and the disappearance and suicides of people he knew.

Through all of this, Freud revealed himself as a man hurt and ravaged, as any feeling human being would be, despairing sometimes, but rising resolutely to his own sense of dignity and self-possession. When, for instance, the Nazi storm troopers invaded his home and the prospect of torture and annihilation seemed imminent, his daughter Anna suggested that, like many other Jews in that time and place, they should commit suicide. "Why?" asked Freud, half indignant, half ironic, "Because they want us to?" Later, brought safely (and wearily) to England, he wrote to Ernest Jones, "Two prospects keep me going these grim times: to rejoin you all, and—to die in freedom."

"To die in freedom"—death freely willed or freely accepted, this is the final measure of human dignity. When Dr. Max Schur first became his physician in 1928, Freud, honest and direct, set up a contract of understanding with him. Schur writes:

> He showed his readiness to establish a patient-doctor relationship based on mutual respect and confidence. Before telling me his history or present complaints . . . he expressed the expectation that he would always be told the truth. . . . He then added, looking searchingly at me, "Promise me one more thing: that when the time comes you won't let me suffer unnecessarily." All this was said with the utmost simplicity, without a trace of pathos, but also with complete determination. We shook hands.

More than ten years later, when he was eighty-two years old, after thirty surgical excisions, scarcely able to chew or swallow or speak, the time came. Schur describes it:

> Freud took my hand and said to me ". . . you certainly remember our first talk. You promised me then not to forsake me when my time comes. Now it's nothing but torture and makes no sense anymore." I indicated that I had not forgotten my promise. He sighed with relief, held my hand for a moment longer, and said, "I thank you," and after a moment's hesitation he added, "Tell Anna about this."

When he was again in agony, Dr. Schur gave him a shot of morphine and another one twelve hours later. Freud did not awaken from his sleep.

So, self-owned to the end, he chose his time to die. And so his good and wise physician helped him to an immediacy of encounter and embrace that is the prerogative of the few. One thinks of the "heroic measures" contrived by modern medicine that mercilessly prolong the labor of dying and, bit by bit, reduce the human person to an agonized animal. And one ponders the thought, rarely spoken aloud in our society, of the responsible human being's "right to die," to cry "Enough!"

No facile interpretations should be put on Freud's asking for death. He had, it is true, hypothesized a "death instinct" in some effort to bring psychological processes into congruence with biological processes, which move inexorably from growth to decay and death. Indeed, his talented and devoted doctor, Schur (an internist who early had been a student and admirer of Freud's and who, after Freud's death, became a leading psychoanalyst), struggles to make some compromise with this (to him) unacceptable hypothesis. He traces carefully Freud's long history of premonitions of his own death time and of his almost superstitious beliefs (under the influence of Fliess and perhaps of Freud's Hassidic ancestry) that certain dates and numbers have life-and-death significance. Schur attributes much of this premonitory anxiety to early cardiac symptoms in Freud and some other physical malfunctions that may have kept the "fear of death" renascent in him. (Anyone who has know tachycardia or other heart symptoms, whether organic or functional, knows death anxiety.) But there may be other reasons, too, why Freud, long before cancer set in, was afraid that his time was running out. He was literally aseethe with ideas, observations, sensory memories and impressions, and electric connections between literature and life, between consciousness and the unconscious, between the individual and the group. He was sensitively attuned to every level and layer of human experience. And, although he worked all day every day and far into the night until well into his middle years, there simply was not enough time for him to pursue all his thoughts, to say what he had to say. So it is surely probable that he was plagued by the constant fear that he would not have time to finish and fill in the grand design and tapestries of the human personality he had begun to weave.

As for the "death instinct": just a few years before his death (and while he suffered constant pain), Freud wrote, "I believe I have discovered that the longing for ultimate rest is not something elementary and primary but an expression of the need to be rid of the feeling of inadequacy which affects age, especially in the smallest details of life." Perhaps that was one of the many ideas he had too little time to pursue.

In his eighty-second year, he wrote to Princess Marie Bonaparte: "The moment a man questions the meaning and value of life, he is sick, since objectively neither has an existence; by asking this question one is merely admitting to a store of unsatisfied libido to which something else must have happened, a kind of fermentation leading to sadness and depression." There, again, spoke Freud the realist. For "meaning" and "value" are surely not inherent in or "promised" by the accident of life. They are subjective interpretations, a consequence of a person's input and the social outcomes of transactions that yield rewards and satisfactions, and/or recognition, and/or gratification—or, unhappily, do not. "Value" and "meaning" are not to be found in passively awaiting their revelation or in renunciations of either responsibility or involvement of the self with other people and tasks. They are, rather, the product of responsible effort and putting one's self "out" and "into" what Freud called "object relationships." Freud knew this experientially as well as intellectually.

Beyond the interest this book holds about how a giant among men faces and deals with dying, it reveals the emotional and psychological problems of aging as expressed by Freud in his personal correspondence with close and loved friends. For that growing army of geriatric specialists today—social workers, physicians, psychiatrists, "senior center" personnel, and so on—it may be useful to look and listen carefully to a great man aging. Freud's aging, it is true, was made more than usually difficult by his being literally eaten away both by cancer and by the necessary repeated cutting-away surgery, to the point where he wryly wondered whether he or his cancers would take over his life. His hearing was damaged; he had other transient physical disorders; his difficulty in chewing, swallowing, and even speaking made him, he felt, unfit to join with others socially; his heavy dependence upon physical ministrations of his doctors and his daughter saddened him; and, finally, in the last year of life, he was torn up from his long roots by the need to flee the Nazis.

One lists all this and knows that, while in its detail it is special, in its general form it is frequently the fate of the everyday man as he ages. If we live long enough, as Freud himself commented, the mind fails the body or the body fails the mind. In either instance, there are the "thousand small disgusts" (Erikson), the multiple insults to the aging person's sense of self and his sources of gratification. Chief among those insults to the personality are the failures of the body—those that cause pain or discomfort, those that cause embarrassment, those that cause a dulling of the senses so that blurred or distorted messages come in from the outside, those that hamper communication and relationship. They have not, it seems to me, been given enough respect and attention by gerontologists. There has been, rather, some tendency to gloss over the usual and almost inevitable decrements of old age with euphemisms and excess cheer, with talk about "golden years," and "hobbies," and "sun cities." These are valiant efforts (and it needs no Freud to explain some of the denial inherent in them) and neccessary, too. Yet, perhaps we need to face the fact that sadness in old age is inevitable, and some disgusts, too. Renunciation (one of the "virtues" of old age that Erikson speaks of) cannot be accomplished without some mourning for what has been lost; frustration is natural, "normal" when the mind's commands are unheeded by nerves and muscles; serenity (which Dr. Schur found characteristic of Freud's attitude in his last years) is often achieved only at the cost of withdrawal of libido and the aged person's disengagement. But let Freud tell what it was like for him:

On his sixty-ninth birthday: "A sense of indifference is slowly creeping up around me. . . . It is a natural development, a way of beginning to be inorganic. . . . The change taking place is perhaps not very conspicuous; everything is as interesting as it was before . . . but some kind of resonance is lacking."

In his late seventies: "There is so much capacity for enjoyment within me; thus I feel discontent with the enforced resignation [due to his illness]. . . . My mood is bad; very little is to my liking; my self-criticism has become much more severe. In someone else my diagnosis would be senile depression."

On a proposed birthday celebration: "The celebration evidently has sense only when the survivor can in spite of all wounds and scars join in as a whole fellow; it loses the sense when he is an 'invalid' with whom there is no question of conviviality."

At seventy-nine, in response to a birthday tribute: "Life at my age is not easy, but spring is beautiful and so is love." And in response to another friend: "Although I have been exceptionally happy in my home, with my wife and children . . . I nevertheless cannot reconcile myself to the wretchedness and helplessness of old age."

But Freud had one great difference from the run-of-the-mill man: aging, he was still a genius. He had been endowed from birth with high and exquisite intelligence, with talents of observation and communication, with creative imagination, with continuously self-replenishing vigor and drive to know, to grasp, to explore, to examine and experiment with ideas. Despite the wounds and scars he had suffered from those who were contemptuous of his theories and/or his ethnic background, he came to his old age having had a life experience of self-actualization and of love, recognition, and admiration by men and women who themselves were acclaimed in the Western world. He aged, moreover, with no sign of deterioration in his mental powers. Despite his losses of hope and energy, he was able still, in his seventies, to write his brilliant *Civilization and Its Discontents;* in his eightieth year, to put the finishing touches on his monumental *Moses and Monotheism;* and, in his last pain-wracked year, to put out his lucid *Outline of Psychoanalysis.* He was, in short, far more than his oldness or sickness. His life thrust, his total involvement in his work, his undiminished intellectual powers were in him superordinate to the forces of decay and disease. Is this, one wonders, given only to the great? Can "integrity" rather than "despair" (Erikson's polar terms for the crisis of old age) be achieved in the last years by lesser men?

Freud: Living and Dying serves to raise these and many other questions and speculations about life in its wintry years. Those who have read Jones's biography, especially volume 3, may find many repetitions in this new book, partly because the author, Dr. Schur, provided Jones with much of the information about the last ten years of Freud's life. But Dr. Schur makes a particular contribution by his focus on the aging process and its emotional freightage, to the disease process (perhaps in its detail of more interest to medical than to lay people), and the interplay (and sometimes incongruence) between Freud's death superstitions, his death theory, and his pre-death personal behavior. The book is a meticulous account by a man who knew, loved, and revered the patient who was his master. It is a book especially for those who know Freud's work and now want to know more deeply the man who, subject to ravages of his all-too-mortal flesh, was yet able to maintain the integrity and nobility of his spirit.

1989 AFTERWORD

I had had the good fortune once to attend a seminar with Anna Freud, when she had come to the University of Chicago to be honored. While I knew that she could not possibly remember me I felt emboldened to send her a copy of the preceding review. She responded at once, with gentle gratitude, but further with the comment that I had written as if I had actually known her father. She had been uneasy that people would not understand (Freud's self-determined choice of the conditions of his death)—but now felt reassured by what I had expressed.

I am sure she must also have been aware of and hurt by the at first insidious and then blatant "debunkings" and bludgeoning of Freudian thought that followed upon Freud's death. Not only were many of Freud's theories being challenged or rejected but some of his personal-emotional and intellectual quirks or misjudgments were being exposed.

It helps only a little to remember that debunking is all but inevitable when one has been made a figure for idolatry. Indeed, it has seemed to me that whether in religious or political or philosophic thought it tends to be from the most blindly worshipful that the scales fall from the eyes with the loudest clatter. And I remind myself that it was Freud himself who had long before foreseen and explained how it is that the sons must kill the father. Perhaps, too, the discovery that one's idol has feet of clay is in part an effort to regain balance between the extremes of thesis and antithesis.

Whatever the reasons, whatever their validity, the fact remains that every one of us in the western world carries some imprint of Freud's thought. The best of it will not be shaken off easily. Even the chaff will be found to hold seeds for further consideration. He will not be silenced.

6

THE CLIENT AS WORKER: A LOOK AT AN OVERLOOKED ROLE

1989 FOREWORD

This essay was written a decade ago, but it possibly holds more interest to social workers today than when it was first published, for reasons that will be touched on further. It was, in fact, the outgrowth of a twenty-year-old chapter on the psychological meanings of work, explored in my book *Persona: Social Role and Personality* (no. 3 in bibliography). That essay was probably the reason for my being invited to become a part of the working group convened by Sheila Akabas and Paul Kurzman which produced their benchmark book, *Work, Workers, and Work Organization.*[1]

As former students and readers of mine will attest (whether with praise or protest), I have for many years searched to identify and analyze the "social" in social work practice, to heighten our awareness of the psychological meanings and impacts that penetrate and shape us as we carry on our here-and-now daily work and love interchanges and transactions. Until recently work had scarcely been examined by social work for its psychodynamic content. Interestingly, it was by Freud that I was spurred to explore the psychology of work. "Work," he wrote, "has a greater effect than any other technique of living in the direction of binding the individual more closely to reality; in his work he is at least securely attached to a part of reality." Then he adds (he, the totally immersed, indefatigable worker!), the "natural human aversion to work gives rise to the most difficult human problems."[2] Is it true? I asked him in my frequent imaginary conversations with him. Is there such a "natural aversion"? And I was tempted to quote his beloved Shakespeare to

---

1. Sheila Akabas and Paul Kurzman, eds., *Work, Workers, and Work Organizations* (Englewood Cliffs, N.J.: Prentice-Hall, 1982).
2. Sigmund Freud, *Civilization and Its Discontents* (London: Hogarth Press, 1949; republished by Hogarth 1963, 1975; also New York: W. W. Norton, 1962).

him—"If all the year were playing holidays, to sport would be as tedious as to work." Instead I went off on my own explorations (some of which will be found in the studies and commentaries listed in notes 3–11).

I was, then, delighted to have been offered the opportunity to join the Akabas and Kurzman group to think on the problems of present-day workers and the connections to be found between these and social work's services and programs.

By now the sociopsychology or psychosociology, the nature and conditions of work and the workplace have undergone what is nothing short of revolutionary changes. The rise and spread of technological and mechanical means and the resultant decline of jobs involving heavy physical drudgery, the swelling numbers of women, wives and mothers among them, claiming their "equal rights" as workers, and spreading the conviction that work outside the home and for money payments is a desideratum—these alone, among other factors, have shaken up many formerly firm beliefs and values. Remarkable for the swiftness with which they have taken place are the changed socially enlightened attitudes of employers who seem increasingly ready to consider and put into effect such working conditions (flexible time, for instance) and provisions (pregnancy leaves, for instance) as will promote family well-being and (it is presumed) worker morale. (I keep wondering if Florence Kelly and Frances Perkins and Josephine Shaw would ever have believed it!)

In the planning and usage and evaluation of such programs and benefits the profession of social work ought logically to be involved, beyond our already established functions as caseworkers with "problem" workers and their families.

A number of schools of social work today offer courses, even specializations, in the "world of work." Moreover it is expectable that marital and parent-child relationships and behaviors cannot avoid being affected, for good or ill, by the many adjustments that occur as an accompaniment of "making a living."

So one turns once again to understand and assess and, when necessary, deal with the several roles that each of our clients carries, not the least of which is that of worker.

It is an interesting omission when you stop to think about it. The omission, that is, of our attention to the objective conditions and subjective meanings of work in the lives of people who become the clients of social workers. Their problems may fester in their self-to-others relationships; in their self-to-task involvements; in their self-to-circumstance difficulties; and work may encompass them all for a major part of each day.

"To be able to love and to work" is held to be the mark of adult maturity. Attributed to Freud, it is a criterion generally agreed upon. "To love" has been central in the interests and therapeutic focus of all of the psychodynamically oriented professions, social work among them. The forms and faces of love manifest themselves in infinite variety and have been explored and explained as subjects of study and clinical help for many decades.

But the many faces of work have had scarce attention. Mostly our attention has been given to the problem of *no* work, or unemployment, enforced or voluntary. No work or irregular work and the complications that result have been a subject of concern in social work, and are seen as a problem of personal or social dysfunction, and the need for and wish for it (in one form or another) have been viewed by us largely in economic terms.

Work has been central in human life since "Adam delved and Eve span." From the time of leaving school (at whatever educational level) to the time of retirement (chosen or mandated), most men and a rapidly increasing proportion of women are employed in paid work. A major portion of their waking time, and energies, and of their conscious effort and attention is invested or absorbed by what we still call "making a living." The forms that making a living—work—take are multiple and varied. The conditions it sets, the demands it makes, the rewards or punishments it metes out, the drudgeries and stresses it imposes, or the stimulation and nourishments it offers—all these are reacted to and coped with more or less satisfyingly by the worker. His or her feelings, attitudes and ideas—about self, about Life (thus, with a capital L), about today and tomorrow, and behaviors, both on the job and in after hours, are likely to be significantly influenced by daily experiences at work.

Published as chapter 5 in *Work, Workers, and Work Organizations: A View from Social Work,* Sheila Akabas and Paul Kurzman, eds., © 1982, pp. 90–116. Reprinted by permission of Prentice-Hall, Inc., Englewood Cliffs, N.J. The version herein has been abridged by cutting and small revisions because of space limitations; however, the main ideas and issues keep their place.

The live human being is an integrated, complex "system" in continuous active interpenetration with the other persons and circumstances. What he feels, thinks, does in any salient segment of his daily life may, in great or small degree and in benign or noxious ways, permeate the other segments of his life. When what he experiences is emotionally charged it reverberates into the inner recesses of his being.

Thus, work may enter the marriage bed. The man who feels physically and psychically exhausted by his day's work may have sexual dysfunctions that are only secondarily related to love or "techniques"; the woman, resentful at having worked all day and then having had to pick up the kids and the groceries and having slapped together some dinner and fed and bedded the children, may be quite unresponsive to her husband's sexual overtures. Work may enter parent-child relationships. The father, bridling under his foreman's watchfulness and criticisms, may take on the tyrant role himself at home. Work may be so taxing, with so few and meager rewards that the family—wife, children, old parents—is blamed for it. They are the slave-lash—"I do it for them." Or, in reverse, work may be so totally engrossing that it all but obliterates interest and emotional investments in other persons who need or reach out for attention and caring.

Until recent years a "worker" was usually a man. In family casework agencies, he was usually the unseen but often complained about husband and father. In child guidance clinics, in school social work offices, in children's hospital wards, he was seen only rarely. He was the father of the child, but his work role seemed to have precedence over his parental role. In relief-giving organizations, it was the husband and father who lost his job and looked for work, but it was the wife and mother (in casework's early days) who applied for "the welfare." In marital, debt, illness, and child-behavior problems, it was almost always the woman who came as applicant for help. She had the time. More important, women's "right" to dependency, to complain, to ask for help was taken for granted. For men to ask for help—especially from a woman—was a disgrace. Their wives went to the social agency, while they sought work or the company of other men who shared the misery of unemployment.

There were and are many kinds of problems for which help is sought that are unrelated to economic needs. The working man was able to keep his distance from them in two ways: (1) he actually could not take time off from the job to come to the agency or clinic; and (2) work—as is often still the case—offered him an escape, a valid defense against being responsible or involved in problems of child-rearing, household management, or the many other difficulties of marriage, parenting, and homemaking that were (and, in certain sectors of the population still are) held to be "woman's business." So, social workers rarely saw the family member who worked.

Another major reason for our scant attention suggests itself. Caseworkers feel—not without reason—that they have little entree into and little power in the world of industry or business. This is particularly true when the world of work is so megapolitan, bureaucratized, rigidly structured—when the individual employee is so remote from his employer—that the work place appears alien and forbidding to the social worker. It is often not even understandable, much less navigable. Our occasional interventions with employers in the client's behalf have occurred when businesses were small and the employer and employee knew one another. This is more rare today. The fact is, however, that there are a growing number of possible intermediaries representing the employer or the union—personnel officers, foremen, supervisors, shop stewards, psychologists and social workers in counseling positions—who, if and when necessary, can be approached on behalf of a client who is an employee. Yet, quite aside from whether such intervention would be wanted or needed, the caseworker often feels uncomfortable in this unfamiliar territory. (Did he not choose his own profession, indeed, in part because he rejected these many aspects of big business—its mechanization, competition, depersonalization, and motivation for personal profit?)

Another major reason for our uneven perspectives and insights into people's experience of work lies in the jumble of paradoxical and ambivalent social attitudes that have arisen about work within the past several decades. Like all other members of their society, social workers are culture carriers, subject to the shibboleths and spirit of the times. So they are often unsure of what they think or believe or even know about the uses of work in the lives of most human beings.

Several decades ago, the worker's reactions to work became a central interest of a number of sociopsychological researchers, resulting in many published studies. One is aware, as one examines these, of a range of contradictory findings, of questions unasked or unanswered, and of sometimes hidden (unconscious) values held by the researchers that might have colored the responses.

Contradictory findings must, of course, be expectable, since "work" is so infinitely varied in its purposes, its conditions, its demands, and its rewards. Add to this the infinite variations in workers themselves, and there are further complexities. One study of workers in industry, for example, found that work was not a "central life interest" for three out of four men.[3] (What was? Nobody asked.) A study of professional nurses, on the other hand, indicated that four out of five considered work and the workplace as their central life interest.[4] The difference in findings are, of course, explainable by a number of variables. Moreover, what a study "shows" may be picked up because it supports a personal conviction and may be cited and widely publicized as though it were definitive.

As for unconscious bias: Is it possible, for instance, that routine or automated jobs disturb the researcher to some greater extent than the worker—and that such aversion is conveyed in the attitudes and queries of the interviewer? Is it possible, further, that questions about gratifications or frustrations on the job have been insufficiently separated out from all those other sources of gratification or frustration that human beings carry? That, for instance, unhappiness at home or about life in general may be projected into the job, with some expectation that work will—or ought to—make up for other felt love-status-reward deficits? Or that for the person who reports dissatisfaction with work there needs to be considered its fantasied and actual alternative? In short—the existent research on work raises as many questions as it answers, and offers support for almost any position taken in regard to work's meaning in present day life.

In the 1960s, on the tide of new views and versions of the human condition, there rose to prominence the concept that work must be "meaningful." "Meaningful" has rarely been explicated for its meaning. "Creative" is another frequently used desideratum, but this, too, has its ambiguity. It poses any number of practical questions, among which would be what prevalence of creative capacity

3. Robert Dubin, "Industrial Workers' Worlds: A Study of the Central Life Interests of Industrial Workers," *Social Problems*, vol. 3, no. 3 (January 1956), 131–42.

4. Louis Orzack, "Work as a Central Life Interest of Professionals," *Social Problems*, vol. 7, no. 2 (Fall 1959). The studies in *Persona* and in *Work, Workers, and Work Organization* are both reprinted in E. O. Smigel, *Work and Leisure* (New Haven, CT: College and University Press, 1963).

is assumed to exist in the population and how many opportunities exist or can be "created" in the world of work for the original and idiosyncratic inputs that creativity implies.

In the introduction to his popular and much-cited collection of interviews with workers, Studs Terkel says that their search was "for astonishment rather than torpor."[5] That is hardly surprising. Which of us, at work or elsewhere, does not hope for that leap of mind and heart at discovering the unusual or experiencing mastery? But realistically, how often can peak experiences—those of astonishment and wonder—occur? There is no question but that certain kinds of work (working with people, for instance) provides far more instances of surprise and unexpectedness than work with things that are routinized, mechanized, completely predictable. But the fact to be faced is that for many essential jobs in today's work, there are only small rewards in the execution of the task itself. The saving remnant may lie in the presence of other sources of "payoff" or satisfaction that attach to the work. These will be touched on later. Here we note only that we tend to deplore situations that fall short of an ideal and run-or-the-mill work is among them.

There is, furthermore, a prevalence of certain obvious inconsistencies in our thinking about work: for example, at the same time that work is deplored as "dehumanizing," "alienating," or "exploitative," there is a great hue and cry against early retirement of workers. Some of the concern about mandatory retirement is due to the financial difficulties the retiree may encounter. But most of it seems to be related to its deleterious psychological effects upon the worker—the loss of role, loss of association with fellow workers, loss of purpose and place. Suddenly, it seems, at the point of retirement, certain vital "meanings" in work make themselves manifest!

A like inconsistency is revealed in the push by and upon women to enter the labor force. Side by side with studies and opinion pieces on the tedium and depersonalization of most work, there stand the persuasions and demands that women be given open access to it. Homemaking and child-rearing are held to be less "meaningful," less "creative" than—what? Selling notions? Being part of a typing pool? The fact is that the roseate promise held out to women about the work world is largely a promise to middle-class, college-educated, "liberated" women. Most women who go to work go into nonastonishing jobs. So do men. Are these meaningless?

5. Studs Terkel, *Working* (New York: Pantheon, 1974), p. xi.

In rough sketch: work is a human being's activity that produces something of value to other people. Needed or wanted by others, it serves a social purpose. Thus it is rewarded by some form of payment—most often by money, sometimes by social recognition, at best by a combination of both.

To work is to carry on certain tasks under certain stipulated conditions. The means and conditions by which such tasks are to be dispatched are provided by the employer, as is the compensation for the time, energy, and expertise provided by the worker. The bigger the employing organization, the more likely it is that this contract of reciprocal rights and responsibilities is explicit, standardized, guarded, and negotiated by the workers' organization—the labor union.

Today's worker enters into highly structured systems. Quantity and quality of goods and/or services must be produced or distributed within a specified time, by specified methods, subject to overview and evaluation by the employer or his representatives. Since most work tasks are interdependent with those done by other workers, timing output, quantity and quality, interpersonal relations, and job-appropriate behavior are continuously subject to requirements, appraisals, and approvals. These characteristic conditions of work in the modern world, often a source of difficulties and dissatisfactions among workers, have been extensively described and documented.[6]

(Note: In the original the complaints and explanations to researchers from workers were set down in some detail. In excising them I list their essence: "robotization"; boredom at repetitive and fragmented processes; expectations regarding rewards unfulfilled; dislike of "bossy" authoritarian superiors; inflexible time schedules; jobs are "dirty" or held in public disdain.)

There is no one among these that does not have some validity. Yet—how is it that most workers, most of the time, grumbling and griping as they go, seem to want to be employed? All everyday evidence supports that conclusion—with, of course, the probability that most workers would welcome a better paying job, a more interesting and less demanding one. Recent studies report that the great majority of present-day workers are "satisfied with" or actually "like" their work.[7] How so?

6. *Work in America: Report of a Special Task Force to the Secretary of Health, Education and Welfare* (Cambridge, MA: M.I.T. Press, 1973), p. 3.

7. In 1973, an "overall response" to polls that asked about satisfaction or dissatisfaction with the current job revealed that over three-fourths of the workers queried reported themselves to be "satisfied" on the job. See John T. Dunlop, "Past

The most obvious gratification that work provides is money. Today's wages and salaries purchase many luxury items—television sets, cars, washing machines. (One is immediately aware of how swiftly yesterday's "luxury" becomes today's "necessity.") It buys commodities that ease drudgery, facilitiate tasks, or add variety to the day's living, and it buys release from work's humdrum by providing vacations, social contacts, and leisure-time occupations.

Other benefits, present and future, are bought by working. Old age and health insurance and unemployment compensation are public provisions; corporations and large private organizations offer pensions and health insurance supplements; and for the unionized worker, there are legal and credit aids, health and housing services, educational and recreational opportunities. Beyond these tangible economic benefits are more subtle psychological ones. "Money talks." It says, among other things: "What you do is valued." While this may be a source of disgruntlement when a worker feels he or she is financially *undervalued*, it is in general a social affirmation of "value received." It has often been noted that among volunteer workers, whose major gratifications come from the rewards of interpersonal recognitions and their inner sense of contribution to the well-being of others, there often crops up some expression of resentment that their work is not truly "valued," because it is not paid for in "hard cash."

Beyond money, work holds a number of further incentives and satisfactions. One is reminded of what Conrad put so trenchantly into the mouth of his Charlie Marlowe: "I don't like work . . . no man does—but I like what is *in* the work—the chance to find yourself. Your own reality. . . ."[8]

"What is *in* the work," is the gist of what follows.

and Future Tendencies in American Labor Organization," *Daedalus*, Winter 1978, p. 89. Similar findings by other studies are reported in Rosabeth Moss Kanter, "Work in a New America," in the same issue of *Daedalus*, p. 54. In a 1965 study of "happiness," nine hundred men averred that "work is of crucial importance" to their happiness. One-third of unemployed men report themselves "not too happy," compared to a little more than one-tenth of employed men. See Norman M. Bradburn and David Caplovitz, Reports on Happiness, National Opinion Research Center (*Monographs in Social Research*, vol. 3, 1965), pp. 14–15.

8. Joseph Conrad, *Heart of Darkness*. Marlow has been toiling over his broken-down old steamboat, and his full comment affirms a further often overlooked truth: "I had expended enough hard work on her to make me love her," he says. He is aware that investment of interest and energy created an emotional bond between the self and an "object."

A present-day social scientist, following his study of over fifteen hundred employed men, writes, ". . . work still remains a necessary condition for drawing the individual into the mainstream of social life. . . ."[9]

Basic to every individual's sense of personal security, of having a place and a purpose in the social system, is the experience of "belonging," of being connected with others in a regularized, reliable, established way. Work offers this sense of social bonding, both to tasks that are held to be socially valuable and to other persons with whom, interdependently, those tasks are performed. There are many facets to this phenomenon.

Companionship with fellow workers is one. As at least one study found, the daily social intercourse with fellow workers was the "most missed" aspect of work by men who had been retired.[10] Even though such on-the-job companionship may be maintained at a fairly superficial level of comraderie, it meets in part the need to be connected with others—whether to share jokes, to vent and share gripes, to counteract loneliness, or, at best, to provide a variety of relationships and a sense of support.

The development of unions and the increase of their power heightens the worker's sense of bonding with a group that is recognized as a force to be dealt with. It is possible that each worker takes into himself some sense of the strength that is provided by union with one's peers.

Away from the job, there are other kinds of social recognition and affirmation in a steady job. Like it or not, an adult in our society is "placed" and establishes some identity by what he or she works at. "What do you do?" "What's your work—your field?" These are questions, abrasive or courteous, that we all encounter early in an acquaintanceship. They are asked in an attempt to establish where a person stands in the social system and are based on the assumption that every adult "works at" something. And the man or woman who does not work (for pay, as volunteer, or self-employment) feels awkward and "out of it."

Students of personality development seem to be giving increasing recognition to the growth of the sense of selfhood and of identity security as a consequence of the active engagement of the person

9. Harold Wilensky, "Varieties of Work Experience," in Harry Borrow, ed., *Man in a World of Work* (Boston: Houghton Mifflin, 1964), p. 148.

10. Herman Loether, "Meaning of Work and Adjustment to Retirement," in A. Shostak and W. Gomberg, eds., *Blue Collar World* (Englewood Cliffs, N.J.: Prentice-Hall, 1964).

with other persons or tasks when what is made to happen is held to be "good," or desirable. The knowledge of the self as a producer, a maker, a provider or facilitator, an agent of some change, gives added dimension to the person when there is some evidence that what is done is needed or approved of by significant others. The sense of self as producing or as enacting functions that are socially valued accrues to one's self-measurement and self-regard.

Work gives form and purpose to the day. It regularizes and stabilizes a significant segment of each day; it mobilizes and channels each person's intentions and activities. Often the time, place, and purpose constrictions that work imposes seem irksome. Yet, as attested to by retirees and persons laid off from work for extended periods, it is common with the loss of work to experience a restlessness, an unsettled, unanchored feeling. The employed worker feels an intensified pleasure in his free time; the person who does no work (study and avocational interests which are goal-oriented must here be included) finds himself "killing time," uneasy about its drag or flight, annoyed to find that his freedom places upon him the burden of choices and decisions about what to do with himself. If work is not too stressful or consuming, it consti-tutes a reliable back-bone in the day of many persons—supporting, as it were, the body of their other, less-regularized activities.

Sometimes for good, sometimes for ill, work serves as an escape, a kind of defense against many of life's vicissitudes. By its very objective requirements, its regularity, or by the undemanding or underpinning relationships with fellow workers, it may serve to bind anxieties.[11] It may dilute the impact of other problems or help to suppress acute awareness of them. This has been suggested as one reason for the difficulty that social caseworkers have had in involving the working man in family problems. Aside from his sense that by his hard work and family support he earns the "right" not to be bothered with domestic affairs, he may also feel the fact that work and the diversions it offers protect him from the impact and import of family difficulties.

In quick sum: For the workers who constitute the four-fifths who report themselves mostly "satisfied," work holds rewards and gratifications beyond (but in no way discounting) money—interpersonal relationships, social status, and personal-identify-

---

11. A study of two matched groups of depressed women showed less impairment of overall functioning in those who were employed outside the home. Myra M. Weissman and Eugene S. Paykel, *The Depressed Woman: A Study of Social Relationships* (Chicago: University of Chicago Press, 1974).

supports, the stabilization of daily life, the provision of tangible benefits, and some psychological privileges. Polls and single-answer questionnaires do not provide insights into what "satisfaction" may exist beyond these rewards. Just as we know less about good health than about sickness, so we know less about the satisfied than about the dissatisfied or unsatisfied worker. We do, however, seem to have enough evidence of the worth and use of work in the lives of adults to be tempted to paraphrase Voltaire's irreverent dictum about God: If there were no work, it would be necessary to invent it.

Paramount in some problems, contributory in others, work penetrates and/or is penetrated by many of the personal-familial difficulties with which social workers typically deal. Roughly categorized, these are the most common:

1. Problems of interpersonal relationships—marital, parent-child, self-to-others, and self-to-circumstances wherein the wage earner's work is an unseen but often dynamic contributory factor.
2. Problems in work performance—where off-the-job circumstances may be cause or contributor, and/or where conditions in the workplace itself may be creating difficulties.
3. Conflicts and stresses in carrying two roles, particularly common for women, whose wife-and-mother tasks and outside employment impose multiple demands.
4. Unpreparedness for entry into the work-role—adolescents, disabled adults, and others.

The first of these problems may be seen in two brief case examples:[12]

Mrs. M came to a family agency for help, she said, in "saving my marriage." Young, attractive, the mother of one child and pregnant with her second, she felt there was "nothing left" of the marriage. Her husband showed only perfunctory interest in her when he came home each evening.

Mr. M did not respond to my invitation to talk things over. He felt marriage counseling was "unnecessary," even absurd. However, in a telephone call, he was persuaded to "take a chance" on one interview. He was a well-put-together junior executive in a large business organization. After my introductory sharing of the problem as his wife saw it, Mr. M still shrugged the problem off.

---

12. "Mr. Miller" was one of several interviews I held which were taped for teaching purposes by the Council on Social Work Education.

Mr. M: To me it seems trivial . . . silly. . . .

CW: Well, for instance—how about doing a sound-movie picture for me of one of your evenings at home?

Mr. M: Okay. When I come home in the evening she wants somebody to talk to, she wants companionship. And the job I have is not taxing physically. But it is taxing mentally, and especially for me, because I am trying as hard as I can to do the best that I can, so that I can get ahead as fast as I possibly can. . . .

CW: Mm—go on. . . .

Mr. M: And when I come home in the evening, I'm *tired*. Whereas she's been alone and quiet. I want an evening *alone*. I have been carrying on quite a bit of conversation all day long, and by this time I'm—well, sort of "sometimey." At work I am forced—not forced—but I mean. . . .

CW: It's in the nature of the job.

Mr. M: Right! I have to, you know, I have to be congenial, naturally, to the people around me. I meet customers and I have to talk to them. And you have to be on your Ps and Qs, and as I say, it's a *strain*.

CW: Um—hm. . .

Mr. M: *Always*. Because I'm trying to do as good a job as I can. At any rate when I come home in the evening I'd like to relax and I'm tired out. . . .

CW: You want to be left alone.

Mr. M: I want to be left alone. And this, of course, is the opposite of what she wants. . . .

CW: I guess you didn't even think of this when you got married.

Mr. M: Well, no, I sure didn't.

CW: What do you do? What job do you do?

Mr. M: I'm with X Corporation. I'm in training right now. [He goes on to describe in some detail his various responsibilities for the supervision and accounting for the sales and service personnel who deal with the company's customers.] At times it's a strain.

CW: You have to deal with other people all day long?

Mr. M: Right!

CW: You try to increase their production? Or. . . ?

Mr. M: I try to guide them—along general lines—I try to keep them on a straight course if possible. And I deal with customers, too.

CW: Do you think your wife gets the picture of the kind of situation you operate in during the daytime?

Mr. M: [Looks thoughtful.]

CW: I mean, have you shared with her what goes on, so she gets some idea of the strain you're under?

Mr. M: She has a general idea . . . but I don't think we've ever sat down and talked it over. . . . I never thought about it until now—to tell you the truth. . . .

Just this far, and the point is clear. This couple's affectional, compassionate, and even sexual relationship have been significantly affected by the husband's work life. It would be simplistic to assume that Mr. M's work requirements and ambitions were the single cause of the marriage rift. (But, it must be said, this is no more simplistic than the "sexual dysfunction" or "lack of communication" that is at times latched onto as *the* cause of a marital breakdown.) What is obvious is that for this man *work* is both a demanding and a consuming interest. It is a potent influencer of his attitudes and behavior. It is scarcely understood by his wife. It might, however, become a shared understanding between them, subject to their mutual exploration, perhaps conciliation, perhaps modifications of expectations and behavior on both sides.

A second brief example:

Mrs. G, my client, married eight years, mother of two children, came to talk about leaving her husband. Increasingly she was finding him "repulsive" sexually, dull, uncompanionable.

Uneducated and unskilled, he worked in a junk yard. He worked "hard" and steadily. He was a "nice" and conscientious man. His earnings were regular, though marginal. Nothing in the course of his work day offered him interest or stimulation; his only contact with other people was when they came to sell or buy the tires, bottles, metal which he sorted and roughly inventoried. He came home every evening exhausted, filthy, depressed, and sullen. Even after bathing, his hands remained cracked with dirt, his nails black and broken. They saw nothing better ahead. She could no longer bear the physical stigmata of his job nor the deadening effect it had had on his personality.

It is scarcely conceivable that this marriage, or indeed the life of the family, could be saved without full consideration of the work of this husband-father-wage earner, its noxious effects, his possible alternative work opportunities—and so on. Here again, work and its impacts may not have been the basic problem in this marriage. But "basic problems," we remind ourselves, are rarely accessible to ready change. Derivative problems, alive and potent in the present, such as daily work involvements, are far more open and reachable for modification. Thus "what's *in* the work" for each man and woman and its repercussions into other life roles cannot be ignored.

Work's repercussions are often seen and felt in parent-child problems. The man whose work day is too full of noise and disorder may demand "*Quiet!*" as he enters his doorway and is greeted by quarreling or even happily noisy kids. The woman who has "put in a hard day," even if it has had its compensations, finds herself furious that her adolescent children have neglected their assigned tasks; or she is too pressed to sit down with the youngster whose teacher has sent a note indicating that he is in trouble, and instead scolds: "I'll whip the daylights out of you if I get another note like this!"

Actually, we social workers need look no further than into our own daily work lives to recognize the often vital effects—sometimes benign, sometimes noxious—that work has upon off-the-job relationships and transactions. It bears repetition: Any role, the work role included, that excites feeling, that is charged with emotion either chronically or at crisis-points, will have its resonating effects into other aspects of a person's daily living.

There is, of course, the turnabout. Just as a person's work life may permeate other parts of his daily experience, so his troubles on the outside may be brought to the job. Worries and angers about relationships, debts and unmet needs, illness, the care and safety of the children—these and other concerns may so trouble the worker that job performance is seriously affected.

It is this concern that is probably the motivator for the growing interest by business and industry in utilizing social workers to deal with such problems. Whether such motivation is less "pure altruism" and more enlightened self-interest is not the issue. Primary is the plain fact that an unhappy, discontented, malfunctioning worker-on-the-job is likely to be an unhappy, discontented, malfunctioning *person*, and this is the concern of the social worker.

How much and in what ways is this work dysfunction due to the actual job realities—to the lack of fit, say, between the worker and his occupational tasks, to poor working conditions, to conflicts with supervisors or work-mates, and so on? How much and in what ways is the work dysfunction created or exacerbated by off-the-job circumstances? These are among the questions that the social worker must ask and answer to assess the work problem and plan for dealing with it.

A major concern to industry today is the high incidence of alcoholism. Whether this incidence is indeed an increase over what it was in the past is a matter for speculation, since facts are not available. What is known is the frequency with which "drink" as the "curse of the working class" has appeared in literature, reformist tracts, and historical accounts over the past few centuries. In any case, modern complex machines and high standards of work efficiency make drunkenness or its aftermath a greater hazard than before. Absences, irregularities, and accidents on the job are the offshoots of alcoholism. Not too long ago, it was assumed that job monotony and stress drove men to drink. Recently, addiction has been attributed to an individual's high levels of biochemical sensitivity to even a moderate intake of alcohol. Almost lost sight of today, however, is the old-fashioned and yet not altogether disposable possibility that problems in family life may play a potent part in the worker's seeking the escape that drinking proffers.

A major concern for social workers is those workers whose jobs may be most often invaded by problems from the outside. They are the most recent entrants into the labor force: women who are mothers of young, care-needing children. They fall into three categories: (1) mothers who seek the gratifications of work, yet are continuously hampered and harassed by home problems; (2) those who must work to meet family needs; and (3) those who are being pressed to work, chiefly because they and their children are financial burdens upon the community.

Despite the advances in recent years toward work equality for women, there remains a persistent inequality between a father-worker and a mother-worker. They may carry equal jobs or positions and earn equal wages or salary. But, with exceptions that are more rare than usual, the home- and child-care arrangements and tasks remain for the woman to take over on her return home from work. They are the traditional responsibilities carried by women: grocery- and meal-planning, clothing and household goods shopping; attendance on the sick or attention-needing child; arranging for dentist, doctor, dancing lesson, birthday party appointments; reciprocal aids and hospitalities and active participation in events, crises or celebrations, in the circle of family and friends. Such trivia can, by their pile-up, constitute a tensional burden that the worker-mother carries to her daily job.

Furthermore, unless there is some surplus of money, adequate home- and child-care services cannot often be bought. To work or not to work may become a nagging dilemma. Mothers who take on paid employment because they actually need the money carry a double burden. The child-care arrangements they make are usually in the homes of other women or in organized child-care centers. Either of these may be at some distance from home or the workplace. The time, energy, and strategies involved in covering these distances are not inconsiderable. The occasional crisis in the care-agent's household, a child's illness, a transportation breakdown—such difficulties cause absence or tardiness that creates tensions in the employer and employee both.

What gains or losses accrue to the children have only been guessed at. The "latchkey child" may run the streets until his mother returns home; the child who attends a well-run nursery or after-school center may be having an enriched learning and companionship experience. But dependable and adequate child-care facilities remain in short supply. At her paid work, the mother's home- and child-management difficulties may fester uneasily under the surface, sometimes causing her to make mistakes, to be irritable to customers or fellow-workers. After work hours, the accumulated stress may play out in family relationships.

Perhaps most problematic to large numbers of social workers is the usually spouseless mother "on welfare." Should she be pressed to work so as to earn some part of her maintenance, if not to get off the relief rolls? Recurrent waves of public opinion push for this, and the social worker is not immune to this pressure. But public opinion, and official social policy, delivers a double message. It says in one breath that child-rearing is a mother's priority task. At the same time, little attention or social approval is given to the work of rearing children, or to the handicaps of single parenthood accompanied by strictured funds, inadequate housing, paucity of educational and recreational outlets, and all the other handicaps to adequate family living that inhere in chronic hand-to-mouth poverty. Further—if mothering is indeed held to be vital to children's well-being, are there articulated, generally accepted criteria for its minimum requirements? Or "crediting" for the efforts—the work—that must go into their achievement? Is there public policy and general recognition that goes beyond mere sentiment for the resources that must exist to bolster otherwise economically and psychologically impoverished family life? And what are the payoffs, the incentives for the "welfare mother" who is urged to take an outside job? She will encounter all the problems of other working mothers. What will her compensations be? Minimal reward creates minimal motivation.

The recurrent issues involved in work for mothers on relief are complicated and of a magnitude that calls for large-scale policy reconsiderations and rearrangements. However, in the individual instances that caseworkers encounter, that need here-and-now help, these questions call for individualized discussion with each mother of the pros and cons, sacrifices and gains, wishes and realities. Essential in such discussion is the social worker's awareness and control of his or her own biases and inclinations and an informed, down-to-earth grasp of the specifics of what work life may offer and what gains and losses may ensue for the individual woman.

Yet one further group of work-related problems remains to be touched on. The persons who bear them are youngsters and adults at all economic levels. Their common difficulty is that paid work for them is blocked by some personal incapacity or circumstantial obstacles.

A heartening number of programs have been developed across the country for the retraining, rehabilitation, and vocational guidance of physically and mentally handicapped would-be workers. Many of these programs utilize social workers as counselors, as "influencers" of the family attitudes and behaviors that affect those of the prospective worker, and as resource persons for necessary services and aids beyond those that are directly work-related.

In hospitals, clinics, schools, and family agencies, social caseworkers frequently encounter patients, students, and drifters whose motivation to work is ambivalent and shot through with self-doubt and fears of others—people who are uncertain about work possibilities or about their own goals. They need several different kinds of help: to examine and come to know their own potential capacities and limitations; to become informed about the existing opportunities that will prepare them for work; to weigh and consider the realistic tasks, the behavioral demands, and the potential rewards in the work world.

Preparation for entry into the world of work ought not be confined to handicapped or unskilled adults. Many young people could also benefit from it. Especially for those youngsters who have spent their school days fruitlessly, "fooling around," "getting by," "serving time," to become a worker is a major role transition. Many youngsters have had few worker models to learn from; many want to earn money but have given little thought to what will be expected of them in return or what they themselves are able and willing to invest.

It is yet another indication of how little thought has been given to the role of work that while there has been a flurry of courses offered to high school students in preparation for marriage and for parenthood, few such courses are offered in preparation for work, which usually precedes those other roles. True, students in some schools do get "orientation" and work-training programs on how to behave in a job interview, how to fill out a job application, and other "how-to" guides. Underpinning these, and potentially of more basic value, there ought to be small group discussions on the facts of work life, of the ethos (not the "ethic") of the work world, of worker rights and responsibilities, of work requirements and opportunities.

No discussion of the interpenetration of work life and other daily life experiences can overlook the many instances of positive, supportive, gratifying effects of work in what may otherwise be dreary or disheartening lives. Two brief examples:

> Mrs. Y, a 55-year-old childless widow, has her ailing, emotionally dependent mother living with her. If it were not for her work (as "secretary" in a large typing pool), she would not be able to pay for the daytime helper who attends to her mother's needs and does the light housework. More important, perhaps, is that without work her daily life would be one of isolation and confinement. As it is, she goes off cheerfully every morning buoyed up by the anticipation, not of the pile-up of the innumerable small and boring tasks she must execute, but of the chit-chat at coffee breaks with "the girls," of the appreciations expressed by this or that user of her services for her speed, her clean copy, or of her new blouse or hair-do, of window-shopping at lunch, of her bowling evening ahead. Work, in brief, brightens her daily life with companionship and variety.

> Mr. Z is an insurance adjuster. At home is his mentally retarded little boy and his anxiety-ridden wife. He carries them both in the pit of his stomach, but during his work day he is relatively free of his dark sorrows. This is because he enters a world where he is regarded by his superiors as a competent and effective company representative. More-

over, he enjoys the variety of the customers he encounters, especially when what he does seems to be appreciated by them and found helpful. He is liked by his coworkers, several of whom he counts as friends, since they are sympathetic with his family problems and, in turn, often turn to him to talk over theirs. In his work, in short, he finds recognition of his capabilities and an affirmation from his superiors, peers, and customers that he is valued. When he returns home to confront its problems he carries in him some sustaining sense of having a back-up source that supports his spirit and steadies his feelings and behavior.

Why, one must ask, would it be desirable or helpful for the Z family's social worker (operating out of the pediatric neurology clinic to help the Z's deal with their damaged child with less anxiety and tension) to draw Mr. Z out about his work at some point in the course of their talks together? What purpose might such an inquiry serve in any case where the problem presented is manifestly neither a cause nor an effect of work difficulties, or where work is clearly an asset to personal and family stability? It is worth consideration. We are generally so continuously focused upon our client's failures and troubles that we seldom turn to encourage him to tell (and thus himself to hear and to know more fully) what his past or present areas of satisfaction are—where he has coped successfully, where he feels "good." Such a shared account, received with responsive appreciation by another, gives a person some heightened sense that he is more than just a helpless problem carrier. So, if it is not flagrantly irrelevant, and if one is in search of some place in the client's life where positives may be affirmed, his work adequacy and satisfaction may be worth talking about as a reinforcement of his sense of self as a "coper."

Whether the worker-client is helped by some social welfare agency or within the workplace itself, the caseworker's helping process is essentially the same. The clear identification of the client's problem for which he wants or needs help, the caring attention paid to his emotional investments or responses to it, the demonstration and assurance that the help is *with* and *for* him, the cards-on-the-table coming to understandings ("contract") about what real and accessible means and actions may be utilized—about who does what and why, the consideration of action alternatives and probable consequences, the guided choice of some next steps—

all these mutually discussed, reflected upon, considered and reconsidered interchanges between client and caseworker are generic to the problem-solving methods of casework. They are shaped, colored, varied by the individual situation, by the specialness of person, problem, and place.

The specialness of each person needs no discussion here. It has had extensive and intensive exploration in social work's value system and psychological knowledge. The specialness of the workplace and its rules and tasks (as is the case with the specialness of a school or a hospital system) and the particular problem centered upon at a given time—these are the substance of specialty. When the problem involves work or the workplace, it is incumbent upon the helper to know and understand its objective realities as well as the client's subjective sense of it.

Valuable as they are, counseling and guidance services are not always all that the client-as-worker needs. His problem often requires the finding and providing of tangible means. It may require changes or rearrangements of the circumstances or conditions that are inimical to his coping. It is often necessary, then, for the social worker to take an active lead in making the linkage or connection between the client and the resource he needs, and to set the necessary changes in motion.

"Active intervention," "linkage," and "advocacy" slip easily off the tongue, but they are processes that involve time, grasp of realities, and skill. There may be several different realities to be grasped. One is the nature and operations of the system to be dealt with. Another is the aims, views, and motivations of the persons who activate the system, since the fact is that all resources and opportunities are conveyed and controlled by people, who must be worked *with* and *through* if one is to influence what they will do and how they will act toward the client in whose behalf we intervene.

Thus the social worker's helping service goes beyond individual or small group counseling. He or she must often reach out to the client's "significant others," to those persons who are or who may be involved in the problem, either as contributors to its existence or as potential contributors to its easement or solution. They may need to be engaged both in some sympathetic understanding of the client and his special needs and in some willingness to lend themselves to meeting them.

It is often the case, then, that social workers in family and child agencies and in a host of other human welfare organizations may need to reach into the workplace both via the client's account of its relation to his problem and in direct negotiations with the employer, his representative, or union personnel. On the other side, the social worker in the union or industry may often need to refer his clients out to such available resources as are appropriate to his problem, and, beyond referral, to enable his client and those resources to successfully connect with one another. At the same time, and often in the same case, he may need to try to influence such persons and conditions in the workplace itself—the work environment, the "system" of peopled roles and arrangements, the "significant others," who, by their authority or attitudes, affect the client as worker.

It is this ecological perspective, this awareness of the continuous input and feed-back between people and the other people and the circumstances we call "environment," and the trained-in readiness and skill to influence the latter as well as the former that may be said to be the distinguishing mark of social work help. Perhaps this is what gives social work its special usefulness in any organization—the world of work included—that seeks to lower the obstacles that block a person's personally satisfying and socially satisfactory functioning.

One hears the echo of Conrad again. "What is *in* the work" for each man and woman, what chance it offers them to find themselves and their reality. This is what we need to know more fully and truly in every case.

7

CONFESSIONS, CONCERNS, AND COMMITMENTS OF AN EX-CLINICAL SOCIAL WORKER

I begin with a series of confessions. For a long time I was an active opponent of private practice because I could not see its social dimensions or roots. I have changed my mind about that. I must also confess that many years ago when I was chairman of the national curriculum committee of the American Association of Psychiatric Social Workers I fought for the abolishment of special psychiatric courses in schools of social work in order that *all* courses on the treatment of people with problems should be infused with psychodynamic knowledge. I have not changed my mind about that. I confess, though, I do wonder sometimes. I have come to wonder whether beyond basic generic preparation, specialization may not be the best way to develop and preserve and articulate higher levels of knowledge. But then when I see some of us, like Stephen Leacock's man, getting up on some maverick horses and riding off wildly in all directions I am prone to let out a primal scream. Where do we think we're going? I wonder, and why? and will we know our way back home?

I ought to confess, further, that some twenty years ago I gave loud voice and my one small vote to the merger of the American Association of Psychiatric Social Workers with the then American Association of Social Workers, in the hope that the professionalization and stature of social work might be enhanced by unification. I have had occasion to ponder on that a bit, too, of late. I was about to confess further, that I had been quite ambivalent about the emergence of societies of clinical social workers—torn between my persisting ideal that social work should be whole and my perception of occurrences less than ideal in the social work arena today.

Presented at the Second Biennial Scientific Conference of the California Society of Clinical Social Workers, October 1973. Published as Occasional Paper no. 5 by the School of Social Service Administration, University of Chicago, March 1974, and in the *Clinical Social Work Journal*, vol. 2, no. 3, Fall 1974. Permission to reprint granted by Human Sciences Press.

But I have come to believe that perhaps this banding together of clinical social workers may be a "saving remnant," may lead to a salvaging and solidification of the professional core of social work. Beyond this I will confess no further sins, whether of omission or commission. There is no time for the luxury of looking backward. So, without further ado I will jump into the cauldron of our today's problems-to-be-worked and from among many I will fish out one major concern. It is a concern to which every clinical social worker must give sober consideration.[1] It is a question to be answered or a problem to be solved for the pressing, practical purpose of interpreting ourselves to others—to legislators whose understanding determines our economic well-being or to the public at large whose understanding determines our survival as a profession. It must be solved, too, for ourselves, for purposes of maintaining or perhaps achieving the self-esteem and security that is a basic condition for a respectable place and status in society.

The question: If we accept the obvious fact that in many ways clinical social workers are like many other people-helping therapeutic professionals, are there any ways or areas in which we are different? Do we have any particular functions, skills, and responsibilities? Any separate, special identity? If so, what are these? If not, what are we? What, in brief, is our unique, differentiated, core identity?

You may feel that these are tired and worn questions and may be impatient at their being raised once again. But they do not seem to go away when they are ignored. Recent events—both the confusions in our own profession and the challenges we are meeting from "the public" to say what is the place of social work in the ballooning pursuit of "mental health"—force our facing these problems. So back into the cauldron.

A recent study of mental health professionals—psychoanalysts, psychiatrists, psychologists, and "psychiatric social workers"—in New York, Chicago, and Los Angeles reveals that while "therapeutic styles differ from person to person . . . the similarity of work style and of viewpoint among therapists is marked." The researchers,

---

1. "Clinical" is used here in its etymological sense meaning, roughly, being at the bedside of the patient, that is, *with* him. Clinical social workers may utilize the method called "casework," with individual persons, or "group work," work with formed or natural groups, or combinations of these in any given problem-focussed unit called a "case." With the growth of interest in the continuous transactions between individuals and their social group or tasks, casework and group work are often alternating or overlapping methods.

finding that psychotherapists among all four professions are more like one another than like those members of their own profession who do not specialize in psychotherapy, then suggest that perhaps there ought to be a "fifth profession": psychotherapists.[2]

Some clinical social workers would welcome this—it might solve many problems. But it might create other problems as well. It is questionable whether those psychotherapists with a medical degree would readily detach themselves from their socially honored medical roots, even if in fact they rarely use their strictly medical knowledge. It is questionable too, whether social workers would be considered equal members in such a fifth profession because, as this same study reveals, theirs is the least costly and the quickest entry into psychotherapeutic practice and (unhappily) they characteristically do less postgraduate study, formal and informal, than do the members of the three other therapeutic professions. So, while there are individual clinical social workers whose special talents have placed them high in the esteem of other professionals there remain questions about whether even an established fifth profession might not have its hierarchies and substrata too.

But put those questions aside. Most of us clinical social workers were born and bred in the briar patch of social work—and a briar patch it is—and we would resist tearing up from our roots. We are too stubborn or too committed to deny our forbears, or we believe too deeply in the mission and purpose of social work in our society and do not want to weaken that one whit. So for us the question is one I have pursued intermittently for the past two decades or so: what is the social work part of clinical social work? What is the margin of our special identity, even though we overlap at many points with other therapeutic professions?

First let us recognize that all clinical social workers are not all psychotherapists all of the time. In a fairly recent study of over two thousand clinical social workers in over two hundred hospitals[3] it was found that most psychiatrists as well as most chiefs of social work staff held two nonpsychotherapeutic services to be the major functions of the psychiatric social worker. One was dealing with people and situations *other* than the patient as they affected his well-being; the other was finding and making accessible the tangi-

2. William E. Henry, John H. Sims, and S. Lee Spray, *The Fifth Profession* (San Francisco: Jossey-Bass, 1971), pp. 180–81.

3. Robert Barker and Thomas L. Briggs, *Differential Use of Social Work Manpower* (New York: National Association of Social Workers, 1968).

ble aids to the social functioning of the patient and/or his family. Of course each of these has tremendous psychotherapeutic influence. But they are not usually subsumed under "psychotherapy." Perhaps more important: within the four psychotherapeutic professions they have by tacit agreement, by tradition, and by practice been considered the special bailiwick of social work. Of this more later.

Beyond this: the "clinical social worker" is employed in many agencies under social, nonmedical auspices: in family counseling and in the many facets of child welfare; in public schools; in institutions for the aged, for delinquents, and so on. In these settings social work and its case-by-case practitioners carry a public charge: to try to engage and help not only people who voluntarily seek help but also those whose problems are complicated by their indifference or by their open, conscious resistance to help. These adults and children are not often candidates for psychotherapy (I have sometimes been frankly envious of colleagues in other professions who have greater freedom to slough off a case as "untreatable" by psychotherapeutic means, or whose majority of clients are educated to the idea of the therapeutic dialogue and are introspective "believers" in the powers of the healer.) To social workers come *some* of the latter for which we give thanks. But it is also true that to social work come, or are sent, people, little ones and big, who need protection, whether from themselves or from others, whose distrust of the helper and the system he represents makes them alienated or actively in opposition, whose personal and/or social deficiencies and disorganizations are so debilitating as to vitiate their coping, whose education and life experience has offered minimal nurture resulting in their stunted or retarded growth. Who shall be the helpers of such people? Thus far the public charge has been upon social work. And thus far social work has tried to shoulder this heavy sector of human needfulness which calls both for more than psychological influence and also for different methods of psychological influence.

I submit that clinical social workers have in the past decade or so given themselves over with heart and courage to the challenge of finding both the means by which to provide the "more" than is contained in the verbal and experiential interchange between client and helper, and also the ways by which deeply deprived, disorganized, disconnected people may be undergirded and enabled to cope with their necessary social tasks. Our literature bulges with articles on "reaching the hard to reach"; on renewed efforts at advocacy and linkage between needful people and the resources present but often inaccessible to them; on the development of new resources; on treatment modes shaped by clearer understanding of the effects of class and culture on what people want and believe; on the necessity to partialize problems for purposes of concentration and focus; on theories of socialization and role as supplements to what had once been monolithic personality theory; on demonstration projects in which great expenditures of time and patience and provisions have resulted in some changes in people's motivation and capacity for coping. And so forth. In short, there is evidence that there has been both broad expansion and considerable modification in the perspectives, the knowledge, and the treatment modes relevant to those particular persons and problems with which social work has long been charged, which we have claimed, and have had public sanction for, as our particular responsibility.[4]

It is a twofold business—that of helping people to want the help they need but cannot or will not use; and that of helping people to use resources that are or seem inaccessible to them, too complex or fearsome to tangle with. Often that inaccessibility lies in the network of services or resources themselves—it is complicated or unyielding or remote. So the resource often needs some workover in order to make it useable by the client-consumer. It is a tough business, this combination of client-advocacy and social brokerage—a difficult one, but our own.

We have always, in social work, talked about the client's "environment." That is a special territory long claimed by or thrust upon us. But we have explored it only sporadically and with small enthusiasm. Conceptually for many years it was taken as a "surround" of one's client or a "background" in which, occasionally, one intervened to arrange this or that, to coax or persuade somebody to do or not to do something in the interests of our primary client. Methodologically it has been largely ignored. One "modified" or "manipulated" it, or negotiated within it out of one's natural abilities and plain common sense. But if a zealous teacher in a school of social work wanted to carry the idea of environmental modification and system negotiations beyond preachment, there

4. The *Casework Notebook*, Family-Centered Project (St. Paul: Greater St. Paul Community Chest and Councils, 1957; out of print); Eleanor Pavenstedt, ed., *The Drifters: Children of Disorganized Lower-Class Families* (Boston: Little, Brown and Co., 1967); Elizabeth McBroom, "Socialization and Social Casework," in *Theories of Social Casework*, ed. Robert W. Roberts and Robert Nee (Chicago: University of Chicago Press, 1970), pp. 315–51.

were no examples recorded of its practice. Case records, exquisitely detailed in their accounts of the dialogue between caseworker and his client, held only brief notations of tasks accomplished or frustrated with, say, the client's school teachers, his landlord, the nurses and ward attendants. Our action upon and within the social environment remains unrecorded, unexposited.[5]

"We have studied man's inner world with unprecedented devotion; yet we assign acutely decisive encounters, opportunities and challenges to a nebulous 'outer reality.' "[6] That is Erik Erikson speaking. To the importance of the "outer reality" social workers have long attested. And yet—.

We have, perhaps, had our hands and our feet in our clients' social environment more fully than we have had our heads and hearts in it. It has not seemed prestigious. So when our common sense told us that man lives twenty-four hours a day seven days a week in life-giving or life-destroying relationships with other people and tasks we would indeed go out to try to affect those relationships here and there. But halfheartedly, as if it were something to be gotten over with so as to get back to the greater purity of the inner sanctum dialogue.

Today the environment is coming into its own. Call it "ecosystem" if you will; call its study "human ecology."[7] Perhaps, despite Juliet's doubts, there is something in a name that may capture us afresh: ecology—the science of the relations between living organisms and their environments.

In psychiatric settings we have characteristically been expected to "gather social history," to "assess the family background," to make the necessary social rearrangements in the client/patient's life-space. The various aspects of child welfare work have required that we observe and assess natural, foster, and adoptive families in their social and psychological environments. The slum flat and streets, the school room and hallways, the hospital ward and clinic waiting room, and, yes, also, the meticulously decorous living room of the middle-class family—these living environments are all known to most of us, known not just as sociological phenomena but in their

5. For a review of the uses and nonuses of "environmental modification," see Richard Grinnell, Jr., "Environmental Modification: Casework's Concern or Casework's Neglect?" *Social Service Review* 47, no. 2 (June 1973).

6. Erik Erikson, "Reality and Actuality," *Journal of the American Psychoanalytic Association* 10 (1962): 451–74.

7. I have taken this term from Carel Germain's article "An Ecological Perspective in Casework Practice," *Social Casework*, June 1973.

psychosocial impacts, their incrowding upon our senses of smell and sight and feel and, in vaguely delineated ways, upon our understanding of their psychological potency.

We social workers were among the first to recognize the family as a dynamic environment, and the first to put forward the idea of the family as a transactional unit of treatment in dealing with problems of role relationships.[8] Yet, interestingly, few of us are aware of this and when documentations and footnotes in social work articles appear on family diagnosis and treatment or on role transactions they are largely credits to non–social workers. I am suggesting here that we sometimes do not know all that we know; that we have not sufficiently valued what we know about "human ecology."

What do we know? We do not, typically, have quantifiable data—our daily involvement with individual instances does not provide for this. There are others whose business it is to study and analyze large group phenomena—whose findings, when we use them, frame and illuminate the individual instances we see. But we social workers know the living, breathing organism in its immediate dynamic transactions with its outer reality—in color, in depth, in action. Except in anecdotes and fragments we have not adequately lifted this knowledge up from the individual instance to extract its dynamic imports and applications.

I remind us that Freud's rather few single case studies were the sources from which vast perspectives in personality theory opened up. Piaget's theories came to life largely from his minute observations of and then cogitation upon the learning behaviors of his own three children. Closer to us: only thirteen families form the group called "the Drifters" from which Pavenstedt, Bandler and others drew and organized knowledge that holds wide and powerful implications for anyone setting out either to treat or to fashion welfare policies for members of this subculture.[9]

Clinical social workers observe such facts, but we have yet to examine and value them. It is only when we understand the

8. For instance: in 1944 Robert Gomberg, a social worker, published the first formal statement about marital and parental roles as the focus for family counseling. See "The Specific Nature of Family Casework," in *A Functional Approach to Family Casework,* ed. Jessie Taft (Philadelphia: University of Pennsylvania Press, 1944). Dr. Nathan Ackerman became consultant to and then a foremost developer of family therapy at the Jewish Family Service of New York, which spearheaded the family treatment movement. Social workers on its staff published extensively on aspects of family treatment.

9. Pavenstedt, *The Drifters.*

meaning of this or that fact that we can begin to attach it to another and so to build an organized, connected body of knowledge. Again we must remind ourselves that the environment is as close in as one other significant person and as far out as what we vaguely designate as "society." And that even people who pay fees for therapy have environments with which they are in continuous transaction.

The most important aspect of human ecology for clinical social workers is the interventive action of *doing*. More than the other helping professions we have been involved in attempts to "influence" and "modify" the person's outer reality when that has been necessary, both the outer reality of significant others and that of significant circumstances. Yet we have not done enough—or well enough. Within the past few years the social work air has rung with calls for "advocacy," "brokerage," "delivery of services." There are a number of questions that rise up. Are there, I wonder, particular action principles that guide us when we deal with "significant others?" Are they the same principles that govern our actions with our primary clients? Or are some different skills involved when we are attempting to affect persons who do not feel hurt, who have their own needs, who are not motivated to be involved with us in the interests of our client? Is the work of linkage between individuals and the complicated bureaucracies and service networks they encounter of small account? Is it chiefly footwork? Or does it require skills to find, select, pursue, and persuade the other side of the transactional seesaw? If so, can we as professionally prepared clinical social workers name and describe the interventive actions called "brokerage" or "ecosystem modification"? Beyond that, can we explain their whys and wherefores so that these action principles can be transmitted and taught to students? to paraprofessionals? And so that such accrued explanations may begin to take their place in the compendium of clinical social work's body of knowledge and know-how? Perhaps the basic question is do we *want* to own this special area of sociopsychological influence? If we do not, then who is to claim it and do it? If we do, how can we become more effective in its cultivation as our special area of expertise?[10]

In sum, I have argued that beyond our valid and inevitable overlap with other psychotherapeutic professions there are two aspects of sociopsychodynamic transaction that mark the particular "turf" of clinical social work. One is the existence of large numbers

10. The effort to work with the client's "others" I have dealt with in some greater detail in no. 6, chap. 9.

of people whose here-and-now problems in social functioning are the concern of a society that claims to want the greatest good for the greatest number. This population, not confined to any one class or ethnic group, may not want or need psychotherapy. But it may want, or need to be helped to want, certain socially supported resources, instruments, and enabling services by which to cope with daily tasks and relationships more satisfactorily and more satisfyingly. This population was inherited by social work at its birth. Secondly, ours is that territory or aspect of human being called "social environment" or "ecosystem" which is the continuous nurturer or depriver, rewarder or frustrater of the individual. From birth to death its penetrations into the person shape not only his external behaviors but his intrapsychic drives and bents, while he, in turn, affects it.

It is possible that when we grapple, intellectually and emotionally, with these several special aspects of human being and becoming, when we place them in the center of our attention rather than on the sidelines we may discover more psychotherapeutic powers within them than we have as yet dreamed of.

More: we will be taking a long step toward being able to explain clearly (so that even a legislator who runs may read) how it is that the desideratum "mental health" is the product of social, not only medical, forms of treatment and provisions. We may, further, come closer to being able to explain both our likeness to other clinical helpers and also what our valuable difference is. We may even be able to explain ourselves to ourselves—which, as you know, is a basic to a person's or a group's sense of identity.

For many complicated reasons we clinical social workers have been in chronic crisis about our identity. Our background history reveals that in early adolescence we rejected our mother, sociology, who appeared to us to have become rather frumpy and ungiving, and we developed a crush on a father figure, psychiatry. And then, when our passionate identification with him had shaped us in his image we found, to our mixed shock and disbelief, that he and our mother were making eyes at one another, even embracing right out in public. Added to our discomfort was the fact that as we came out into society we were never considered the most beautiful or lovable of its children. And, as if this were not enough, we have found ourselves inundated by a conglomeration of relatives—half-brothers and half-sisters, parasiblings or subsiblings—demanding recognition, guidance, and sometimes our place.

Identity, to quote its foremost expositor, is the accrued confidence in one's inner sameness and continuity "at the same time as one is developing a defined personality within a social reality which one understands."[11] And further, "Identity connotes the resiliency of maintaining essential patterns in the process of change."[12] Two ideas here: To know and feel a secure and stable identity there must be the sense of continuity with one's roots, with a central core. From this there results the confidence that is basic to the resilience and adaptability that makes it possible to both tolerate and engage in change. Identity can never be wholly achieved through imitation or me-too identification; nor is it achieved by the denial and cutoff from one's sources. So we must attend devotedly to the recognition and nourishment of our roots, to those special areas of understanding and action that have long been assigned to and shouldered by social work, to the clarification of how we are like those from whom we have incorporated knowledge and of how we are different.

Mature identity whether in a person or in a profession is characterized by degrees of differentiation. To know and to value the core concerns and knowledge of social work, the core concepts and principles that underlie effective help to people whose social-psychological functioning is impaired or hampered—these constitute the basis of our identity. From this, differentiation and specialization may occur. Without commitment to our roots, without that psychological spinal cord, change can only result in splintering and diffusion.

One last confession. I have become a common scold. Like most common scolds—wives who nag their husbands, parents who chew out their children—I defend myself by saying, "But it's for your own good. It's for clinical social work's own good." The fact is that my identification with clinical social work is so long and so strong that I cannot remain neutral and aloof. I am irrevocably involved and committed. I am committed to the belief that the good society must provide services to individual persons and families whose inner powers and outer means for carrying their daily love and work tasks break down, or are deficient. I am, then, committed to the development and the public support of a profession whose understanding and skills are concentrated upon the social-psychological transactions between those inner powers and outer means, transactions

11. Erik Erikson, "Identity and the Life Cycle," *Psychological Issues* 1 (1959): 89.
12. Erik Erikson, *Insight and Responsibility* (New York: W. W. Norton, 1964), p. 96.

between person and person, person and his role tasks, person and the complex social organizations and services he needs and finds wanting. There, I believe, lies our particular identity as clinical social workers.

One final word from Erikson. As one resolves the identity crisis, he says, one is ready to face the task of adulthood. That task is "how to *take care* of those to whom one finds oneself committed . . ."[13] That, it seems to me, is the on-going task in clinical social work's "transition to tomorrow."

1989 Afterword

In September 1986 the Clinical Social Work Sector of the National Association of Social Workers held its first national conference (San Francisco) and chose to honor me for a "lifetime of passionate commitment to human welfare" along with several other gratifying, if not entirely deserved, kudos. I was asked to comment on my "view of clinical social work today."

Here I excerpt a few paragraphs that seem relevant to the foregoing paper.

> An old friend of mine announced many years ago that he would not attend another social work conference. "Because," he complained, "they all end the same way: 'social work is at the crossroads.' It is time we put our teeth into some concrete steps."
>
> Here we are again at the crossroads. Again we are in search of those concrete steps onto which we can put our *feet,* not our teeth, firmly. If it is any comfort to have company in misery I remind us that a number of other professions, older and more firmly entrenched, are also facing questions of their directions and goals, are also being buffeted by unpredictable social, economic, political rough winds. Moreover, it is a recurring and expectable phenomenon of human living that solutions of many problems seem, paradoxically, to breed a host of new ones.
>
> My view of clinical social work is that I am *for* it. I am for it because its aim is the enablement of human beings in their struggle to deal with one or more of their problems in coping with daily life tasks in ways that empower and enhance their sense of the self and of at-oneness with their fellow-men.

13. Erik Erikson, *Identity: Youth and Crisis* (New York: W. W. Norton, 1968), p. 11.

Further, I concluded it was not too forced an act to move from the Greek root, 'klinikos', meaning 'at the bedside of' to 'clinical'. All that was needed was to move the bed. One could still be "at the side of," in compassionate attention to the needs of the client/patient.

The designation "clinical social work" does seem to imply professional knowledge and know-how. It suggests that its practice is the product of accredited preparation and carefully scrutinized practice. When "social" follows on "clinical" the combination affirms the inextricable connections between individual persons and the social climates and circumstances with which they are in dynamic transaction, and which frequently must be addressed. So I have come to be comfortable with this changed title.

There are, undeniably, some advantages in its use. Among them: it promises more ready access to political and economic supports that ensue when expertise is defined, certified, and demonstrated. Already, advances have been set in motion by the carving out of firm standards of practice preparation, by our active pressure for licensure, by our organized drive to be paid for our practical and therapeutic services by that ever-powerful "third party" who holds the public purse strings. Such active efforts promise far greater public understanding and acceptance than we have had.

Our need remains to clarify our special and not-to-be-minimized identity. We are more than simply a "me, too" therapeutic profession. I go forward with the determined hope that our profession will be more robust and respected when we can articulate and demonstrate that educated, clinically oriented, skilled caseworkers are, in many situations, the profession of *choice* not of chance. We are the profession of choice when there is recognition that the person's social surround, the living social matrix of his daily life is significant to the creation and/or solution of his problem(s). And also when those who need but fear intervention must be reached out to, engaged in moving from distrust and resistance to some motivation towards change, whether in themselves or their situations or both. Engaging the "hard-to-reach" is one of the special crosses social workers have to bear. At the least it deserves our thoughtful consideration and our inventive effort.

In the course of my professional pursuits I have often been fatigued, discouraged, anxious, saddened, angered.

Moreover, I claim that I have been consistently under-paid, and over-worked.

But the rewards have over-balanced all that. I have been richly nourished by some inspired teachers, both in psychiatry and social work, the colleague of many tal-ented, original, stimulating peers, both among the true believers and the heretics. I have never been bored, be-cause while "the same old problem" may come along, it is never the same person who bears it, nor the same so-cial situation which bears upon him. I have been heart-warmed by occasional recognitions—such as you give me today; by the sparkling eyes of a child whose face was once stony-cold; by a client's actually *doing* a difficult thing we had rehearsed over many hours. I have repeat-edly known the gladdening experience of what I've called "instant motherhood" provided me lovingly by students who, within nine months, grew from neonates into the beginning of competence as professionals. And I remain deeply grateful to my clients, people of all ages and classes, through whom I have vicariously experienced the manifold aspects of being and becoming.

Thus my own one life has been tremendously vivified, varied, and enriched. Somehow, I feel more whole as a person than I could otherwise have been, more free to feel at-one with others, still full of wonder at the marvels and mysteries of the makeup and behaviors of all of us human beings. All of which, in the final analysis, explains why I am glad and grateful still to be connected in colleagueship and questing with each and all of you!

PART TWO

TEACHING—GLADLY AND OTHERWISE

8

THE CHARGE TO THE CASEWORK SEQUENCE

1989 FOREWORD

Out of my eight published articles on teaching (nos. 10, 12, 15, 16, 24, 41, 53, 72 in the bibliography) I have chosen four for this section. My choice was determined partly because I still liked them (which, sadly, does not always happen when one reappraises one's brain children!) but chiefly because requests for copies of them even today indicate their apparent usefulness to others.

As I have said, there has probably never before been such widespread need for teachers of social work, especially for those knowledgeable in the practice and theory of what is by far the largest sector of its practice—casework and group work. Across the country numerous colleges have inaugurated courses and programs for "entry levels" of social work practice. How are the teachers to be prepared? Recognized for their practice competence, for their know-how skills, many social work practitioners have been catapulted into the arena of education, thrown to the lions—or is it the lambs? The assumption has been that they will "just naturally" be able to transmit to others what they themselves know.

Many are so able. For others, however, it is a big and hard-learned leap from the work on individual cases with particular kinds of problems to identifying guiding principles and theories that must be found and articulated in order to make learning transferable from one instance to others. Moreover, the exacting business of shaping meaningful assignments and learning tasks, of formulating testing means that will reveal not only the students' grasp of necessary knowledge but the teacher's own competence in providing it, the discipline of culling out selected references and sources rather than overwhelming students with staggeringly "complete" bibliographies—these and many other basic adjuncts to learning and testing and retention and connections in the minds of learners are too often allowed to "just grow," like Topsy, well or poorly.

One may take comfort from a wise observation Gordon Hamilton made many years ago: that casework operates in some middle ground between therapy and education. There is, I firmly believe, a great deal that is methodologically transferable from casework whether with single clients or with groups, to teaching, such as setting the basic climate between teacher and students— that of acceptance combined always with expectations and requirements; that of the encouragement to exercise imagination and speculation, along with the demand that a position be supported by relevant facts or reasons. In short, as some French sage put it, good teaching and thence good learning combine both *rigor* and *tenderness*. In that respect a good caseworker-groupworker is well-prepared for teaching in certain basic ways; beyond basics most of us have much yet to learn.

Further—and in development—are the programs of guidance, consultation, teaching aids, and standards offered by the national Council of Social Work Education. A number of graduate schools offer short-courses and seminars on field and classroom teaching. To those efforts I hope the four pieces included herein may add in some small part—to offer challenge and some security to the new teacher, and to the seasoned teacher perhaps some support or expansion of perspective.

This sober subject must be preceded by a sobering fable. It is the story of Neolisha Richmond.

Professor of social casework in the Generic School of Social Work, known to her familiars as Neo Richmond, she met her untimely end one day recently in an explosion of smoke and sputter. Her colleagues report that on the morning of her passing they had become aware of sounds of small explosions coming from behind her closed door. However, since Neo had recently taken to express-

Presented at the annual meeting of the Council of Social Work Education, in Toronto, January 1964. Copyright 1964, National Association of Social Workers, Inc. Slightly condensed, it is reprinted with permission from *Social Work*, vol. 9, no. 3 (1964): 47–55.

ing herself in fairly violent expletives, these noises roused no more than some mild amusement. But suddenly there was the sound of great shattering. Whereupon Neo Richmond's colleagues rushed into her office to find to their horror that a complete disintegration had occurred: to put it bluntly, Neo had "gone to pieces."

It is true that Professor Richmond was known to have had some eccentricities, but in the eyes of her non-casework colleagues, these did not exceed those of any casework teacher. When a professor of medicine was rushed in to examine the remains, he was frankly at a loss and vacillated between calling in one of the university's alchemists or one of its atomic physicists. He ended by gathering up the pieces and other bits of evidence for further study.

Among these bits was a daybook in which Neo Richmond had been writing when her disintegration occurred, and by a series of fortuitous circumstances this book was placed in my safekeeping. I share some passages with you in the belief that they hold a lesson for us.

The book opens on a date of a few months ago, and the opening passage expresses Neo's high resolves and spirits.

"*October 1*. The year's at the fall," she writes, "the campus dew-pearled. I feel all refreshed after my month's vacation, in which I did nothing but sleep and eat and rework the syllabi and bibliographies in my courses and catch up on this year's publications in psychiatry, public health, social psychology, anthropology, and, oh yes! social work." She goes on, still ebullient, "The eager students are all here and my heart leaps to think that again I am to have some part in leading them to become effective professional social workers!

"*October 5*. At Curriculum Committee today we spoke of the necessity to integrate and synthesize knowledge across the board. The research faculty believes that more research-mindedness needs to be inculcated in the students. This can best be done in casework courses where knowledge needs to be differentiated from opinion, tested hypotheses from speculation, etc. This led the social welfare policies and services faculty to wonder whether in casework courses we show enough of how social policies and services affect casework. Then our lecturer in human development in the social environment said he feels strongly that the casework courses should integrate all the information in his course. Everyone agreed that the cross-fertilizing, integrating, synthesizing experience our students need must occur in the casework sequence. I'm sure all of us casework teachers," Neo adds, "should be proud of this faith in us.

"*October 8.* This was a hectic day with one phone call after another. Miss Silver of the Golden Age Bureau urged that we put more cases of aged people into our casework courses. Students, she said, need to get the conviction that 'the olden years are golden years.' Mr. Brown of the League for Exceptionally Retarded Children phoned—wants us to put in some cases of exceptionally retarded children since students need to get the feeling that retardation is normal except in extreme cases. Mrs. Black of the Association for Emotionally Handicapped Youth between the Ages of 15–17½ called to say that they have scholarship money or research grants or both to promote interest in EHYBA of 15–17½.

"*October 10.* At the Community Fund Luncheon I sat with Miss Green of the Family Agency. She questioned how many marital cases we have in our sequence because our recent graduates don't seem to understand much about neurotic marital interaction—at least judging from the last student she hired. Mr. White, Public Welfare Commissioner, made a stirring luncheon speech. He said casework courses at schools are becoming so effete that students don't understand about money as a medium of exchange or why budgets must have 25 percent slashes. He urged that casework teachers concentrate on making public assistance an exciting prospect for students. One of these days I must find time to talk to my fellow casework teachers about all this.

"*October 18.* Meeting with field teachers and classroom teachers to discuss how to dovetail our efforts. There was considerable discontent expressed by the field instructors because it is already three weeks since the quarter began and students do not seem to know how to conduct an interview yet. We asked ourselves where this might best be taught—and the field instructors were unanimous in the conviction that the casework classroom is the place for it. Moreover, it was suggested that role-playing would be a good method to use in casework classes since it would involve the student not just as a mind but as a whole personality. I must confess," Neo goes on with her refreshing honesty, "there is something about this that makes me _____ . [It becomes hard to tell whether the next word is "uneasy" or "queasy."]

"*November 12.* I had a disconcerting experience today. There is so much talk abroad about intervention for prevention in social work. Everyone seems agreed that the casework sequence is the place in the curriculum where this ought to be taught because, after all, this is where students learn to become 'doers.' So I worked far into the night last evening preparing a lecture on our responsibility as caseworkers for preventive intervention and I delivered it this morning. The class seemed enraptured. (What a joy it is to feel you mold these malleable young ones!) After class young Miss Brainard came up to me, batting her great blue eyes, and said, 'Miss Richmond, I *want* to do interventive prevention. That's why I came into social work. But my supervisor seems dead set on meeting problems that are already *there*! How do I begin to prevent?' " And here, in Neo Richmond's characteristic frankness, is the notation, "I did not know what to tell her! I think we need a subcommittee to discuss this.

"*One week later.* Meeting today with the dean and executives of child welfare agencies. They report a tremendous rise in the incidence of preschool, prepsychotic, precocious children. There is an inadequate supply of child psychiatrists, and a dearth of training facilities, and little treatment theory for this group of children. So the consensus was that casework courses should . . . and so on. I am," Neo adds parenthetically, "beginning to have the mild frontal headaches and nausea from which I suffered last spring.

"*December 2.* It is urgent, everyone says, that we incorporate cases into our courses that show family interaction, diagnosis and treatment-wise. Our social science consultant tells me that communications theory, small group theory, and transactional theory are absolutely essential to this. I've arranged to have lunch with him so that he can quickly brief me on these. I cannot understand why I feel so dizzy these days. . . ."

There is one further entry having to do with a meeting of casework, group work, and community organization faculty for purposes of developing a course in which all three methods will be merged into one generic practice method. In the midst of this entry the handwriting becomes difficult to decipher. There is a blot of ink, a smudge of ash—and this must have been the moment of Neo Richmond's disintegration, her end.

This is the end of the fable too. Its point was that in most schools of social work the casework sequence has been charged with, has had thrust upon it, or has taken to itself a greater profusion of learning-teaching tasks than its able and competent teachers are able or competent to carry.

This is probably why the subject to which this paper is addressed recurs again. "The charge to the casework sequence" has been worked over time and again. It has been succinctly stated in the "Curriculum Statement" of the Council on Social Work Education. It has been spelled out in imaginative detail by casework teachers, particularly and admirably by Charlotte Towle, and in committees at local and national levels. In spite of this the question remains perennially unresolved. In part this is as it should be. In a changing curriculum, sensitive to a changing world of need and knowledge, the casework sequence must likewise be subject to continuous change and modification in content and emphasis.

But part of the question about our charge is the expression of our uncertainty and discontent with what we do. This uncertainty and discontent has sources outside our own push for excellence. One such source is the great diversity of demand that comes from many places: colleagues in other sequences, special interest groups, field placements, and potential employers, each of whom sees his area of operation as the universe of social casework. Another source of discontent is awareness of the overwhelming recent proliferation of knowledge about human beings, no part of which is alien to casework. And a third source of uncertainty lies in our own backgrounds: we have been caseworkers, working in the fine-point techniques of the miniature. When we become teachers, it is clear that we must change our art form: we must become muralists, painting in the large for many students to see and understand, and this transition is not an easy one. These several demands—to adapt to too many external stimuli and to changes of role—carry considerable stress.

Stress calls up varied efforts to cope. One is retreat into what is most familiar and what is most safe. For the casework teacher this means teaching cases: this case shows this, that case shows that. Another coping effort is responding to all stimuli, but when these are multiple and variegated the coping efforts are often diffused and fragmented. The result of either maneuver is a casework sequence that resembles a smorgasbord. It may indeed be highly attractive and stimulating to the appetite both of instructor and student. It offers a taste of that and a bite of the other. The trouble is, it doesn't quite add up to solid nourishment; it doesn't stick to the intellectual ribs. In either withdrawal into the confines of "the case" or in setting forth to incorporate everything, the casework sequence often becomes a collection of fragments, of pieces—bright or dull, as the case may be—but not fitted or held together by the firm tissue of conceptualization.

The primary and priority charge to the casework sequence is that it provide students with a central core of casework knowledge. This central core consists of the basic facts, ideas, and principles that govern and inform what the caseworker does in practice. It is *what* we know (or believe or assume), *how* we operate, and *why* we believe, assume, and operate as we do. *What* we know, or take as known, has to do with people and their problems, viewed within the purposes and programs of the social work profession. *How* we operate has to do with our value system and our skills of intervention. *Why* we believe, feel, and do as we do is concerned with the connections between what and how. The charge to the casework sequence is a charge to its teachers to name, identify, formulate, and connect those ingredients.

Schools of social work have eighteen months or less as education time within which to turn a college student into a professional person who is to wield power and influence over the lives of other people. Within these eighteen months the casework teacher has only a very small part of the student's time and attention. Our task, then, must be to use that time to the utmost, most economically, with greatest effectiveness. I suggest that to identify what must be taught and learned in casework within the narrow margins of the master's casework sequence we would do well to start our thinking, not with our eyes on the far horizons of ideal objectives, but with a frankly nearsighted question, such as: What does a student need to know in order to be for one hour alone with a person who is disturbed by a problem for which he needs casework help?

This is a beginning question. As you tackle it, you will find quickly that the answers begin to fan out into a range of subjects. Our preliminary focus must be upon the anatomy of knowledge: *What* is the basic content I must teach to prepare a student to take his first steps in casework? As we grope for the answers to this little, myopic question we will perhaps move more logically and realistically toward our ideal.

I have a recurrent daymare. I am at Convocation proudly presenting my students to the university's president for their master of arts degrees. Suddenly he turns to me and says, "By the way, what *is* this body of knowledge you certify you have taught this student who is about to receive this honored degree?" I shake off the anxiety this daymare rouses in me by taking pencil to paper in the effort to add my all too slowly developing answer, but I confess that I am not yet free of stammering.

There is no implication here that casework teachers do not have knowledge. We do, in abundance. But often it is more in our bones than in our minds, and we have yet to lift it from "feel" to thought. When it is in our minds it is often in such unarticulated form that it is more readily exemplified than explained; we can show it in a case better than formulate it in a generalization that is transferable from one case or situation to another. Often it is knowledge that is experiential—which, indeed, is the truest knowing for each of us. But if it is to be useful and enabling to a student, its rationale, its "why-for" must be found and explicated.

This, then is our charge, I propose: to ask ourselves and to answer—what does the social caseworker on the job have to do? From this—what does he need to know? Then—since what he needs to know is greater by far than what he can possibly learn in his all-too-brief sojourn with us—the casework teacher must make some ruthless selections from his large body of knowledge. Criteria for such selections are probably these: what seems most essential for the caseworker's usual job-to-be-done, what is most relevant, what most immediately useful, both in today's student practice and in tomorrow's practice as an agency employee? And then we must take our lists of concepts (which is to say our "big ideas") and our facts, and our theories (which is to say the explanations of observed phenomena), and our principles (which is to say the laws that govern our decisions and actions) and pattern them in some organized, connected ways. We will then have identified and formulated the core body of knowledge to be taught over the casework sequence.

It may differ from teacher to teacher or school to school. It may differ by what is emphasized, by what is considered most relevant or useful, even by underlying theory or conceptual system. The seeds of diversity and enrichment of our knowledge lie in such differences. What needs to be alike is only this: that we all involve ourselves in the like effort to identify and formulate and organize what we hold to be the practice theory of our subject matter, casework, and its connection with the rest of social work.

How can we go about this task in some more effective ways than we have thus far? My suggestions fall far short of my convictions—it is always easier to point the problem than to solve it—but I offer them for whatever they are worth.

First you must find a room with a door that closes and a telephone that is disconnected. Alone, or in the company of a few colleagues, you go into this room with what in effect is tying your hands behind your back: you go in without any case material. Now ask yourselves: "If I had no cases to teach from, to start with, to fall back on, what would my casework course consist of? What would I teach?" You will find yourself unnerved by this question. Perhaps more than we like to admit, we have used cases as substitutes for the more solid stuff of sequential ideas and connected constructs. I must hasten to make clear that I am not advocating that we give up the use of cases in teaching casework. But I am suggesting that we torture ourselves a bit with that idea as a way of forcing ourselves to come out from behind the drama, color, diversions, human interest that cases provide, to ask, "If I had to teach casework by extricating and explaining its constant content, without using cases, what would I say? Can I identify the big ideas, explain them, and then explain how and why they are valued and useful in casework practice?"

If your answer to these questions is "yes"—then the work to explicate begins. One small example will have to serve here to indicate what this work consists of.

Take the concept of relationship. It is an idea talked about from the first day of a caseworker's professional life to the last. It is an idea of the essential emotional and psychological connectedness between two people, basic to any process by which one person attempts to influence another. I must ask myself, "What do I know about relationship? What are its components, its dynamics? Can I explain them, not simply describe them? What are the likenesses and differences between natural and professional relationships? Why is relationship a potent factor in casework? What principles can be derived that would govern the establishment and management of good working relationships?" And so forth.

Remember, we are still not using cases—we still have our hands tied behind our backs. In our self-discipline we must find our answers, not by dodging into the examples that cases so obligingly afford, but by rigorous efforts to state what we hold to be generally true or generally workable or generally accepted. These formulations take sweated labor.

But we are not yet done. Because now we must set down what becomes apparent as soon as one begins to explore any vital part of casework's knowledge. That is, what I do *not* know about relationship—or diagnosis—or whatever the subject may be. "What I do not know" falls into two categories: that which is known to others, but not to me, and that which no one yet knows. For the former there are remedies. One looks up, bones up, or resolves to do both at the first available library hour. For the mysteries that remain unplumbed, the teacher's honest recognition of the unknown or the uncertain in his subject matter serves several good purposes. It frees teacher and student both of anxiety and pretenses. It unites them in that partnership of curiosity and wonder to search.

The drudgery of identifying our knowledge, small piece by small piece, and viewing each piece in its relation to other pieces has several rewards. An immediate one is that when you examine a "big idea," turning it about in your mind to view its various dimensions and asking yourself, "How so?" "Why so?" "What for?" you find a number of spontaneous connections occurring. You find you are "integrating," seeing, and connecting up the relationship of one piece of theory with another. These connections occur because it is in the nature of generalizations that they embrace groups of ideas or facts, and that they suggest either likenesses or the exceptions that prove the rule. Moreover, the perpetual questions of "Why is this important?" and "How is it useful?" and "So what?" force us to view each subject within casework in relation to another, and to the surrounding frame of social work.

To use relationship as an example again: Relationship in casework is a concept that has evolved over the years. It has a *historical* dimension that can be used to show the student that, like the many other concepts in social casework, it is the result of developments in psychological knowledge and changes in social attitudes. (An example is the remarkable democratization of caseworkers' attitudes to their clients brought about by the economic catastrophe of the early thirties.) Relationship has an *ethical* dimension, related to professional values and standards. *Social and cultural class expectations* bear upon the forming and content of relationship. Relationship is affected by the fact that casework is an *institutionalized practice,* that it takes place in certain kinds of organizations. It is affected by the *individual genetic endowment* and *personal life experience* of both client and student. It *occurs in every human transaction* in which the student is involved—with his instructors, schoolmates, clients, colleagues, all—and its assessment and understanding of all these varied transactions is subject to certain same approaches and same laws of self-management.

When the casework teacher can affirm that he is teaching a solid subject matter rather than extracting what he can from a series of cases, then he is ready to untie his hands and reach out for case material. But now he will view cases differently and use them differently. His chosen case will provide the vivid, live examples of what he is able to present to his students (or will, by his focused queries, draw from them) in the form of major concepts and guiding principles. He will not "teach the case," nor will he milk it for everything of interest it may hold. Rather, he will use those pieces or phases of a case that exemplify or illustrate his points. Or he will use several cases comparatively, parts of each, to particularize, to show the diversities within the generalizations he is attempting to convey. What is important is that the generalization should be on tap in the teacher's mind for presentation, explanation, testing, argument, whatever—as the substance to be retained for further use.

The charge to the casework sequence today, then, is that we find, name, and formulate our major central body of practice theory; that we say what it is within our particular bailiwick we know or hold to be true, what we believe to be desirable, how we operate as agents of help and change, and why we operate as we do. These constitute the basic concepts, assumptions, assertions, and practice principles that, when organized, form a body of social casework knowledge. The questions of how to provide sequence, continuity, integration, and testing follow on this. The problems of class and field integration and their differences cannot be viewed except in the context of what we consider to be our most relevant, and useful core content. The recent insistent proposals that practice among casework, group work, and community organization is increasingly overlapping and that therefore there ought to be one "generic methods course" cannot, I submit, be reasonably thought through until at least one of these methods (preferably all, but at least one) bears out and formulates not alone the conceptual framework of social work that embraces us all, but also the specific concepts and especially the specific practice principles that are characteristic of a specific helping method.

Our reluctance to engage ourselves in this heavy task of identifying and articulating our working theory is understandable. Especially in casework there is some history of deep-lying resistance and distrust of articulated knowledge, of "knowing" that has been lifted from the bloodstream to the brain. One sees this attitude repeatedly in the juxtaposition of "art" and "science" in casework discussions. Repeatedly there has been implied the primitive fear that if we name what we know the magic will vanish from it, that if we eat of the Tree of Knowledge, the Eden of intuitive arts will be lost to us.

This has so often been used as one rationale to avoid grappling with conceptual knowledge that, at the risk of being ridden out of our closed "thinking room" on a tangent, I beg to touch on this point. As far as I know there is no evidence that science is death to art. There are therapeutically potent people—social caseworkers as well as witch doctors among them—who cannot tell what they do or why it works. There are, at the other pole, intellectually potent people who can tell, but cannot do. And there are, happily, people who combine both healing talents and intellectual clarity. We hope casework teachers are among them.

When one examines the arts—both the creative and the performing arts—one sees that all artistry is based upon science. (I use the term "science" now in its only valid sense when it is associated with social work, as meaning a systematized body of knowledge and action.) Michelangelo studied and knew every sinew and bone in the human body before he brought life out of stone. Picasso was an impeccable draftsman before he began to break the rules in order to create new forms and modes of expression. The point is, he knew the rules he was breaking. Like all geniuses, he created new knowledge, new rules, for other artists to use. Great musicians, whether composers or performers, know—because they have had to study, analyze, and incorporate and drill themselves in the theory of harmony, counterpoint, sound, acoustics—the principles governing their particular forms or their particular instruments. Genius or talent was born in them, but it was given discipline and direction by knowledge. So I cannot believe that when a caseworker or a teacher of casework sits down and tries to tease up out of his intuitive "feel," out of his viscera the "knowing" that must be lifted to his mind to become conscious and fully possessed by him—I cannot believe that this throttles spontaneity and sensitivity. Knowledge possessed is the guide and disciplinarian of art.

This brings us back to poor Neo Richmond. It is true that had she worked at the charge proposed here she would have found it a rigorous, demanding, exhausting, and never-quite-finished job. She would have had to be assured that no one of us has as yet adequately met that charge and that she had much company in her professional misery. She would have had to persuade her dean that she needed more time for scholarly study.

Now, she might still have met an untimely death. But she would have died whole, not by disintegration. Her students' memory of her and of what she had taught would have been of a viable, put-together, connected subject matter. Moreover, she could then have had a decent burial—which is the very least that a good casework teacher deserves.

1989 Afterword

My initial reaction on being asked to present a paper on "the charge to the casework sequence" was a negative one. How stand up before my fellow teachers of casework–group work who, for a number of reasons, tend to be the most beleaguered members of any social work faculty, and utter pious "we must" and "we should" clichés?

Then I reminded myself that one of the most useful defense and coping strategies is the use of humor—gallows humor though it may be. I had just read that recent medical speculation had advanced a physiological basis for this phenomenon: that laughter seems to release some of the body's own pain-killers— endorphins—and thus ease pain. So I invented poor Neo Richmond, the prototype of the teacher of casework.

It was interesting to observe: as, in dead earnest, I read aloud the first two paragraphs of this fable to the several hundreds of teachers who had gathered to hear it, there were some minutes of anxious attention and puzzled concern. Then smiles and bursts of chuckles leaped across the room, ending in a roar of appreciative, empathic laughter. In our humorous recognition of our troubles we were united.

Alas!—these same troubles crowd in on us today, more than two decades since this paper was presented. I name a few of them in some stubborn belief that they are more modifiable than they have been assumed to be.

Today's Neo, male or female, must do what every teacher of any subject matter must do: read, think, cull out and set down the objectives of what is to be taught, the main ideas and directions of the course, the materials and learning experiences that will achieve these, the ways in which the students' (and certainly the teacher's own) effective grasp may be tested.

Outside the classroom students are having other planned, as well as unanticipated, educational experiences. They are being involved in practice with clients, patients, other professional personnel in "field placements." If there is to be some reasonable coherence between what they learn in class and book-study and the work with real people who have real problems under the supervision of another teacher-in-the-"field," there must be fairly frequent and substantive communication between the classroom and field teachers. Even in schools where there is an overall director of field-practice, the Neolishas find themselves in frequent telephone or in-person communications on a whole range of small and large problems. Whether it is about a single student's "putting his head together," or about differences between what is taught in the classroom and what is being taught in the field, the reality is that if some reasonable integration is to be achieved between theory and practice, class and field must keep in touch toward mutual agreements. It is a never-ending process—because no sooner has Neo and her ilk established firm and silken working understandings with an agency than a new person takes on student supervision, and the process starts over again.

Meantime, back at the school: along with courses in practice with individuals and groups, students are taking a number of other concurrent courses—on, say, theories of human behavior, history of social welfare, social policy, administration. Many students, unfortunately, are too accustomed by their previous educational experiences to "take" their disparate subject matters and tuck them into sectioned notebooks or into separate mental compartments. Somehow it seems to fall upon the shoulders of casework teachers to do the job of helping the students to seek and to see the connections and relationships between these courses and what they are learning to think and experiencing in practice. Why and in what ways are these other courses useful to them? Why are they being required to read research critically?

What linkages exist between carrying a caseload, interviewing often difficult people in difficult circumstances, developing caring relationships, devising means and ways of aid—and the study of public policy? Attention must be paid. Connections must be made.

Unless I am quite mistaken the responsibility of making social work education whole and meaningful rests most heavily upon the shoulders of the Neos. Why? Is there not opportunity and need for other courses in the curriculum to make something of this same effort—to lift the student's eyes to see the application and relevance to the individual case of social planning, policy issues, administrative operations and problems? Is this made more difficult when the teachers of those subject matters have known nothing of social work in practice?

The publication of "The Charge to the Casework Sequence" brought a letter from one of my most influential teachers, Gordon Hamilton, in which one point bears on the task of any teacher of practice: that of the continuous movement from the generalization to the particular, from the principle to the specific instance of its application. Hamilton was a master teacher. I had quickly recognized this when first I was her student, and then became her colleague. What I had appreciated and attended to closely was her ability to move swiftly and surely from the particular instance to the general principle that governed it, from abstraction to theory, then to its practical application or, at other times, its lack of "fit."

Gordon had drawn away from me during the struggles between the "diagnostic" and "functional" schools. She stood as the protagonist of the former, while I had begun to incorporate a number of the functionalist ideas into both my practice and teaching. (I confess I was reminded of Leonato's comment in *Much Ado About Nothing:* "There was never yet philosopher that could endure the toothache patiently" to which I silently amended, "Nor never yet the philosopher-teacher that could endure a favored student's nay."

However, on reading about Neolisha, Gordon wrote warmly. Her letter, in relevant part, said: "Just a line to tell you how much I enjoyed it. It is both witty and sound. I wish you had (in your cradle) written that when I started teaching. I think I always knew quite a bit about social work one way or another but—I never *did* learn to teach, except perhaps for principles. . . . But how well you put it to us!"

She was mistaken. She *did* teach principles brilliantly but also their application to the individual instance. That was what was so refreshing and useful at a time when casework was so frequently taught case by case, each full of pieces and bits of revelation, but with little linkage from case to case. Gordon "connected," not only by identifying common elements among cases but by identifying the relationships between casework and larger social issues. It was Charlotte Towle, however, with whom I came to work later, who not only had had rich clinical experience but had the ability to see the universe in a grain of sand, who made "integration of theory and practice" a high art. Of which more further.

One further grateful note on Gordon Hamilton. I once uneasily confessed to her that even though I had by then taught long enough to have developed a sense of security, I found that I never approached my first session in any course without a tumult of butterflies in my stomach. "Me too," she said. "And let me tell you—when that no longer happens, it's time to quit teaching!" That was a comfort. So the butterflies arose again and again, but now to my gratification.

9

THE USE OF THE DISCUSSION METHOD

In these days of the frantic effort to communicate with one's fellow-men before it is too late, the discussion method is used as widely and sometimes as indiscriminately as vitamin pills. From solving problems of world maladjustment to personal maladjustment, from deciding "Shall we have a larger national defense system?" to "Shall we invite boys to our party?" from promoting good legislation to promoting good fellowship, from fostering good leadership to fostering good learning, the discussion method is held to be a means. It is readily understandable that, with a means so widely used for so many diverse purposes, there results some rather loose thinking and loose applications of this method of problem-solving.

Gather a group of teachers of social work theory and practice together about the subject of classroom discussion, and there will be general and warm agreement that discussion is a good teaching method and a good learning means. But one of the surest ways to bring conversation about "discussion" to a dead stop is to ask, "What is a discussion?" The origin of "to discuss" means "to shake apart." To "shake apart" both the silence and the question, this attempt at descriptive definition is offered.

Discussion is thinking out loud together with others. Or, to put it more formally, a discussion is a reasoned verbal communication between two or more persons. (Emotions may be involved or may underlie the reasoning, but the conscious effort is to hold emotion in the check of intellectual processes. If emotion breaks loose,

A condensed version of "Teaching Casework by the Discussion Method," *Social Service Review*, vol. 24 (September 1950): 334–46. © 1950 by the University of Chicago. All rights reserved. Reprinted in *Education for Social Work*, ed. Eileen Younghusband (London: George Allen & Unwin, 1968).

rational communication breaks down.) A discussion proceeds from a point of mutual clarity and agreement as to its focal issues or facts or assumptions; these constitute the framework of reference and gauge of relevance. There must be, further, mutual agreement that the significance of these facts, issues or assumptions is open to question or interpretation or differing judgment. Discussion begins with a question of opinion, of differing interpretation of accepted premises or facts. The activity in a discussion is the exercise of minds in an effort to "shake apart"—to explore, analyze, evaluate and come to some conclusion or judgment of a situation, idea or act. The conclusion may be that a conclusion cannot be arrived at, that the issue remains one of preference, opinion, personal value— but this will have been established by communicated thought rather than by impulsive espousal. All discussions have these elements in common.

The classroom discussion, however, poses some special considerations. It is a method used towards a specified end: that within a given period of time students will have incorporated a certain content of knowledge, certain habits of thought, and certain ways of operation. Within a university, as in any formal school system, a sequence of courses leads to a terminal point at which it is certified that the student has mastered certain experiences and has arrived at a certain point in his development. Within any one course a certain section of knowledge and certain exercise in the use of that knowledge must be experienced and learned within a limited period of time. Classroom discussion is, then, a bounded discussion. It is bounded by what is to be learned within what period of time.

It may be argued that discussion which is "freewheeling" and which comes to have content and take shape via the group's own recognition and self-disciplined efforts is in the long run the richest and truest learning experience. This may be true. It may be argued that discussion wherein members of the group are free to say that which they are moved to say is "democratic." This may or may not be true, depending upon some definition of "democratic" and its differentiation from "anarchy" or "laissez faire." It may be argued that discussion, better than other teaching methods, can be paced to the students' learning rate, which does not necessarily conform to the quarter or semester system. Both these statements are true, provided "should" is not slipped in for "can." But the reality of the ends to be achieved within the limits of given time is implacable. No one knows better than the teacher how brief is the life of a course and how fleeting time. Today the neophyte gives hail; tomorrow the graduate says farewell; and in the span of a few deep breaths the teacher and the former student are on the same platform (each with some mixed feelings), each performing as a discussant of a professional paper.

If it is accepted that classroom discussion must be controlled by considerations of what is to be learned within what period of time, then the role of the teacher in classroom discussion begins to come clear. He cannot beguile himself into thinking he is just a "catalytic agent." Nor is he a "group leader" in the general sense of nurturing, over an unspecified time, a group's capacity to achieve its self-determined ends. He is a "leader" in the explicit sense of having the authority and obligation to guide and to direct and often to require. He is an "instructor" in that at given time and place he must inject some knowledge by means of which the class can go forward. He must take responsibility both for stimulating discussion and for controlling it, both for releasing the students' energies and for insistently directing them to the task for which they have been freed. He is responsible not only to promote movement but, literally, to "steer the course" so that direction is not lost. He must not only keep the class going but help it arrive.

It cannot, then, be happily assumed that in classroom teaching discussion is good for the soul. Whether or not it is a good means of teaching and learning depends upon the teachers' clear understanding of what it is, what its relation is to the specified educational goals, and finally upon the teacher's working out such ways and means as will promote and manage the use of discussion in achieving these goals. What follows here is limited to the use of discussion as a method of teaching. Its specific content is that of the use of this method in the teaching of social casework, but it may have some wider applications. To observe a good discussion is to be impressed with its apparent spontaneity, freedom, the combustion of ideas among the participants, and by the keen skill of the leader both in provoking new thought and drawing its varied strands together. One tends to think of this teacher or discussion leader as a "natural." Perhaps he is. Or perhaps his readiness is the product of preparation, and some skills have become second nature to him which were once carefully learned and incorporated by prepared practice.

Many of these skills are those which the casework teacher learned and practiced in the one-to-one discussions of the casework process itself. Transferred with necessary modifications to the class group, they remain familiar to him. One of these skills is attentive listening, not just to the words being said but to the import of what is being said. Following on this (and in the experienced discussion leader it is virtually spontaneous with it) is the effort to make connection between that which has been said and that which preceded it or that which might logically follow it. This sequence or interplay of statements and questions the discussion leader must relate to the major questions or issues in discussion. The ability to do this is the ability to maintain focus upon a nuclear idea at the same time as its radiations are followed and then drawn back to the central body. (This, too, is a skill well known to the caseworker. The client's story may lead into labyrinthine paths, where both he and the caseworker will be lost except as the caseworker has learned to maintain a central focus and to help the client relate himself and his involved discussion back to that.) The discussion leader, then, must be able to focus discussion so that, for all its diversity, it maintains an essential wholeness, a basic unity. The awareness of basic unity needs, of course, to be shared with the discussion participants who, in their involvement with one or another idea, may have lost the direction. Periodically, then, the discussion leader pulls together related parts of the discussion; if discussion is visualized as the spokes of a wheel radiating from the hub, the leader may be said to "rim the wheel."

Within its unity a good discussion must have movement. It must progress. For all that it may eddy about a question or idea at any given moment or at other times leap across logical barriers, it must move forward in a progression of clarification to the resolution which is being sought. The leader of a good discussion must be able, then, to help the group keep aware of where it is going, whether it is getting there, and when it has arrived. This means that the leader himself must have a good sense of direction and a clear perception both of immediate and of more remote goals. And when, as sometimes happens, the release of tension through self-expression leaves the discussants feeling content, the leader must goad them one step further—"So what? Where does that get us? To what conclusion do you come?" (Thus, too, though in different manner, does the caseworker help his client take the step of coming to grips with the implications for his action of that which he has come to understand.)

That a discussion should have unity, direction and movement can reasonably be assured through the instructor-leader's advance preparation; and, if he is not a "natural," he may come to act and feel like one. Discussion in casework classes most frequently arises out of consideration of the specific case material at hand which has been studied in the light of certain reading or foreknowledge, from these materials general understanding and principles of the life-process and the helping process are sought. Each class period partializes the whole of the progressive sequence of cases and their teaching content. Each class period requires of the instructor, then, that he structure its major teaching points, related to the structure and content of the course in its entirety. The casework teacher comes to his class not with a case which, by virtue of its drama and interest, is bound to evoke many reactions from many students. He comes rather with a case whose teaching values and principles he has been able to extract, formulate and relate both to that which the student already knows and to that which he is to come to know. He has set down his major teaching points. These are the points around which the student's learning is to spin itself.

If discussion is to be the means toward that learning, then the questions which will provoke thinking in the desired direction can be formulated in advance. Immediately as this is done, possible student responses and reactions suggest themselves. In the quiet and safety of his own office the discussion leader may have that fantasy rehearsal which prepares him to expect even the unexpected and to be able to deal with it. Perhaps it is needless to say that this is no mere rehearsal of the posture and the technique. It is the anticipation of the possible ideas which may be evoked by the central questions. It enables the leader to plan how speculation can be encouraged or curbed, how movement may be propelled from generalization to the specific or the other way about, and so on. Finally, the discussion leader may prepare by setting down some rough formulation of the possible conclusions to which the class may come. By this means he has his goals in mind, and at the moment of summation he is not desperately dependent upon memory to serve him in rimming the wheel.

One danger may inhere in such careful planning—that of overplanning and subsequent rigidity. Driving for the answer in the teacher's mind, insistence that the class move from Roman I to Arabic 1 in the teacher's outline, although all the class push and excitement is focused on what is Roman II, Arabic 3—this is rigidity which may lay the cold hand of death on a discussion. Let the students discuss Roman II, Arabic 3. They are impelled to do so, and impelling energies must be captured and harnessed for learning. If the logic is inevitable that Roman II must follow Roman I, this will make itself manifest as discussion boils, or the instructor may point it up: "But you'll notice that we haven't established the evidence on which to decide this," or "You're assuming that thus and so is the case. Are we agreed on that?" Life as the student lives it does not occur in outline form. Perhaps the most persuasive instruction in the need for logical thinking is the students' experience of becoming enmeshed in a melee of reactions and impulsive ideas and a demonstration by the instructor of how logical process may serve to extricate them.

The teacher who uses discussion without a working outline runs many risks. Unless he is an old hand at the method, his own sense of comfort, that equilibrium in him which is essential to his being able to listen to others, follow and remember their arguments, will not be steady. Even the outline which after being set down is never used is reassuring, like a portlight in a storm. Without an outline it will be difficult for the teacher to maintain clarity as to where the discussion should be going and when it has arrived. Along with his students he may be swept away by colorful or dramatic details which are interesting but irrelevant. Or he may find that he and the class have followed a tangent and that they are about to fall off into nothingness. Or the unexpected ring of the hour bell signals the end, and thoughts are left loose and ravelled. Bells may call the close to even the best of discussions, of course, but the prepared instructor is able to take hold of even that last moment to say, "Here is where we are; there is where we have yet to go; that is where we will begin next time."

There remains one further and important value in the instructor's advance preparation of discussion. He can help the student to come prepared. At the first class meeting some learning task is set for the student. He will prepare for class with more thoughtfulness and selectivity if the major problems for consideration are posed for him by the instructor. The book will be read not in order to store away a batch of knowledge but instead it will be put to immediate use to illuminate the problems that have been set before him. The case will be read, not for its highlights of human interest, but in the search for such understanding as will clarify the problems posed.

Even the prospect of continuing discussion will be anticipated and mentally prepared for within the perspective and focus of formulated questions. Outside the class, then, the questions or problems posed by the teacher provide stimulus and focus for learning. To the ensuing class the student comes already chewing on the food for thought which the teacher has set before him.

So much for what goes on behind the scenes on instructor's and student's part in preparing for discussion. Its acting-out takes place in the classroom. Communication begins. It begins with the eyes. The leader of a good discussion must begin by looking at the discussants, must say to each with his eyes, "I see you, I recognize you, I am content (and often glad!) to be with you."

Not much time should pass before the instructor should have identified his individual students and should be able to address them by name. Everyone of us knows the gratification of being recognized and named in a group and, conversely, the annoyance at being considered anonymous. Beyond the good human relations involved is the effect such recognition has upon a student's participation in the work of a class. To be simply a nameless person in a classroom offers an easy "out" from responsibility; to be specifically known to fellow-students and teacher is to be impelled to live up to the concept of ourselves with which we invest our names. In the small group this presents no problem. In the large class the instructor who is to know his students must develop devices by which to do it. The use of a seating chart for a few sessions so that a student stays "put" long enough to be identified (and students are pleased to conform to this when they know its purpose), the calling of roll, not for an attendance check but with attentive taking in of the distinctive features of the respondent, are among the means by which "the student" may quickly become "this particular student" to the instructor, and anonymity may give way to responsible identity.

All participants ought to be apprised of the purpose and the rules of the game. These do not need repetition from class to class once the pattern of classroom learning behavior is established, but at the students' beginning in a course sequence it is well to share them openly. Details and exceptions are best left out; they will not be remembered because the students are too busy dealing with their feelings about whether they do or do not like the person, clothes, voice, etc., of the instructor. Some simple general statement of how we will function together and what will be expected of the student in the way of classroom participation (along with other general requirements) and to what purpose we operate as we do helps to ready the student for his responsibility and role.

Caseworkers have long operated by the adage, "Accept the individual but not necessarily his act." This is readily applied in the classroom situation. Each student is listened to with equal attentiveness and respect. His right to difference from the leader or others in the group is given full recognition. Except as it is manifestly not true (as with the student who momentarily feels mischievous or negative), the motivation behind what the student says is assumed to be his honest wish to clarify his own thought or to contribute to group thinking. There is no place here for a show of the annoyance or impatience or downright despair which the leader may sometimes feel in response to a student's comments, nor place for the caustic or witty thrust at what seems ludicrous or absurd. The leader would be less than human if he did not feel these and other emotions in response to what he hears. But, like the disciplined caseworker, he subjects his feelings to vigilant control. His business is to help others to feel sufficiently safe and accepted that they dare to move forward.

The probability, however, is that the teacher of casework tends to err less in the direction of attack and more in the direction of over-protection, of accepting the student, his act, and his communication too wholly and too uncritically. Trained as he has been in the tradition of handling people with care, dealing with them so that hurt is not knowingly inflicted, giving them personal support while they struggle to work on their problems, the caseworker-turned-teacher is likely to come to the classroom trailing clouds of "treatment" in his wake. He is likely to sidestep correction of an erroneous idea or to challenge an illogical opinion for fear that he may hurt feelings or undermine the student's self-confidence. And the result may be the discussion where everyone, or nearly everyone, has expressed himself, everything or nearly everything has been accepted as "right," and there is a temporary glow that "we are as one." Until the student leaves the classroom. Then he, who proposed that $a + b = c$ and he who suggested that $a + b = x$ begin to argue as to which was right and they are left to their own confusions.

The teacher's clarity as to the difference between the discussion as a therapeutic experience and as an educational experience rests upon clarity as to the purpose and content of a school course and the function of the teacher in bringing that purpose and content to life. An understanding of the nature of growth and learning leads to the recognition that while the student must be accepted, not everything which he produces need be.

The fact is that all human growth is stimulated by *acceptance and expectation*. *Acceptance* provides the benign climate within which safety and nurture are experienced; *expectation* provides the stimulus and challenge to reach out, strive, struggle, "come one step out of safety." Implicit in casework (and perhaps progress would be hastened if this were more often made explicit) are certain expectations by the caseworker of the client; acceptance is the support and nurture towards this end. Within the educational situation expectation is open and explicit. Consistently, certain tasks are set for the student to master, and they are progressively demanding. The student's ability to perform them is matched against standards and within time limits. The teacher must expect, then, as well as accept, and in courses which prepare the student for professional excellence the expectation is that he will learn to think straight, to see inconsistencies, to use words accurately, etc. Therefore, while the student is sustained by acceptance, his utterances must be dealt with so that discussion will not be simply an experience in self-expression but an experience in self-reaching for further learning.

There are a number of ways by which the instructor can support the integrity of the individual student at the same time as the irrelevant or rambling or erroneous contribution is directly dealt with. The warmth of good humor provides an equable climate for comfort. Good humor is tolerant and understanding, and the laughter that occurs within it is laughter *with*, never laughter *at*, the person. The depersonalization of that which might be interpreted as attack is helpful toward maintaining the student's self-respect: "I'm sorry to have to cut you off, Miss Black, but time's the villain of the piece, you know." Universalization of fault (when this is valid) helps the student feel that he is not different, that his error is a common one: "All of us are prone to vague generalizations when we've not thought something through. Mr. White has said what a lot of us were probably thinking." Or, "This is a natural and understandable mistake you're making, Miss Brown. I'm glad you brought it out so that all of us can work on it." Maintaining the student's sense of his group membership, that he is always part of group effort is reassuring: "I'm afraid we're going off the track, Mr. Green—it's a temptation for all of us. But let's hold ourselves to the point." And, of course, the accrediting and support of that which can validly be used to promote problem-solving serves always to buoy up the student's self-esteem: "I'd seriously question the conclusion you've come to, but some of the points you've made along the way are good. Let's look at them."

An important means in all learning is by imitation and identification. Student attitudes, not only towards that which they are learning but towards those with whom they work together, are subtly but surely shaped by the attitudes of the instructor-leader. Vital to the students' professional performance will be an ability to hear others out with attentiveness, to control their negative feelings against a speaker, and to deal with what is being said rather than with the sayer. This grace of human relations and this foundation for clarity of thinking comes in some part to be consciously and unconsciously incorporated by class members as it is seen and steadfastly maintained by their leader.

Even with the best of discussion management, however, problems are likely to be encountered, troubling to the instructor and sometimes to the class group. Every teacher knows those extremes of the active-passive class curve. The consistently quiet student is often troubling because he creates dead spots in discussion, difficult because impassive silence defies interpretation—(is he with us? beyond? behind?)—and because he is not carrying his share of responsibility. The over-active discussant, on the other hand, takes more than his share of time and attention, may race ahead of the class, or bog it down in his own personal mire, or put other students to flight. Within these two problem spots in class discussion are differences which call for different handling by the instructor. The aggressive discussant may be one of two distinct types. One is an active, eager, searching learner, thirsty for knowledge and impulsively running towards it. His feeling is that learning is good, he wants to partake of it freely, and sometimes his greed overcomes his awareness that others may also want to share. Because this person is with the instructor (wants to be with him too much), because he feels positive toward his learning experience, it is only his behavior and not he himself that needs dealing with. Within the discussion situation this can be dealt with, firmly and good-humoredly, by his being asked to hold on to himself, to give others a chance, or even by passing over his insistent hand with a friendly glance of acknowledgement. He is likely to understand and accept limitations on himself.

The other type among the over-active discussants is the student whose approach to learning is by mobilization for fight, whose feelings of suspicion, potential danger and negativism are roused by the new or the different. He must attack or spar with each new idea or the purveyor of such ideas. As a person whose first feeling is *against* (though he may come eventually to be passionately *for*), he is often unloved by class and teacher. But he may serve a very useful purpose. The gadfly and the doubting Thomas are antidotes against the smugness or slickness which may develop in a class or in an instructor. The probing quality of a hostile mind may take a good poke at frozen formulations. Furthermore, this one individual's expression of negativism or doubt may be the echo of what was in the minds of many in the class who lacked the courage to say so. When this is so, it can be seen in the brightened eyes of the other students or in the readiness with which they'll move into the fray. If, on the other hand, this is a one-person problem, this too can be known to the observant instructor by the manifestations of the elaborate patience or the cooling interest which appears in the class. The problem of repeatedly expressed negativism or fixed ideas can be dealt with in only a limited way in the classroom. Again, the rules of discussion are invoked. "Is anyone else concerned with this issue? If not, let's not take class time for it." Or, "I'm going to interrupt you, Mr. X, because we can't thrash that out here. I'll be glad to discuss it with you after class though." The more troubling problem is whether this student will ever be able to arrive at feeling at one with the subject matter he is to master and the persons with whom he is to operate professionally. This question will have to be faced with the student in individual conference, and his ability to change his classroom behavior will be partial test of his ability to become a professional person.

Among the silent ones, too, two different types are to be found. The one is the submissive learner, students who have been drubbed into passivity by their previous learning experience, whether at home or in school. They take what is fed them obediently, uncritically, and if they are resistive, they are not conscious of it. They taste without particular pleasure, often swallow whole, and tend to be resigned to some of the miseries of indigestion. They are troubling to the instructor, not simply because they may be a passive load to be carried by the rest of the class, but, more, because of the question they pose as to their eventual ability to give nourishment to their profession.

The second major group of students who do not readily participate in discussion are those who are active but introspective learners. Their mental activity during discussion is readily seen in the responsiveness of eye, in the lights and shadows which play across their faces, in the quality of alertness in their very posture. Sometimes, as only written assignments will reveal, the most deeply thoughtful, critical, insightful students are to be found among those silent participants. Here the problem is less that they do not make themselves vocal but more that they work as lone operators rather than in co-operative venture. However, the classroom is not the most vital testing ground of their ability to co-operate in relationship with others. For these students as well as for all others, active field work practice, client-worker, worker-co-worker, worker-supervisor relationships are the test of ability to give of one's self and take in of another.

But so long as the use of the discussion method in the classroom aims at the development, through practice, of certain behavior, it is incumbent upon the instructor-leader to attempt to engage the non-discussants, be they the silent-passive or the silent-active ones, in open participation. There are several ways by which this can be done. While a course which is to use the discussion method starts with the instructor's sharing with the students the ways by which they will operate and the wherefores of such ways, it may be necessary to repeat something of this as the course goes along—"You'll remember we talked in our beginning session about the values for our professional development in sharing our thinking, in working together at difficult problems. Right now about three people seem to be carrying the lug." Sometimes the silent student can be called on. This should happen not when he is likely to be caught unprepared or unrelated but rather when the opportunity for response offers him easy range (as "What is your reaction to. . . ?") or when his face makes plain that he is at one with the ongoing discussion. Sometimes the instructor may respond to the communication from the student which comes via the written paper by adding to his comments the suggestion or the wish that the student share his good thinking or his interesting ideas with the rest of the class. And sometimes, again, the problem needs to be dealt with between instructor and student in individual conference with the instructor's attempt to understand the meaning of the student's nonparticipation and to help the student understand the value to his own growth of risking himself.

One must not be seduced by the happy active noises of discussion and the spread of participation into believing that this in itself is an educational experience. Communication is not enough. Planned education requires that the student learn by doing certain things in certain ways. Classroom discussion has as its major purpose the establishment and the exercise of given ways by which professional communication may be assured. These ways are based on habits of sound thinking, and the teacher leading discussion must hold himself and his students to the exercise of these habits.

Thinking begins with an observed or perceived fact, situation, or condition. Whether data will be observed or perceived accurately or not depends in large part on whether mental vision is clear. Its most frequent dimming or distortion is due to emotions or attitudes which come between the observer and that which is perceived. Spontaneously with perception comes ideation—that which is seen is "read into," that is, inferences are drawn. From among these speculations some selection is made and a supposition or hypothesis is formed which invests the data with meaning. Now the validity of this meaning is taken apart and tested by such facts or knowledge as may be brought to bear on it. In this process of analysis, account is taken of which is known, what is inferred, what is supposed, what can or cannot be validated, what remains to be known and what can be put together into a synthesis called judgment or conclusion.

Obviously, every problem we encounter in our personal or professional lives does not demand for its solution the whole of this thinking process. Even when it does, we are often not conscious of having taken these steps because of the spontaneity and speed with which they may occur. But teaching and learning from the materials and processes of casework make particularly necessary the carefulness and the disciplined habits of mind which assure good thinking. Casework, concerned as it is with understanding and helping live human beings in live social situations, tends to rouse in the student considerable subjective involvement, impulsive assumption, prejudice for or against, emotionalized thinking. These reactions will distort or blur the clarity of his perceptions and his judgment unless he has become habituated by practice to the discipline of thoughtfulness. What the student thinks and how he thinks can best be known and best dealt with as he communicates and shares his thinking aloud in class discussion. To differentiate fact from inference, to separate what is known from what is felt, and what is felt from what is thought, to widen and deepen the range of ideas, to develop and test meanings by pooled knowledge and experience, to scrutinize interpretations in the light of knowledge, to weigh pros and cons, to arrive at considered judgments—for all these purposes the discussion provides opportunity and offers experience and practice in the communication, sharing, testing and synthesis of thinking.

Discussion provides this opportunity. Whether it will be used depends of course directly upon the teacher. To his assumed ability to think around a point and then *to* it he must, as a discussion leader, bring a store of ready energy and patient persistence in order to spur on and yet hold his students to the rigorous demands of sound thinking and clear communication. [In the original publication there followed here a rather long and perhaps obvious illustration of some of the points made above. In the need to meet space limitations I have not included it here. I have a reasonable hunch that every teacher could put forward her/his own example of a pointless or pointed and fruitful discussion.]

To rim this many-spoked wheel. The educational value of discussion is the exercise of the student's mind in habits of clear thinking and clear communication. Within a given course of study the use of the discussion method is affected not alone by this purpose but also by considerations of content to be learned within a given time unit. By virtue of these several factors and of his necessary perspectives as to direction and goals of study, the teacher must be both prepared and active in his role as instructor-leader. His preparation consists of seeing and using each class session as a forward-moving unit of the whole course structure and of formulating and sharing the essential questions to be "shaken apart" toward their resolution. His activity consists of conveying to his students his understanding acceptance of their feelings and foibles and, at the same time, his understandable expectation that their interest and efforts will be brought to working on problems of common concern. Within this tempered climate which the teacher sets, he must repeatedly and continuously encourage the students' exercise in those habits of shaking-apart, evaluating, reorganizing and sharing their thinking. By these means discussions which began as verbalized reaction may develop into intelligible and responsible communications of knowledge and ideas.

1989 AFTERWORD

Is this food for further discussion?

10

VALUES: BELIEVING AND DOING IN PROFESSIONAL EDUCATION

Ages ago I entered the first grade, a teacher's dream of an open vessel thirsty for knowledge and, yes, for values to be poured into it. Every morning the gong rang at nine and some twenty of us rose up and put our right hands upon the general area of our hearts and pledged allegiance to our flag and to the country for which it stood. By about the fourth grade and some 796 pledges later I had begun to wonder about my flag and the country for which it (and we) stood. Why did we say that same thing every day, and then abruptly flop into our seats and turn to doing our sums and tables? What was it for, I wondered; what did it have to do with the other things we did? And, because I could not fathom its use or its meaning in relation to anything else we did, it became for me, and probably for my fellow pupils, a kind of nonsense chant like those we used when we jumped rope or bounced ball. Perhaps it had the unifying value of a group ritual, but little more, because it was largely mouth-talk even though it emerged from touchingly pious-looking faces.

I suppose mouth-talk from pious faces is common among us all even as adults when we talk about values in the blue—in their remoteness from action in specific situations, when we "pledge allegiance" to those values that are so abstract and so lofty that no one would gainsay them. Peace, equality, freedom, and justice, all are pure gold values, and everyone treasures them. The dignity and worth of every human being, the right to self-determination, the reciprocity between man and his society and between rights and responsibilities—these are values reiterated in social work—but

Presented at the Centennial Symposium of the Jewish Family Association of Cleveland, May 1975. Originally published as "Believing and Doing: Values in Social Work Education," in *Social Casework* 57, no. 6 (June 1976): 381–98. Permission to reprint herein (with a few deletions) given by Family Service America.

they are not exclusive to social work. They are espoused by every politician from far left to far right; they are popular slogans inscribed in our national documents and upon our national monuments. They are so high level as to be safe and impregnable. They are also so general and abstract that they may be subject to radically different interpretations. No one would be against them. What is subject to argument, to opposition, or given to violence, is how they should be operationalized, by what instruments and means they may best be achieved. As soon as any one of us is pushed to move from belief to doing, from abstract to concrete, from the ultimate to the proximate values, then the conflicts and the differences and the varied interpretations of their meaning begin.

I am, then, about to make a flat-footed value judgment. It is that a value has small worth except as it is moved, or is moveable, from believing into doing, from verbal affirmation into action. A value—defined here as a cherished belief, an emotionally invested preference or desideratum—has small worth if it can not be transmuted from idea or conviction into some form, quality, or direction of behavior. The power of a value lies in its governance and guidance for action. If values are to serve as action guides, they must be "drawn down to earth." They must be "operationalized," changed into instruments that fashion and direct our doing.

It is usual to speak of this level of values as "lower," but there is nothing disparaging in that term. They are "lower" in the sense that they are grounded in the hard realities of time and place and person-in-situation. Their pure gold may have to be alloyed with some baser metals, to be sure, but that is toward fashioning them into firm and strong instruments available for everyday use.

It is these operating, instrumental values, those that guide and govern what we do in our daily living, to which I will attend, relinquishing with reluctance the headier pleasures of the pure and the absolute. Our question is: How, in education for a profession—social work in this instance—can values be taught and incorporated and applied so that they serve not as defensive shibboleths, but as guides to professional action in its daily, commonplace forms?

It is necessary as a prologue that we recognize and understand that the very existence of social work in the special forms it has taken in this country is the expression of some ultimate values. We did not make ourselves up. We were, and are, created by our society that says, "we hold these human welfare values to be essential."

Social work then is our society's invention of an instrument, publicly and privately forged and supported, by which its averred goals for human welfare may be actualized. What social work *has* invented are the ways and means, the strategies, the models of *action* by which these values may be realized. Social work's specialness, then, is at the level of proximate instrumental values. Our specialness lies in the particular knowledges, skills, and resources that we have developed or organized by which the over-arching values may be drawn upon, reached for, and actualized. What is better, rather than worse, for this family or person whose worth and dignity we affirm? How, faced by internal and external constrictions, may this person yet be helped to become self-determining? What means and resources must be found, created, or made available in order that people may be readied to give care and be responsible to their families or community? These are some of our practical questions in pursuit of our cherished ultimate values.

We begin with the recognition that students come to professional education for the practice of social work already deeply imbued with values. They are value-carriers, whether they know it or not, even those who have recently encountered and espoused the "value" called "neutrality" and "scientific disinterest." Like every one of us, the social work student is often quite unconscious of the values that silently and powerfully guide his internal and external behaviors. The "still small voice" of our long-ago incorporated consciences, and the more accessible and articulated pushes and pulls of our ego- and social-ideals have all been taken in through our pores, so to speak. They have been absorbed from the inputs of influential parents, friends, teachers, books, and other media, taken in and made our "own" because they have had emotional power and meaningfulness at times of our emotional impressionability, or vulnerability, or openness.

When a value, belief, or commitment becomes part of us, we tend to take it for granted. It is "natural" or "normal"; we are scarcely aware of how it affects how we see and feel things, how we judge them, and how our actions are shaped by those perceptions and assessments. Then, at some moment, we are brought up short by an uncomfortable awareness of a grinding of the gears, a blockage between a cherished belief and a situation that challenges its purity or its practicability. It is this sudden awareness and questioning of long-held values of self and of the social work profession, that the student of social work experiences acutely, both in the classroom and in his agency practice.

It is a discomfort which in moderation is much to be desired. It is necessary to the modifications of thought, feeling, and action that constitute the connections between believing and doing; the passage from seeking knowledge because it holds interest or is self-enhancing, to seeking it in order to be of use to others. To these ends the teacher in social work education, whether of social work's helping processes or of its problem-areas, whether concentrating upon the individual or the society, whether in the classroom or in the social agency, must, in alliance with the student, grapple with the ends and means of social work values.

One of the most valuable attributes of any teacher is that he should remain somewhat uncomfortable, and paradoxically, that he should be comfortable with his discomfort. I speak of the discomfort that is the product not of personal anxiety or malaise, nor of some sense of personal inadequacy, but the product of intellectual and emotional grappling with the facts of disparity, discrepancy, and distance between what is known and what is yet to be understood—between what we value and the demands of situational realities. It is the condition the poet calls "divine discontent," divine, I suppose, in that it serves not to yield merely to griping and grumbling or despair and resignation, but rather in that it acts as a constant spur toward searching for what is better rather than worse, toward discovering the lesser of evils or the greater of goods.

So equipped, the teacher begins with one necessary condition for influencing another: that of being a "model." Among other attributes and behaviors it involves a constant searching for congruence between believing and doing, for identifying those proximate values that are in the direction of ultimate ones as well as those that violate them; it includes honest recognition of the relativism of many values and the frequent conflicts among them; it demonstrates tolerance and humility in the face of the imperfections of human beings, including that of being a social worker.

Such "modeling" is easier said than done. It is probably easier in the protected ambience of a classroom than in the hurly-burly of practice when what is done must often be done quickly—and thought about afterwards, often in the dark of sleepless hours. But the honest facing up to not knowing and the uncertainties and conflicts about values as they are carried into action, whether at the level of personal help or political strategy, that shared recognition of the gap between "ought" and "can," "should" and "shall," forms a strong emotional bond between teacher and student. And, as has been said, beliefs, attitudes, and ideals are best incorporated when such a bond is alive. So grappling with values is central to the emotional and thought changes that professional preparation involves.

The "modeling" of honesty, of awareness of gaps between the ideal and the real, of the consistent effort to reconcile them when that is possible, and to face inherent conflict when it is not, to recognize incongruences between them and actions that seem imperative at a given time and place, ought to characterize teaching in every part of the social work curriculum.

One of the instrumental values that social work education claims and cherishes is that professional education should be an integrating experience, that the student should consistently be challenged and helped to see the parts in relation to the whole and the connections between ends and means. This goal is valuable because the subject matters of social work are diverse and complex, and among the surest ways of binding us together, of, for example, directly helping the community organizer and the caseworker see and feel their kinship, are our commonly held values. It follows that all good teaching, whether in class or field, requires that every abstract notion or idea that is held to be a guide or precept for action must be examined for its implications for what is to be done. And, conversely, that every decision about what and how to do must be scrutinized in the light of the values to which we claim allegiance. The questions are simple ones: What good is this? For whom? What is problematic about it? Why is this more or less desirable than that? What consequences are likely to be the outcome of this position or action? The questions are simple: the answers are not. But the grappling with ambiguities, conflicts, and irreconcilables, the exercise of thought and responsible choice and decision is the essence of professional education. In these efforts the teacher must take active responsibility.

How do teacher and student decide and choose among values? What makes us believe something is good, desirable, better for people's well-being? What makes us move in the direction the belief points to? We make a value judgment. I know this is anathema to many so-called social scientists who aim for scientific purity and total neutrality in their researches. There is probably not a class or field teacher of social work who has not had the student who, on hearing that the teacher believes one thing rather than another, will say, indulgently or indignantly as the case may be, "But *that* is a value judgment!" As if to say, "But you are violating a sacred scientific tenet!" (I have thus far been able to control my impulse to say, "And so are you!" Because *he* is valuing too, except his value is total neutrality and mine is a commitment in a given direction.) Whether even the purest of sciences can ever be "disinterested" is open to at least a quizzical eyebrow.

In a profession one must stand for something; one professes to certain desiderata and standards; therefore one is charged with the responsibility to analyze, to assess, and to make judgments. No doctor hesitates to make a value judgment when he encounters a disease; no lawyer desists from making a value judgment when he encounters crime or lesser conflicts; no teacher can avoid making value judgments as he examines his school program and the individual students who grapple with it. And no social worker committed to enabling human beings to carry their work and love tasks in personally satisfying and socially acceptable ways can avoid the continuous facing up to the judging of what seems, at this time and place, to be better or worse, desirable or noxious to individual, group, or community well-being.

Clearly, there must be some safeguards to such judgments so that they are not simply the product of personal passions or subjective preferences. That is where teachers in both classroom and field practice agency have vital educating roles beyond that of encouraging free inquiry.

There are three sources which the teacher draws upon for the clarification, as far as possible, and objective consideration of values and their implications for action. One is the body of empirically established knowledge; another is the body of experiential knowledge; and the third is that of such theory as seeks to explain and to order observed phenomena.

Within the biological and behavioral sciences there is a rapidly growing corpus of research which supports, or in many instances changes, social work's conceptions of what is good or better or necessary for human well-being. Our working value judgments may then be based upon established facts. Perhaps it goes without saying that the teacher needs to know and impart, or at least point the way to, those facts.

A number of research experiments show, for example, that the capacity to love, to respond affectionately, and later to "socialize" with others stems from early body contacts and emotionally gratifying communications between a mothering person and the infant. A number of other researches reveal that moderate quantities of sensory and muscular stimuli from a nurturant environment—talk, play interchanges, and playthings—arouse and exercise many perceptive and responsive capacities in young children. The implications in these simple but important findings are that a caseworker sees mother-child closeness as "valuable," and that value is placed upon creating gratifying responsive transactions between a baby and the people and objects in his environment. What the caseworker then does, arranges for, counsels, and suggests is shaped by this firm knowledge. And how a community worker or organizer draws his blueprint for a child-care facility, for instance, will be in consonance with these values derived from research.

The second foundation undergirding social work's instrumental values is that of its vast store of experiential knowledge. Here again the teacher is responsible both to transmit and to guide and involve the learner in becoming familiar with it. Over years of repeated experience with certain forms of human difficulties and social problems, social work has accumulated (though, unfortunately, has not always articulated and systematized) a deep and wide knowledge of the interchanges between the individual psyche and the social conditions within which it develops. No professional group, for instance, has had as much experience as has social work with money—or lack of money, or having to ask for "unearned" money as have social workers. None has experienced as many people from foreign countries and cultures trying to gain a new foothold in a strange and complex land. None has known as many children suffering neglect or actual abuse. From these and like experiences we have developed a number of instrumental values which point the way to our professional behaviors. We argue adequacy of money grants and housing arrangements not just on the lofty basis of our valuing equality of opportunity. We argue it further on the basis of our valuing man's initiative and social responsibility, a value that emanates from our experience that chronic deprivation tends to result in apathy and alienation. Further, we have repeatedly experienced, for example, that a child removed from his parents, vicious or inadequate though they may be, still yearns for them and carries some idealized image of them in his mind and heart. So the social worker values the child's own family as his best environment until the situation proves untenable. Thus, our initial effort in child welfare work is to influence and change conditions within the child's own family. When that effort fails, as it often may, the value of the child's feeling connected with his blood-tie family creates the delicate balance between the caseworker's commitment to affirm and protect the child's need for roots at the same time as he may have to be moved to grow in new soil.

Connected with the value-creating and value-shaping knowledge of research and experience is a third foundation stone. It is theory—the attempt to explain psychological and social phenomena, the propositions put forward by thinkers, whether in social work or elsewhere to identify some commonalities or principles, or to make some order out of their often variegated first-hand observations. Such proposals offer temporary guides to what appear to be the formulation or re-thinking of instrumental values. That the teacher in class or field must provide the means by which such explanatory theory and its implications for believing and doing become part of the student's professional equipment is obvious. What is not always equally obvious is that such teachers must also alert the student (perhaps himself too, now and then) to the fact that this is indeed a body of theory, useful toward systematizing thinking and in illuminating understanding, but subject to further inquiry and meticulous observation.

The propositions of theory say "perhaps," "it is possible," "for the nonce it seems" that this explanation holds directions for what we do and what we should value. The problem in these tentative propositions occurs when we do not recognize that they express probability or possibility. Rather, out of some need for certainty we grab onto them as "the truth." The whole course of the use and abuse of Freudian theory, for example, might have been different if people had not so passionately leaped to aver that the idea of the oedipal complex is "absolutely true" or "absolutely false," is a sacred idea or an insane one. So would a whole set of instrumental values that evolved from that complex proposition—values, say, about the nuclear family versus communal group living, or about what is desirable in sex education of children. Perhaps it is in this area especially that the teacher himself must remain rigorously self-aware, that his predilections for this or that theoretical construct or fragment not thrust him into over-valuing its "truth" or power. In this most uncertain of all worlds, there is nothing for it but to say, to ourselves and to those we teach, "as of now," "at this time," "it is proposed," and "it seems to be the case" that this, rather than that, will produce the better, rather than the less good, consequences.

The reality is that even those values that have arisen out of rigorous research findings have often been turned topsy-turvy by some contradictory and equally rigorous research. Each day's newspaper carries the report of some new findings in the most precise of physical sciences that prove that what was thought to be "good" or "essential" for health last year has now been shown to be malignant; from the less precise but respectable behavioral sciences, that certain educational modes guaranteed to prepare a child for college turn out to be destructive to his creativity; that what was held to be a potent environmental influence has now been established as secondary to genetic endowment. We must face the fact, therefore, that knowledge itself is far from immutable. It changes, and with it the instrumental values that are its derivatives.

Yet another fact of reality requires that we keep flexible and continuously at work in assessing, weighing, making choices, and tolerating uncertainties. It is a fact that the further one moves down from absolute values, the closer one comes to specific persons and specific conditions, the more do values become relativistic. That is, the more do they require that the judgment of what is or is not desirable must take a number of variables into consideration. (Even at the level of absolute or ultimate values there are such questions to be faced. For example, in a given society or for a given person, is justice or compassion the higher value?) Certainly, as one moves toward the earthy levels of everyday life there occurs a loss of purity, an increase of relativism, and often an emergence of conflict between and among values themselves.

As examples of such conflicts: We hold human life to be precious and we exult in this century's advances in saving children whose physical-neurological conditions, were they unattended by medical science, would result in early death. And at the other end of the life span, we value the extension of life in the aged. And yet, and yet. We grow aware that many of those "saved" children become a life-long misery to their parents and to themselves; that extended old age may become mere vegetation, burdensome to the senile person himself, to his children, and to the community that can not build fast enough or well enough the means to house and care for him.

These are value conflicts for all of us. In social work such examples abound of clashes between values. Whose well-being do we hold to be of greater value: the psychotic patient or the people whose lives he may affect? Do we put him away into a hospital to rehabilitate him or to protect those he may harm? When he is judged to be ready for discharge, and he is my client, I become his advocate. I become passionately concerned that his achieved, if frangible, state of mental balance should be maintained, and that his family should readmit him to its bosom, that employers should open jobs to him. When I am his family's caseworker, however, I become their advocate, I resist his return to them because his "cure" is precarious, because the group welfare is of greater import than the single individual's, because they may need protection from him. And so on, in all our thinking about the individual and the group, about parental versus children's rights, indeed about almost any social problem, because value conflicts inhere in most of them. (One is tempted to echo the comment attributed to H. L. Mencken to the effect that there is no social problem for which there can not be found a solution that is simple, neat, and wrong.)

The recognition of the relativity of instrumental values does not at all mean that "anything goes." Nor does it allow us to shrug off a conflict with a cynical "that's the way it is." If indeed we "profess" to striving for the greater well-being of the many people whose lives we touch, it requires that we struggle to clarify our means in relation to our avowed ends, our beliefs in relation to our behaviors. It requires that we be able and willing to mentally juggle a number of considerations at one time and to make responsible and often admittedly imperfect choices among them. Those choices are responsible when they are made in the light of what is currently known or held to be true, and in awareness of what valued end is being reached for. To develop this responsible behavior the social work teacher must help his student exactly as the student must learn to help his client: to face, to taste and to chew, to consider, weigh, and choose those adaptations between self and conditions, between what is wished for and the demands of reality, that are the essence of living. Perhaps the mark of maturity, whether in a professional person or in any one else, is the recognition that in an imperfect world the most cherished values themselves must contain imperfection, and that decisions and choices of action must take into account both what is most to be desired and the specific limitations and possibilities of this time, this place, and this person. It is both a delicate and difficult job. Students of social work come to us afire with idealism, and it is important that we do not douse that fire but, rather, use it to forge the instruments that are to be its product. Most of the values with which the student comes are at high levels of ultimacy. Some of them are unrealistic outgrowths of myths that have been circulated in the recent culture of the young. Many have been passed around and espoused during college bull sessions, accompanied by a sense of superiority over the benighted state of the rest of the world. Few have been tested in the blood and sweat of living them out or helping others to do so.

"I believe," says the student, "in the individual's right to self-actualization." Good! So does social work. It values human worth and human potential. That is why we work at putting together opportunities and processes by which self-realization may be exercised. Now, "self-actualization" (or "self-realization" or "self-determination") means in real life, that is, what exactly? Does it, do you feel, mean "rugged individualism?" Does it allow for stepping on someone else? In a particular case, for instance, does it encourage a husband and father to abandon his wife and two babies because they seem to be in his way? They *are* in his way. Whose self-actualization are we concerned with? And, further, do you believe any responsibilities accompany a person's rights? What ways do you see of coping with the lifelong struggle between a person's rights and his obligations? Are any compromises possible? or necessary?

What is illustrated here is clear. It is, first, the teacher's affirmation of an ultimate value which everyone treasures, to which our hearts leap up. But then there follows the forcing of thought, the exercise of discriminative judgment about the actual operation and instrumentation of that value—its explicit meaning as it is carried into action, the limitations and complications in it as soon as the individual is seen as joined with others, whether in marriage or parenthood or any other form of social contract, its sometime conflict with other cherished values, and so forth.

Such questions and conflicts in our value systems must not be glossed over. They require thought that weighs and balances, and that includes openness to compromise. Compromise is hard for the young, but it is an ever-present necessity of life if beliefs are to be translated into action. One may need to compromise with the time it takes or the detours that must be traveled to go from where one is to the goal one reaches for, and certainly often with accepting some less than ideal solution.

"Going to college is a middle-class value," says the student (whose own college education has conveniently supplied him with that concept). "And I don't want to impose my middle-class values on my client." His client is an intelligent, black adolescent, the only son of a mother whose hopes have been shattered by his recent drop-out from high school.

"That's good!" says the social work teacher. "I mean about your not wanting to impose your values on another person. Because that would run counter to a basic value in social work—the individual's right to make his own decisions. But we must talk about that ideal and its meaning. Whether, for instance, self-determination includes acting on impulse or whether it means making a considered, knowledgeable choice. And we will need to talk also about whether there is a difference between imposing on and influencing people. But first let's look at this business of middle-class values. What are they, anyhow? Are they bad because they are middle-class? Does the economically lower-class person necessarily subscribe to a different set of values about everything? Does that class value ignorance? Or failure? Do the poor want to stay poor, or do they hope to move up in the world? Taking your young client as an example—what does he value for himself? Do you know?"

What is briefly illustrated here is again the several-fold approach to the examination of values both in definitional terms and in operational outcomes. What has been called to the student's attention is that the unexamined value is not worth holding. And, that beyond saying what a value means by definition, it must be scrutinized for its probable consequences as it is translated into action. Further, it can not be assumed that so-called class values or culture values are carried in the same degree or kind by every individual within a given group. Indeed, true valuing of a person requires that *his* particular values, *his* desired ends, should be drawn out and considered if along with respect for the person we value his self-awareness and self-direction.

Several years ago I developed and taught a course on "Utopias and Human Welfare." My original objective was to help students to see that they are part of a long and often radiant tradition of reaching for a more perfect society, of the fashioning of social blueprints for the betterment of human existence. To both my own and the students' surprise, a second objective rose to predominance: the need to identify, face, examine, question, reevaluate, and restructure a whole complex of values that they, and I too, unthinkingly, had carried, believed in, and now found ourselves confronted with.

The students start with a zealous commitment to the idea of a society that offers the greatest good to the greatest number. So they support such legislation and regulation as will insure this value. Then they go first to live in Plato's *Republic*, later, in its modern counterpart, B. F. Skinner's *Walden Two*. Suddenly they are acutely uncomfortable with the infringements upon their own taken for granted individual rights. They are passionately attached to the notion of individual freedom. Then they become suddenly aware of the actual narrow boundaries which curtail their self determination in their everyday lives. Now they argue and tussle with questions such as where *laissez-faire* should end and social constraints begin; with the relation between freedom and control.

Again, they are firmly for "excellence." What other value could one hold for one's chosen leaders? Yet (reluctantly recognized) this desire implies elitism. On the other hand, does egalitarianism tend to have a down-grading effect, the risk of valuing mediocrity?

Some warmly approve of communal living arrangements; yet few are personally ready to give up the pleasures and pains of the nuclear family. "Happiness" is unanimously valued. But what is it? What does it mean, exactly? There is considerable "unhappiness" about the shallowness of all human feeling induced in Aldous Huxley's *Brave New World,* where the avoidance of pain is a governing value. So questions fly about, asking whether "happiness" as a constant state of being is possible, whether creativity requires some soil of discomfort, whether our culture's valuing of "happiness," undefined and unexamined, has not created a great deal of personal unhappiness.

And so we go—shaken up by our recurrent awareness of the paradoxes and conflicts in our own value system, rocked by the embarrassed laughter at the recognition of the jumble of often incompatible values we have carried, and with the earnest struggle by each of us to find some workable adaptations between ideal and real.

What I illustrate by these few examples is the need for all of us to put our guiding and often unrecognized values under the scrutiny of their implications for action; our need to recognize how two or more high-level values may, at the point of being tanslated into action, be in sharp conflict; the fact that values infuse not only those segments of social work education that deal with the understanding of and direct service to individuals and small groups, but also those subject matters dealing with large-scale organizations, with policies and planning. The need for conscious awareness of the values that influence our doing applies at every level of social work. Not only may subjective and unanalyzed values motivate the case- and group-worker, but community planners, researchers, indeed, all of us are pushed and pulled by often unseen value assumptions and commitments. Only as we continuously raise these assumptions and commitments to full consciousness can we take possession of them. Otherwise we, and consequently our practice, are possessed by them.

Thus the identifying and examining of action-guiding values ought to be part of every learning experience offered in social work education. This belief is a personal "value-judgment" and I admit it, cheerfully. It is a judgment based on an educational value stated earlier: that preparation for a profession should be an integrating experience, to enable the learner to see parts in connection to the whole, the ideal in relation to the possible, the cherished belief in its effect upon action, the "truth" and its consequences. Such questioning, probing, assessing, and exercise of judgment, such conscious decision-making dialogue between what I believe and what I do, must go on both within and between teacher and learner until it becomes an ingrained mode of thought for each of them. It is the distinguishing mark of a professional helper that he not only is knowledgeable, that he not only is skillful, but that he is constantly striving for a "fit" between what he believes in and what he tries to make happen. Further, it is our values that bind us together, those which we all stretch to achieve even as we share together the uncertainties, the conflicts, the ifs, ands, or buts of the instruments and processes by which to grasp at them.

In today's world, and certainly in that of social work, we desperately need that dogged search for a sense of congruence and connectedness between what we believe and what we do. Under the present day's shifting and splintering of values there lies a two-forked temptation in every profession to escape looking at its dilemmas. One is the escape into easy cynicism and the other is the escape into techniques or technology.

"A cynic," said Oscar Wilde, "is a man who knows the price of everything and the value of nothing." One ponders on how a cynic is made. It seems to me that he was once an idealist whose illusions have been shattered. He was a person who once believed beyond belief, who admitted only of absolutes, whose values were such over-blown bubbles that they could only burst in their contact with the dirt and crosswinds of reality. "All or nothing," he said in effect. "What is not all good is no good at all." So, protecting against his inevitable sense of defeat he turns to contempt, and abandons all consideration of values. He does what he does for want of something better. He seeks a professional degree only as a kind of "union card." He knows the price of everything and the value of nothing.

A tempting by-path in the search for certainty and security in our disordered world is toward technology worship, that of the hope and faith that certain techniques, or tricks-of-the-trade, will provide the panaceas, and will turn the screw of personal or social miseries and malaise. Chiefly, technology asks, "Does it work?" Its proponents tend to assume that "If it works, it is good." They do not always ask, "Good for whom?" or "Toward what end?" or "Relative to what other possible alternatives?" Thus, there often ensues the experience of finding that some technically perfected machine or method that "works" turns out to be noxious, "bad for people" in unanticipated ways, creating or carrying new problems in its wake.

Social work is not free of this push into technology—the search, sometimes frantic, sometimes funny or troubling, for some foolproof technique that "works," some way of helping people faster, more easily, more dramatically. In the one-tracked quest of "how to do it," the "why," the values, may be lost to sight. There may, for example, be many needful people who do not fit into the mode of a given technique, so they may be cast off; there may be quick cures of small symptoms with calculated or naive ignoring of the malaise or malady they express; there may be manipulation of people in ways that undermine human rights; there may be schemes for social reform that carry within them, unnoticed, seeds of social destruction. And the professional person himself may become, in Max Weber's phrase, a "specialist without spirit."

Every profession has its cynics and those who hold technique to be both their most valued instrument and goal. But no profession survives or thrives because of them. We survive as a profession when we represent and carry into action our culture's valued beliefs and commitments. We thrive as a profession when we can forge and demonstrate the ways by which those desired and desirable goals may be approached, reached for, and occasionally grasped and actualized. To this on-going task of giving life to the ideals of social work education we must continuously translate believing into doing, must continuously search out the integrations between what we profess and how we act. This task is the essential condition for a profession's wholeness, and, certainly, it is a condition for the mental and emotional wholesomeness of its practitioners.

1989 Afterword

What a rare pleasure it is to find one's self in unambivalent agreement with one's self after more than a decade! But what a lot of unfinished business remains to be done; what self-scrutiny and rigorous realism must be held to by any one of us who presumes to "teach values," to transmute ideals and principles into practice and our beliefs into behaviors!

11

". . . AND GLADLY TEACH"

The thought of moral virtue filled his speech
And he would gladly learn and gladly teach.
CHAUCER

Still mourning the death of Char-
lotte Towle and remembering our long years of association in which
I knew her as colleague, as friend, and as great teacher, I came to
ponder that perennial question: What is a great teacher? What is he
made up of? What attributes, what modes of relationship and
communication, lift him to a special place in the minds and hearts
of those who learned from him? Is there any point, I asked myself,
in talking about it at all, in trying to analyze the practice of teaching
past the point of paying tribute to those few who, like Charlotte
Towle, lighted up the sky for some of the fortunate among us?

The probability is that most great teachers are born, or shaped in
childhood. There is a charisma about them, a giftedness that is
grounded in some secure sense of self. There is some generosity of
mind that is the result of an inner life so abundant and rich that it
spills over to give its content to others. There is some free and open
receptivity to encounters with new knowledge or ideas or people
that makes them able to take them in with interest and delight. And
there is their obvious pleasure in the exercise of mind and action
that continuously shapes their subject matter to the needs of the
students they teach. These qualities are gifts of person and are not
to be had for the wishing; nor by self-command. We cannot wake
up in the morning and say, "Today I simply must be creative"; nor
can we adjure another to "go develop a sense of humor" or "be
ingenious."

Presented at the Plenary Session of the Council of Social Work Education's Fiftieth
Annual Meeting, Salt Lake City, Utah, January 1967. First published in the *Journal
of Social Work Education* 3 (Spring 1967): 41–50; reprinted (abridged) as "Great
Teachers" in the *University of Chicago Magazine*, November–December 1968, and
in *The Social Work Educator*, ed. Joseph Soffen (New York: Council of Social Work

One remembers the attributes of great teachers as they have been recounted by their admiring or loving former students, and remembers also that those that go into published essays are, by this mark, the accounts by gifted or at least highly literate students. I sometimes wonder how the run-of-the-mill student perceived Socrates or Mark Hopkins or those fabled Oxford dons who regularly tore their students to ribbons and thus, so the stories suggest, produced masters of logic and literary form. One reads descriptions of great teachers—Barzun, Highet, Edman—and others, and at the moment of vicarious identification, one gets some heady sense that "I too have some part of this." Then the book is closed, the class hour approaches, yesterday's carefully developed notes look deadly, and one thinks, " 'and gladly teach!' But *how?*"

The problem for a teacher who would gladly teach so that his students might gladly learn is this: How can he become a good teacher by the exercise of his conscious intentions? Indeed this is the problem for schools of social work today. New schools and departments of social work are springing up everywhere overnight. They arise not because the profession stands in full readiness to transmit its developed body of knowledge, but rather in response to a clamor for social work practitioners. The scramble for teachers results in faculties that, depending on one's point of view, may be called richly diverse or oddly assorted. In either case, the new recruit and the old hand both, in those lonely moments behind the closed office door, when they face only their teaching notes, ask themselves, "How?"

Portraits of model teachers are posed and haloed. So rather than describing these, I ask myself what I believe is a basic question: "How do adults learn, anyhow?" Most educational theory stops short of adulthood. Yet students in schools of social work are adults, and even if we find that numbers of them are still involved in the identity and role confusions of adolescence or the natural work and love problems of early adulthood, it is still probable that their learning patterns are fairly well set and their capacities for change are neither as flexible nor as plastic as they were before all those other teachers made their impress upon them. (Many of those other teachers, including parents, have done rather remarkable jobs, incidentally, in stretching and exercising growing minds and in supporting confidence in self-and-other.) But, even for the good

Education, 1969). The present version, slightly abridged, is reprinted here by permission of the Council on Social Work Education.

learner, the tasks of professional education—and particularly social work education because of the many psychological hazards in social work itself—demand and challenge the young adult to a new kind of learning. It is not just that he learn more about this, that, or the other; he is equipped to do this as his transcripts confirm. It is that he must winnow, rearrange, and reorder everything he has already learned, plus what he is about to learn, into new configurations, shaped by questions of "So what is its use for social work? What does it say for what I or others ought to be and do?" Moreover, he must, at once, risk himself in using his barely grasped knowledge and know-how in the interest of others, and in this uncertain endeavor he will be subject to continuous scrutiny and evaluation. So his teachers both in class and in field face the task of changing the perspectives and affects and behaviors of all but grown students with all but settled learning patterns.

Recently, several perspectives on the dynamics of personal change have emerged that bear upon learning and teaching of adults. Among them are the crisis and stress studies which show that at crucial points in an adult's life he is most vulnerable to, or accessible to, influence from "powerful others." "Crucialness" is inherent in the risks and shifts and investments of self that both career choice and the impact of field work force upon the social work student. "Powerful others" are those persons who are assumed to possess the means by which one's gratifications or goals can be achieved and who, further, proffer (or withhold) the nurture of love, safety, and recognition along the way. A number of recent inquiries into the core dynamics of learning in children point to the basic essential: a relationship that combines potency and affectivity, power and love. We are concerned here with learning in adults, but it seems probable that here, too, though in diminished degree, *power and love, within a context of crucialness, are the dynamics of both unconscious changes and changes by conscious effort in our students.*[1]

Power and love are vested in—or are perceived by the student to be vested in—the role of teacher. The intensity with, and degree to, which these attributes are felt or sought in the teacher will depend, of course, on how much the student wants what the teacher has.

---

1. Orville Brim, in his essay "Socialization through the Life Cycle": "It appears that if society is to undertake basic re-socialization of adults . . . it might well institutionalize in some form the high power and affectivity characteristic of childhood learning." Orville Brim, Jr., and Stanton Wheeler, *Socialization after Childhood* (New York: John Wiley, 1966).

One further conceptual perspective, derived from ego psychology and put forward notably by Robert White, adds to our view of teaching and learning. That is the concept of an innate drive for competence, which suggests that motivation in the human being consists not only of finding means to relieve tension and to achieve surcease of anxieties, but also includes an insistent urge toward mastery and toward experiencing the self as effective and competent. When the teacher believes this to be true (not, one hopes, because of its oracular source, but because it confirms what he already has observed), he will take a certain position or view of the student that will affect his teaching content and relationships.

These several ideas—of power, of love, and of competence-motivation at a time of crucialness—are significant for the teacher of adults and for what he must do and be.

What is the nature of the power that students perceive and seek or sometimes fear in a teacher? The power that is feared is easy to identify; it stems from the teacher's having the right and responsibility to assess the student as a learner. This has heightened meaning in a professional school because such assessment may shape the career goals of the student and affect his future. So grades and evaluations are touchy things in a professional school despite the graduate student's having learned to say that he knows grades "don't really matter." But this evaluative power is not what infuses the student-teacher relationship with its major significance.

The power that is held by one who is to be an influential teacher is that of knowledge and know-how. The teacher must be seen to possess knowledge of the subject matter he teaches—possess it not in the sense that he has simply boned up on it, studied and crammed it, but that he has made it his own. He has come to possess it by mulling it over, having given the time and thought to view it in several perspectives. To use a physical analogy, he has incorporated his knowledge by long and careful tasting and smelling and chewing of it, and by "listening" to the tastes and textures of this food for thought before he has swallowed and digested it. He has made it his own by connecting it with what he already knew and believed, by a continuous process of mental shuttling between the special subject matter of his knowing and the general subject matter of his field; and between this and its import and uses in the profession; and between these and their relation to man in his daily life. His knowledge, then, is not a rigidified body of relevant facts and theories that spills forth on call like a tape from a machine; it is, rather, ordered, shaped, selected, lighted up, colored, and infused by the workover it is continuously undergoing in his mental and affective processes and in his interpretations of life experience. He becomes a *person* full of knowledge, not simply what we call "a brain." A "knowing" teacher knows his subject mentally and feelingly. He knows it not "by heart" but *"in the heart."* He warms it and warms to it continuously by his exercise and play with it and by his caring about whether it is well put together; he tends to its gaps and thin spots, and tries to weave it whole. This kind of work to attain and expand knowledge is akin to loving.

In the academic situation, the teacher is held to have power when he "knows his stuff." His power of influence widens when he can show his students how to know theirs, how to grasp what they reach for. In the professional school, a further consideration marks the teacher of influence. It is that knowledge must be actually *demonstrated* to have power, that is, that it must have quick and apparent relevance and application to the learner's aim, which is to put knowing into action. In the professional school, then, the teacher's power must include not only knowledge but know-how. The student of social work must experience his teacher as someone who could, on call, apply the principles of interviewing he is teaching, construct and conduct a research project in an area of obfuscation, advise or testify before a legislative committee on social policy. Nowhere more than in a school of social work must there be the evidence to refute that dusty canard that he who knows *does* and he who knows not *teaches.* Its persistence stands as a reminder to us all that to seem powerful to the student the teacher must show his know-how as well as his knowing. One reason for the field teacher's influence being more potent than the classroom teacher's lies in the student's imputation to him of greater know-how. One problem for the teacher who has no direct social work experience is that there is often evident some missing trackage between his knowledge and its application.

I think back now to Charlotte Towle as a powerful teacher. She was a little woman; physically she always had to look up to her students. She was modest and unassuming in her bearing and manner. Fired by conviction and pushed by strong belief, she would speak out loud and clear and without compromise. But there were other times when she was uncertain or weary or tentative or simply self-contained. Yet I do not believe there was a single person among Charlotte Towle's students or colleagues who did not experience her as a major influence upon them. Wherein did her power lie? It lay in her knowledge and her know-how.

One could not be with Charlotte Towle for an hour without recognizing what a store of knowledge she possessed about the individual personality and the human condition, about all the living transactions between man and his social environment. She did not just "know" these things in a static way; what she knew was constantly at play in her, lighted up, now in one area now in another, by a continuous lively intelligence and probing curiosity. It was constantly being added to—not in some monolithic accretion, but in sifted, reshuffled, reorganized, and newly connected ways— by her continuous study combined with wide and varied nonprofessional reading, and by her insightful taking in of every new person and situation she encountered. Continuously she wove, unravelled, and rewove her ideas and observations and learnings so that the fabric of her knowledge was elastic and always in growth and change. You knew, when you opened some subject with her, that you were in the presence of a person who *possessed* what she had learned. Because she had made it her own, she felt comfortable with it, with neither the need to display it nor to feel uneasy when she was faced with a gap. When she said, "I don't know," it carried neither embarrassment nor annoyance, but rather some pleased sense that there was something new that deserved exploration.

Charlotte Towle also had know-how. One sensed this not simply because she could explain principles of treatment in the classroom or because she had been highly regarded as a practitioner; one knew it with immediacy and validity in the encounters with her as teacher, consultant, colleague. She knew how to draw out and to feed into a person's own potentials and strengths, how to free initiative in others, how to empathize and support, how to differ without rancor or threat, and how to criticize without either hedging or attacking. She had the know-how, in short, to deal with another person in ways that undergirded him at the same time as he was being influenced to change. She demonstrated this in her everyday contacts with students and colleagues.

Some of this power of knowledge and know-how was, of course, inherent and unique to the person of Charlotte Towle. But much of it was worked at by her, cultivated over the years of self-disciplined open-mindedness and responsibility. It is this combination of self-discipline, open-mindedness, and scholarly responsibility that, I believe, can be emulated and learned by those who aspire to be potent teachers. It does not matter that one may never match one's model. What does matter is that the essential attributes of the model are understood and may serve as a constant inner touchstone against which to test and change one's own operations as a learner-teacher.

To be potent in changing the minds and behaviors of adults, there must combine with knowledge and know-how the power of love. In what sense does a teacher love and show love? At the least, and fundamentally, he must love his subject matter. That is to say he must care about it; he must feel strongly that it is important, or that it matters, or that it has value. He must pour himself into it in some "heartfelt" ways. He must enjoy the pleasure of its company, of playing with it and examining it from all perspectives. He must see its faults and lameness. But, like the parent who pensively views his less-than-perfect child and forgives him for his imperfections and affirms his becoming more and better than he is, the teacher who loves his subject matter must be able to admit to and deplore its imperfections while at the same time affirm and defend its present and potential values.

A teacher's loving investment in his subject matter is a contagious thing. I suppose love is always contagious, warming to the people who come near to it, even though they may not be its direct recipients. All of us remember with warmth some teacher who affected us in benign ways, not because he was a brilliant theorist or a charismatic teacher, but because he was so obviously in love with what he taught. And all of us remember with distaste the hack who found no further delight or interest in his subject matter and served it up dead cold.

A second aspect of loving infuses influential teaching: love of the learner. The teacher who loves his student does so in ways appropriate to this particular role relationship. It begins with receptivity to the person and the intent of the learner. It moves forward with the acceptance of his ambivalences (because all new learning tasks excite some "no" as well as "yes"), his doubts, his knowledge deficits. This acceptance is not total. It must combine with the expectation, held firm and clear, that the learner has the motivation and the capacity to grapple with subject and self. Loving involves affirmation of the person and his potentials. It involves feeding in to him generously, with attention to his capacity for intake and with willingness on the part of the loving teacher to invent ways to engage him. But in the teaching role there can be no lowering of expectations and standards because both teacher and student are, by their implicit contract, engaged in an unalterable pursuit: the development of the student as a representative of a profession. When a teacher invests love in both the subject matter and the learner, his constant endeavor is to bring them happily together.

Having said this much about warming and freeing the student with love, I recall again all the stories of tutorial systems in English universities, which contradict my claims. They recount one-to-one sessions between teacher and student, consisting time after time of a ruthless tearing apart of the student's efforts, an often sadistic criticism, a wracking attack. And out of these experiences came some of the most brilliant, effective, clear-thinking philosophers, writers, and statesmen of our times. How so? What of love? One answer lies, I think, in recognizing that we have the testimonies of the survivors of that system; those who went down under it do not boast of it or commit it to print. A second explanation may be that those who went into this system and survived it were already strong, fortified by mastery of all the stressful experiences that abound in an educational system that was set up to discipline and train an elite. They already felt power within themselves, and their sense of union and identification with their tutors derived from the devotion of both to the subject matter and the students' ambition to claim it for his own.

Students of social work are not typically formed of such stern stuff. Moreover, their subject matters, while often less intellectually rigorous, are more experientially demanding. For these reasons alone, the social work teacher's power of knowledge must be warmed by his reception of the learner as competent (until proved otherwise), as being appreciated for all his own unique qualities of mind and style, and as warranting respect for his intent and efforts, if not always for their outcomes. Criticism there must be, but it should be accompanied by guidance for change (or decision that change is not possible) and by concern for the learner's own integrity.

When I speak of the teacher's love of the learner I do not for a moment mean that engulfing, dependency-creating overseeing of every sentence the student speaks, or that anxious rehearsal of every move he is to make. I speak rather of that interest in the individual student, in receiving him as someone who has a style of his own, a potential for shaping it, and as a person who must risk himself and therefore who will be expected to make some mistakes, and who must be allowed to be foolish at times.

The influence of Charlotte Towle through the several kinds of loving spoken of made its deep impress on those who learned from her. She poured herself unstintingly into her several subject matters. Her class preparation, her consideration of how to meet student need, how to select, shape, and phrase her knowledge so that it would be meaningful and retained for use by the learner—these considerations were her central concerns.

She loved learners as she loved learning. Her comments on student papers were running dialogues with them, praising or taking issue as the case might be, never simply marking right or wrong, good or poor, yes or no, but spelling out the issue that was overlooked, supplementing the undeveloped idea, pointing out the alternatives. She took delight in all growing things and their nurture, and her students and those others of us who learned from her were among them.

Can loving be imitated and learned? Can a person who undertakes to teach set his jaw and determine that he is going to love his subject matter and his students and then go and do so? Perhaps; but only to a limited degree. Certainly there are days for each of us when the appearance of another book on our special subject matter makes us recoil in self-defense, protesting that we don't want to know one more thing about penguins or people or processes. There are days when each of us thinks that a university would be a marvelous place to work if only there were no students in it. But these days are few and far between and, if they are not, they are the surest signal to the teacher to find his niche elsewhere. Perhaps this negative criterion is the most that one can say about the loving aspects of teaching. One cannot command loving either of knowledge or learners. One can only say quite surely that if there is not a fairly continuous sense that what one teaches is vital and important and even beautiful in some ways, and if, from this, there is not some wish and urge to share the pleasure of this matter with others and to bring others to want it, then as a teacher, one will have very little influence upon students.

The teacher's powers of knowledge and its uses and his demonstrated investment in both the learner and the field of endeavor are, then, two major forces in transforming the student into a professional person. The third force drives within the student himself. But it needs the teacher's recognition, support, and stimulation to find its fullest and most appropriate expression. I speak now of the drive for effectance, the motivation inherent in each of us to strive for mastery, self-actualization, competence.

These different terms—effectance, mastery, self-actualization, competence—have been put forward in recent years by various ego psychologists (Hendricks, Hartmann, and White among others) to name a phenomenon that earlier psychodynamic theory had left underdeveloped.[2] It is the phenomenon of an innate motive beyond what is explained by the concepts of libidinal and aggressive drives: the drive for pleasure that is experienced in the exercise of the ego—of its powers of muscle and mind—in the pursuit of higher levels of effectiveness and sense of competence.

The concept of the innate drive for competence as present and developing in the autonomous ego (rather than as some neutralization and sublimation of more primitive instincts) is a concept that seems particularly useful in the educational situation. In essence, it affirms that our students, selected by us because they have proved their capacity to learn, carry within them strong thrusts to explore their world beyond what they have done thus far, to learn more and better and for an avowed purpose, and to use their minds and complete selves either for the pleasure it gives them now or for the promise of pleasurable competence ahead or both. There are exceptions to be sure. There are those among our students in whom capacity turns out not to match drive and those in whom the competence drive has been checked or warped by long-standing emotional barriers. Not all graduate students are free to pour their energies into learning. But, conservatively speaking, it seems that if a teacher finds the idea of competence-motivation compatible with his own observations and experience, it may serve as a useful stance or viewing point for his relationship to the learner and that of the learner to the subject matter.

This stance promises some fresh perspectives on teaching and learning. The idea of a competence drive shifts the focus of teacher attention from the student's dependency needs to his coping capacity. It focuses less on his expectable inadequacies in a new

2. Applicable to educational endeavors as well as to those of casework practice (see notes on the essay "In Quest of Coping," herein) are the theories or newer thought on ego psychology: see Ives Hendricks, "Work and the Pleasure Principle," *Psychoanalytic Quarterly*, vol. 12 (1943); H. Hartmann, *Ego Psychology and the Problem of Adaptation* (New York: International Universities Press, 1958); Robert W. White, *Ego and Reality in Psychoanalytic Theory*, Psychological Issues, vol. 3 (New York: International Universities Press, 1963).

situation and more upon undergirding his potential, waiting-to-be-tried competences. It suggests that classroom teachers might well raise their expectation levels and expand opportunities for the students' greater freedom of inquiry and greater exercise of originality. Perhaps we have not recognized or treasured enough the driving initiative and ideals and the impatient push for action with which so many young students enter our schools today. Perhaps we have not been ingenious enough in modifying our instructional methods or curriculum arrangements to match and make the most of the students' robust, even though brash, drive to become and to do better as quickly as possible.

How fully and pleasurably a student experiences the exercise of his powers of thought and action depends heavily upon his teachers. The opportunity he is afforded to take risks; the support he gets for using his initiative; the respectful consideration he gets for his ideas, far out though they may be, not in uncritical acceptance of them but in acceptance of his intentions while his notions are subjected to the light of greater knowledge or cooler reason; the expectation that he is capable and competent as a learner until he proves otherwise; the freedom he is given to try himself provided that he is within the boundaries of his professional role and purpose—all these opportunities may be opened to the student by the teacher who views him as a learner striving for actualization as a professional person.

Charlotte Towle knew this intuitively. In her usual disciplined way, she lifted her bone-and-marrow knowledge to her conscious consideration. When ego psychologists were only beginning to put forward their propositions about the autonomous ego and its conflict-free functions, Charlotte Towle had already written, "There is evidence in human behavior that, in contrast to the tendency towards resistance to change and regression to the past, there is also a strong and inevitable impulse toward progression . . . the human personality in the process of maturing begins to reach out beyond itself."[3] Until some learning or self-management problem showed itself she presumed her students to be motivated and able to work and reach beyond themselves.

Before the perception and affect-changing powers of cognition were given full recognition by most psychologists or educators,

3. Charlotte Towle "in person" may be clearly seen in her own writings, especially some of her early ones (1935 and on) reprinted in *Helping: Charlotte Towle on Social Work and Social Case Work* (no. 4 in the bibliography).

Charlotte Towle had observed and articulated these powers. She wrote some years ago, "in an educational situation the means to the end of effecting change in feeling is through the intellect. New ideas, new intellectual orientation may bring a change in feeling, thinking, and action in the context of an influential relationship." She did not for a moment forget the dynamic matrix of the supporting relationship that provides the learner's safety island. But she was also clear about the difference between an educational and a therapeutic focus and in the former she understood the many aspects of ego strength, including the cognitive, that empowered the learner.

Never was the learner her creature; he was seen, rather, as a self-motivated source of potential professional power. The dialogue between Charlotte Towle and a learner—whether that learner was a first-year student or a colleague—was a matter of respectfully shared knowledge, opinion, and judgment. If in the end you disagreed, there was no threat to her or to you. She took pleasure in seeing difference asserted and therefore left one free to be himself. This is probably the truest mark of the great teacher: that he gives generously of his knowledge and notions and attention to the student and then, having offered such nurture, he does no violence to the independence of the learner; he leaves him free to be himself. In some part it is caring for the individuality of the "other" that enables a teacher to leave his student free, and in some part it is belief in the learner's own drive for competence. Charlotte Towle combined this caring and belief.

To return now to the question posed at the outset: is there any point to studying the model of a great teacher? Is there any purpose in examining those forces and attributes that account for the quickening and illumination of communication between teacher and learner? After all, teachers, like students, must essentially be and act themselves. And teachers, usually older by some years than students, tend to be long-patterned in their ways of operating. But it is also true that teachers, like students, are moved and shaped by powerful and loving relationships and by their competence motivation.

The powerful "other" that moves the teacher is usually in the nature of a professional ego ideal. That ego ideal may be incorporated in the living person of an "other," a colleague, for instance, who demonstrates and stands for what one would like to be able to do and be. One can never replicate him but one can emulate him. One can observe what he does that is good, what seems useful, what is admirable, and what makes him effective, and, from his repertoire, it is possible to borrow those parts that fit into one's own and that promise to enhance one's powers. Or the professional ego ideal may be shaped and colored by teachers in one's past, or even those only read about who, in their teaching role, acted in ways held to be admirable or potent. Through identification with them or the taking in of parts of them one's sense of strength and of responsibility as a teacher grows. When one looks closely at the great teachers, one sees not only their innate gifts of intellect and communion, but also their disciplined engagement with their subject matter and with its transmission. The "power" we impute to the great teacher is some combined mastery of an area of knowledge and mastery of self as its interpreter.

This is where love comes in. It must be there to warm the teacher's stretching powers. If he is to be an interpreter of the subject matter in which he has invested he must also invest himself in attentive reception and nurture of those who are to receive his interpretations. He will need to become a matchmaker, if you will, between his subject matter and his "object matter," the students.

To some degree love *can* be worked at. Indeed it must be—even that loving that leaps in us spontaneously as between a man and woman or parent and child. There are those moments or phases of a relationship where, because of transient rejection or indifference or antagonism, one must work at rearranging one's self, acting with patience though one may feel only irritation, acting the wish to understand though one may feel only anger, reaching out to receive the other though one may feel like slamming a door shut. All love must be worked at now and again. The behaviors of affect and actions that convey "love," or, if you prefer, "I like and value you," become infused with genuine feeling when they are rewarded by responsiveness.

When, through these efforts, the teacher achieves a happy engagement—when a student's eyes light up with new understanding, or he cries "aha!" or, less dramatically, he merely affirms by his respectful attention and dogged study that he has faith that this is good and useful—then the teacher gets his reward. He will find in himself some stir and change in his feeling toward the student or the student group that is embarrassingly close to love. We simply cannot help loving that upon which we have some benign influence, whether it is a homely, scraggly ivy plant on an office desk that finally puts forth a shoot because we have tended and watered it or a thorny student who suddenly lights up one day and becomes a learner. That small reward for the hard work that loving often requires is a powerful incentive for further effort on the teacher's part.

All of us, students and teachers alike, strive to be the cause of some "good" effects, the cause of some changes that are held to be desirable. This is what the concept of motivation for competence expresses. And this is what pushes us as teachers to stretch our sights and our efforts: to read, study, discuss, wonder; to turn the merciless light of question upon cherished beliefs to see if they are true or only comfortable; to shake up and blow the dust off old ideas to see if they are still relevant; to continuously answer the nagging questions of utility to professional responsibility and practice. This is what makes us want to lend ourselves to the student and then to support and stimulate him toward his own actualization as a member of our profession. This ideal of ourselves as being a "cause" in the development and change in a new generation, toward its achievement of what we hold to be good, is what drives us to develop and change ourselves, to invest ourselves in study and students toward our own greater competence. This is what sends us back year after year to ponder on teaching and, despite the grind and the groaning, to gladly teach.

1989 Afterword

It was heartening to me that the senior physician chosen to speak at the annual meeting of the medical staff and students of the University of Chicago's Department of Medicine and its hospitals asked to use this essay as the basis for his address on the "model" physician teacher.

PART THREE
AFTER HOURS

12

MILTIE AND ME

1989 FOREWORD

I suppose there is no professional person directly involved in help to individual human beings who does not carry one or two of them home after hours.[1] Doctors, lawyers, teachers, social workers, clergymen, practitioners of the several professions that proffer advice, counsel, one or more of the range of physical and psychotherapies—all leave our offices, close our doors, ready to turn to families and friends, to nourishment and re-creation of body or spirit, to escape to changes of pace, place, persons, pursuits.

And suddenly we find that one or more uninvited presences are with us. We may have looked forward to some activity that promised re-creation—reading a book that by its subject matter or literary quality refreshes the drained mind or draws us into other lives in other times and places. We may involve ourselves in some physical "work-out" that not only allows but requires aggressive competition. We may seek sheer escape—sitting in stupefaction before the TV—or, if we are lucky, we may be lifted out of ourselves by seeing or hearing some spirit-elating performance of dance or music or theater.

Still, with all these and other re-creations, there may linger within us some partial or whole re-play of the day's encounters, often to plague us, sometimes to please. All these in the privacy of our own minds, of course, gnawing at our "innards" or swell-

1. Those few among you who know the writings of our professional "mother," Mary Richmond, will recognize that I have taken the title for part 3 from her book *The Long View,* which holds a group of her on-the-side writings. In it you may still find some pleasurable after-hours. See *The Long View,* by Mary Richmond, collected and edited by Joanna Colcord and Ruth Mann (New York: Russell Sage Foundation, 1930).

ing our sense of well-being, or glimmering about like fireflies that light up but elude capture.

We have different ways of dealing with these after-hour residuals. They include defenses of escape, postponement, substitute involvements, or mental review toward gaining perspective. We have imaginary conversations, which, come morning, seem rather less astute than they did when we turned off our bedside lamps. Some of us jot down reminders or adjurations. A few of us spell out (perhaps "spill out" is the more accurate term) in talk or in writing an account of what happened, in some effort to "get it out of my system," or for the corrective experience that re-view or distancing often provides.

I am one of that latter group. Sometimes I am not sure what I feel or understand until I set it down on the neutral surface of a blank sheet of paper. Then, often, a sense of sadness becomes compassion for all of the human condition; unease of mind or conscience materializes into a resolution to "do something" toward constructive coping; anxiety or anger may dissolve into irony or laughter, because human beings, including myself, are really funny people.

As a small diversion from the stresses and unavoidable complexities of your day's work and study, I decided to include herein a few of my after-hour writings, all of which in one way or another relate to the business of social work. Fleshed out and fashioned into readable form, they are the after-hours afterthoughts of one social worker, not too different from her fellows, who at this point is at work on the business of putting an as yet unfinished, vivid, rewarding life together.

I have never quite forgotten Miltie. He was about five years old when I met him, and he would be—yes, unbelievably—well into his sixties now. I look for him now and then when mug shots of crime suspects are shown, or when I see one of those piteous, bleary, tattered old men half-lying on wintry street curbs. Perhaps he's sheltered in one of the back wards of a state hospital. On the other hand—who knows—maybe, what with the caprices of fate and circumstance, he's become a grandfather, taciturn, unreachable, who yet takes his grandkids off to fish now and then.

Miltie and his family were assigned to me when I first entered social work, at twenty, right out of college. Do not for a moment think I knew nothing about social work. I had taken a course in "rural sociology" (because it happened to fit into my overcrowded schedule) and its title held a kind of bucolic promise. Moreover, I had read *Oliver Twist* and *David Copperfield* and *Les Misérables* and other tales of the worthy poor of the nineteenth century, so I was at the least ready to bleed with them and to try to make up for their dreadful deprivations of mercy and justice.

Miltie was the youngest of the Golden family and I was to be the family's caseworker. Some months before I had arrived Mrs. Golden had applied to the agency for help, explaining that she could not raise her three children on the five hundred dollars of insurance money she had been paid upon her husband's untimely death. Financial assistance had been instituted. Rent arrears and a cycle of colds and mumps among the three children had all dwindled into insignificance as Miltie emerged from his diapers (rather belatedly), and began to "climb the walls," but literally, his mother reported tearfully. Neither she nor her two pensively obedient little girls could control him.

I made my first home visit to meet Miltie. I had been sure (as most beginning social workers are) that I "loved children." But not Miltie. His eyes were a hard blue, as if enameled, the kind of eyes a clumsy toy maker might have put into a doll head. His hair, a tumbled mass of soft golden curls, was like that which Italian renaissance artists painted on their fat cherubim. His lips were thin and tight, like those of a mean old man. It remains hard for me to describe him because even his features did not fit together somehow; they looked as though they had been taken from other faces and stuck randomly onto his pasty face. I could not find love in my heart for Miltie.

On my second visit Mrs. Golden said she couldn't stand it anymore. Miltie had climbed up onto the icebox to reach for an overhead gas pipe and a large section of the ceiling had crashed down in showers of plaster. Against all tenement-house custom, the landlord was about to sue the tenant for the fallen plaster, instead of the other way round. For me the last straw came about ten days later. A cat, an impoverished alley animal, had slunk its way into this unfortunate family, and had been taken over by Miltie. For once obedient to his mother's request, Miltie went to fetch the cat to show it to me. "It's another mouth to feed," said Mrs. Golden wearily, and I thought I must ask my supervisor if relief budgets allowed for pets.

Miltie returned, dragging the cat by its tail. Then, with the faintest of smiles, he picked it up (by its tail, the cat screaming) and he slammed it hard against the wall. Within several days I was hustling Miltie and his bewildered mother off to a psychiatric clinic.

The psychiatrist was a frayed and shaken man after his session with Miltie. He ignored Mrs. Golden, and addressed me. He said I must "Try to make *friends* with Miltie. Get to *know* him," he said. "Show *interest*." Well, I *was* a beginner, and he *was* a psychiatrist, maybe an apostle of Freud. So that was how I decided to take Miltie to the aquarium.

It was probably one of those thrusts of the unconscious that made me choose that particular place for our first "friendly" encounter. If you've ever been to an aquarium you've noted, no doubt, that when you look directly at a fish—any fish—you're met with a cold, supercilious stare, and silence. Some movement of the bitterly pugnacious lips, perhaps, but no real responsiveness. Another reason, less subtle, was that a streetcar ran about half a block from the Golden's flat to a short walking distance to the aquarium. Decided and done.

Miltie had been stuffed into his leggings and galoshes and now he was all mine. At first I was tremulously grateful to him. He had made no audible or visible response to my tentative trials at conversation, but neither had he kicked me or bolted away. He sloshed just behind me as we walked, looking something like a walleyed pike in a tassel cap. There was a moment, in fact, when I thought he *was* a walleyed pike. Up rose the uneasy memory of the duchess in *Alice in Wonderland* and the lullaby she sang to her pig-baby: "Speak roughly to your little boy / and beat him when he sneezes!" Pig-pike—but I controlled myself.

Once we were inside the aquarium I felt more comfortable, and in the gentling twilight there we moved from glassed-in tank to tank.

I began by being cheery. I made noises denoting wonder, surprise, delight as we stopped to view each fish. Miltie was unmoved. I changed tactics; I became engaging. Which fish would Miltie catch if he had a pole? Silence. How would Miltie like to ride on that big turtle? Miltie remained a stuffed pike. With some sag in my spirits I became pedagogical. I told him the one fact I knew about the electric eel, and I touched ever so lightly on the sex life of the salmon. He did not blink.

I became aware that as each fish noticed Miltie's nose pressed against the glass of the tank it would dart off into a corner of the tank, obviously terrified. This made me uneasy, and finally I suggested that Miltie must be tired. He moved to the next tank. As he stared into the water a small school of herring flashed upward in an agony of fear. He moved again to put the evil eye on the next tank.

I summoned up my courage and decided, aloud, that we would go home now, and I began mentally to compose my letter of resignation from the agency. Abruptly Miltie came to a full stop. He was fixed at a tank of Japanese goldfish, and they were in a flurry of wrapping their red-gold draperies about them and going up for a breath of air—or an escape. Miltie opened his mouth and spoke. "What's dem?" he asked. Suffused with pleasure, I told him. "I want one," he said, stonily. I explained about aquariums. "But I want one," he repeated. I thought fast. There was a new Walgreen Drugstore at the corner where we would get our streetcar. It was luring customers in by giving away two goldfish in a bowl with every dollar's purchase. I didn't need a dollar's worth of anything that day, but two goldfish for Miltie were not to be brushed aside by practical concerns.

The sun seemed unusually bright as we came out of the dark of the aquarium, and Miltie's face seemed effulgent with light. In a way I felt a stirring of love for him. Something in him had responded to the most beautiful fish in the aquarium, and he actually had reached out to another creature!

In the drugstore I bought a toothbrush and some talcum powder and asked for my free goldfish. Miltie looked with cold eyes at the two orange-colored slivers languidly floating in the bowl. They did indeed look very skinny and lonely compared to the radiant Japanese group we'd left behind. So I suggested we'd buy some pebbles and a small castle and some plastic greenery to put into the bowl. The fish took on new spirit. The clerk suggested fish food, and I said of course, Miltie would want to feed his pets. To this Miltie nodded. I exulted. I would be able to tell that psychiatrist that the child had shown an interest. And he was concerned to nurture another creature!

We celebrated with chocolate sodas. Over our straws I picked up the thin threads of our new-found relationship. "What are you going to name your fishes?" I asked. "Nuttin'," he said. I put forth again, "Shall I come and visit you and your fishes sometime?" "Nah," he said. In the pause that followed I felt inexpressibly tired. "Don't you like the fishes?" I quavered. Miltie pushed a blob of ice cream into his mouth. "Nah," he said. "I don't like no fishes. Dem," he added, as he dipped his creamy spoon into the goldfish bowl, "is for my cat."

I've never found my way back into an aquarium. Somehow I stayed in social work. Maybe it was because not long afterwards I was transferred to another district with a whole new caseload. I hasten to add that it was not in the nature of a reprimand but rather of a reward—for what I am not sure. But every now and then I wonder about Miltie.

13

BALLAD FOR OLD AGE
ASSISTANCE, 1954

POLICY: *At the time of application, reapplication, or redetermination of eligibility for Old Age Assistance, information shall be obtained from the insured regarding his life insurance, including the name of the beneficiary. Also discuss his burial plans, preference of funeral director and ownership of cemetery lot or burial space.* (Official Bulletin No. 53.63, Illinois Public Aid Commission, December 17, 1953.)

What are your plans for dying, little man?
Whom will you choose to shroud you, head to foot,
How will you pay for decent tears and prayers,
Which is the piece of ground where you'll be put?

Say, even as you stretch that stringy hand
To grasp such warmth and nurture as you can
To bind thin bone, faint pulse, and hope together,
What are your plans for dying, little man?

Taxes are high, remember,
Chiselers will lie, remember,
We must all die, remember—
Remember, little man?

What is your name, your number?
What is the point of crying?
Living and feeling are costly—
Come, sir,
What are your plans for dying?

Social Service Review, vol. 28 (March 1954): 90. © 1954 by The University of Chicago. All rights reserved.

1989 Afterword

The first-century Roman poet-satirist Juvenal is quoted as having said that "it is indignation that leads to the writing of poetry." Certainly to his, though certainly not to all forms of poetry. But his saying held true for my verses above.

14

PEOPLE ARE CRAZY ALL OVER

"Oh, dandelions!" she exclaims in a kind of shy elation. "Yes, dandelions!" I repeat. "All over the place!"

We close the hospital door behind us and set out together to cross the street where, in the vacant lot, hundreds of dandelions bloom, their faces lifted to the sun. It is an April afternoon, and under the gently uncertain blue sky the ground is starred with the profligate affirmation of yet another springtime.

"I'm glad you like them too," I say to Tillie as I pat her sweatered arm. She does not draw away but smiles tentatively.

"I wonder where they got that name," she murmurs, and I tell her that in French "dente de lion" describes their jagged toothy leaves. "I like that," she says.

This is her first outing from the women's ward since she was brought in several months ago by her mother. She had been Queen of the Nile then, holding her head high, making imperious gestures to unseen courtiers, raising her voice occasionally above a mumble to speak in some arcane, unintelligible syllables. In our clinical diagnostic conference we—several psychiatrists, a psychologist, a nurse, and I, a student psychiatric social worker—were in full agreement on the obvious diagnosis, and on what our separate and joined functions were to be.

Her mother, "an odd and withdrawn person," as reported by the psychiatrist at Admissions, had suspected Tillie was "going crazy" for some weeks. She had just "sort of floated out of it." Smart, her mother had said, very, very smart. Reading all the time. Good books, like Shakespeare and history. But saying nutty things like, "Shall I abide in this world? Is it a sin to rush into the secret house of death ere death do come?" (In preparation for our conference I had paged through *Anthony and Cleopatra* and found the sources of Tillie's eloquence, all but word-perfect.) "I will eat no meat, I'll not drink, sit—I'll not sleep either." She had repeated these lines on her first few days of wandering about the women's ward, refusing all but minimal food and drink, agitated and unseeing. Although she was not quite fifteen years old it was the women's ward to which she had been assigned, partly because of a free bed there and partly because she was already physically overblown, heavy-hipped, breasts straining against her too-tight blouses that gaped at their buttonholes.

"Why do people call them weeds?" she asks. "They're really flowers, I think!" Now she is looking at me, eye to eye, trustfully. I tell her that she is saying what I had always thought. She smiles and stoops to pick a handful. "Maybe somebody will discover how to domesticate them," she ventures.

"Maybe you will," I say, "when you go back to school, and maybe study botany." A vague look in her eyes tells me I am moving too fast. So we bend and pick, and finally sit us down upon the ground and begin to braid the sticky stems into a garland.

As we pluck and weave I say let's talk about what she'd like to do together with me when we go out. I know Dr. Powers has told her how well she's doing, and that soon she'll be well enough to leave the hospital. And I'd like to make going back into the outside world as pleasant for her as possible. What would she like me to do, with her, or for her? She concentrates on her braiding. I say maybe we should just take it easy—take a bus, go downtown, look at windows and people. She nods. We agree that little by little we'd start exploring, and little by little we'll talk over what she feels and thinks about going home and returning to school. And we will be honest with one another. Now she looks at me directly, and with a mischievous smile she places the wilting dandelion garland on my head. "You are Queen of the May!" she says.

"Let's be done with queens," I say lightly, "and just be our own selves, looking around us for interesting or funny or heart-lifting things—like dandelions." Her knowing look tells me she gets the idea.

Over her several months of hospitalization Tillie had begun to let go of her hallucinations and delusions. Whether it was the feeling of safety that the neutral walls of her hospital room gave her, or the regular therapeutic sessions she had with the caring, compassion-ate, unperturbable Dr. Powers, or those biochemical changes in the brain which remain unfathomable still—who knows? Tillie had improved remarkably, and plans for her discharge had begun. Mine was the role of linker between the hospital and her gradual reentry to home, school, and outside interests. That would involve, of course, my preparation of all those other people whose understanding and behavior would support her recovery.

First among them was her mother, with whom I had talked—reporting, explaining, sympathizing—on her regular visits to Tillie. She was a tightly-held-together little woman, spare in figure and speech, neither asking nor giving out. Her husband had left her some years ago, taking Tillie's younger brother Stanley with him. No, Tillie didn't seem to miss them. Her husband was regular in his monthly support payments, so she couldn't complain. But it was hard. She had once been a machine operator in a slipcover and drapery factory, and now she did sewing for neighborhood people when she could get jobs.

Naturally she was worried about Tillie, especially since she had been such a smart kid. Too smart maybe? Maybe her brain got overworked, like a fever? That's what she thinks made Tillie crazy. Stanley got along fine, but he wasn't very smart. Well, you can't have everything. Some people are lucky, some not. (She had a way of closing off discussions with aphorisms.)

I had also talked with Tillie's homeroom teacher, and we had agreed to plan further about what special arrangements could be found for tutoring or summer school so that Tillie could catch up with her schooling. I'd try to find where possible tutoring money could be had, she to find whatever other resources there might be. Maybe the not-too-far-away Neighborhood House had summer recreational as well as educational possibilities.

But Tillie would have to be readied for all this. She and I took several more walks about the hospital neighborhood, looking at and talking about ordinary things—watching kids' zest and grace as they jumped and danced through the flying arcs of jump ropes, ambling along the riverside, marveling at the varieties of boats and ships, and thinking how, since antiquity, they had tied the world of people together. Generally she was quickly responsive, appreciative of humor, almost gladdened at times.

When I suggested that one day we might go to the Metropolitan Museum she lighted up. She'd like that! She had been there before, especially to its Egyptian section. I cut in to say let's look at things she hadn't seen much of, like let's go breathe in the beauties of the trees and mountains and landscapes of some of the French Impressionists. She agreed, more docile than enthusiastic.

We move among Cézannes, Monets, Derains. "Beautiful, very, very beautiful!" she comments, and she giggles at my pretending to breathe in deeply for flower fragrance or clean blue mountain air. She is drawn to some Van Goghs. I tell her that he spent several years of his life in a mental hospital and had painted some of his most passionately beautiful works during that time. She looks more attentively at his painting. I say that what it shows me is that a whole person is a lot *more* than his or her sickness. She looks at me intensely. "I like that," she says. "It's true."

We pass some Picassos, and she stops, abruptly. "You know what I think? I know Picasso is supposed to be a very famous artist and all that. But I think he's really crazy."

"But why?"

"Because," pointing to a cubist composition, "he chops up everything into pieces. Or else he makes people look—well, like crazies. *Nobody* has two eyes on the same side of her face!" This is no time for an art lecture but I find myself wanting to make some room for a touch of craziness. "Maybe some of us see things differently from others," I propose. "Maybe," she grants. "But he is *really* crazy." So much for Picasso. Then, with a rare expansiveness, she adds, "Why I like the Egyptian things is, everything's in order. You know?" Yes, I know—all those triangular skirts, those mathematically correct hair and headdresses, that measured, profiled walk.

Back at the hospital where we part she says she enjoyed that, and I remind her that there is so much yet to explore in this world. "See you!" she says, with a brief wave of the hand.

Late that afternoon Dr. Powers stops at my office doorway to tell me that he is turning Tillie over to a new resident who has just come on. Partly it is to ease his own too heavy caseload, but partly he hopes it will widen Tillie's ability to relate to other people. That hope has been strengthened, he says, by her manifest "connecting" with me. Then he introduces me to Dr. Newcomb, and we two go off for a cup of coffee in the staff room so that I can fill him in on details.

Dr. Newcomb's big brown eyes behind big round glasses give him an owlish look, but his soft speech and gentle attention as he listens and questions me make me feel sure that he will not threaten Tillie.

"I'm going to have to learn a lot in this place," he says, and then he blurts out that he himself is in psychoanalysis. Not only is it personally helpful to him, but it is teaching him a lot. Of course, he adds, he'd do most of his learning when he got to his didactic analysis. We agree that one of the rewards of working with troubled people is that there is no end to learning.

Shortly afterwards, a friend gave me two tickets to an afternoon concert at Carnegie Hall. Tillie clapped her hands with pleasure when I invited her. "I love music!" she said. She appeared on time, with her pale lank hair plastered down, and in place of her usual straining blouse and skirt she wore a neat shirtwaist dress her mother had made. Its mustard color accentuated her sallow skin, but as the concert went forward she looked lighted up from within, her face suffused with excitement. During intermission, in a rush of confiding, she said she used to take piano lessons. She had loved it. But she quit when she realized she was "not good enough." "Not good enough for what? Not for your own pleasure?" "Not even for that," she replied. "Because I love music, and I hate myself when I spoil it."

After the concert, in the warmth of shared pleasure, I suggested that we make a real party of it and have tea at the Russian Tea Room. She drank her tea and ate her tea cakes (plus one of mine) with her eyes shining and her pinky stuck out for elegance. It was worth every dollar I'd had to spend out of my own limited student purse. When we'd finished she leaned across the table and said, shyly, "Another thing—I don't think the composers would like what I did to their music." We laughed, and then I said she had the upper hand over most of the composers. They were stone dead, and she was full of life. She grinned. "That's true," she said. "Very true. You always say true things." When we parted she gave me a quick, crushing hug, and fled.

The time Dr. Newcomb had set for his first session with Tillie turned out to be the time Tillie's mother usually made her visit. So I phoned her and said I'd visit her at home, since I would be in the neighborhood anyhow, to talk to Tillie's teacher about school plans.

"Very nice," she said. "Save me a trip."

Out of the street's bright sunlight I came into the stygian first-floor corridor of the Bronx apartment house, and all but felt my way to the door at its end. Tillie's mother admitted me, gaunt and wraithlike against the darkness behind her. "Come in, come in," she said, and hurried to her windows to pull back the drawn drapes.

We were in the living room. It was crowded with three pieces of bloated furniture, a heavy overstuffed sofa and matching chairs that faced one another across a little glass table with bowed gilt legs. Against one wall was what I later learned was an upright piano and its stool. I blinked to be sure I saw what I was seeing. The two windows, the three-piece set, the piano and stool, and the now lighted lamps perched on small tables that flanked the sofa, every one, were slipcovered or draped with fringed "throws" of a sinister darkly glowing purple sateen. "Sit down, sit down," Tillie's mother said, patting a place on one of the chairs. I obeyed, and was engulfed in its purple depths.

As lightly as possible I say I can see what someone's favorite color is. "I'm glad you like it," she replies. "I love purple. It's supposed to be a kind of noble color. You know?" I knew. "It's practical too," she goes on. "Doesn't show dirt. The material's good and strong." She explains that a friend owned a dry goods store, and had bought a bargain job lot of bolts this purple sateen. She reminds me that she had worked making slipcovers. So, she got a good price, and "made myself a new place, practically." Now, in one corner I recognize by its protruding iron-claw legs a humpbacked sewing machine, shrouded in purple. Then Tillie's mother rises up and proudly shows how she, with the janitor's help, had enclosed the piano with a drapery that covered it from top to bottom. Its curtains were on draw cords, like window drapes, and "if you want to play" you can part them. I express admiration of her ingenuity.

Has Tillie seen all this? No, not all. She had only begun to work on it when Tillie started to get sick. Did she think Tillie would like it? "Why not?" she asks. "It's neat. Keeps the dust out. Moths too. You know, moths like to eat the felt inside pianos." So I'd heard. But maybe that's not as important as some other things? At this she gets up and draws the window drapes closed again. "The sun fades the color," she says.

I ask if I may see Tillie's room. She leads me to an open alcove across from the living room. Its one window gives on the air shaft between this and the next building. Dominating the room is a heavy, busty bureau with an oversized mirror. It faces the living room, so its mottled glass reflects a purple haze. A whitewashed iron bed is covered with a faded chenille spread. Bedside is a small bookcase, crammed with books, and as I bend to look at their titles she repeats what she has said before. Too much reading strains the mind, she thinks, and she looks at me fixedly for confirmation. We return to the living room, and I say that it's very hard to know. Even the experts are not sure what causes mental illness. But I think we do know something about how to help people make a comeback. "That's good," she says. Then, urging "Sit, sit" she all but pushes me back into the open jaws of the purple whale. "You know what I think? People are crazy all over. The whole world is getting crazy. I see them everywhere, on the street, in the subway." She looks at me intently.

I had been about to suggest that when Tillie returns she should pull back the draperies on the piano and leave the keyboard open for Tillie to see. But when I open my mouth all that comes out is, "You've had a really hard time." Her lips twitch, but she clamps them together, lifts her bony hands and drops them into her lap in utter helplessness.

Suddenly I feel panic rising in me—a clutching at my bowels, a pounding of my heart. I feel shut-in, breathless, smothered, shrouded, entombed—as in a sarcophagus—in some combination of claustrophobia and hysteria. I have a sense that something bad is happening. I wriggle up and out of the chair, and say I must get to the school before it closes. She says, "Oh, too bad, I was going to give you a cup of tea." I thank her and promise a next time and I make for the door. Down the hallway I take hold and turn to wave her a reassuring goodbye but her door is already shut.

I race to the subway. As the train roars and rackets through its tunnels I rehearse what and how I shall report to my supervisor and Dr. Powers. In a way, I begin to see, this calls for gallows humor—it's a purple-black comedy, a hilarious-bitter story of interior decoration and interior meanings. Should I reveal the craziness that possessed me? Or should I just play it cool, and write down on my trusty legal pad, objectively, factually, my observations and next-step recommendations? What is the truth? ("What is truth?" asked jesting Pilate.)

Rushing to my office I almost collide with my supervisor. "Oh! I'm so glad you're here," she says. "I'm afraid I've got some unhappy news for you." I settle down with elaborate care at her desk. "It's Tillie. She's in Egypt again."

"What do you mean?" I am trembling now. I am possessed by such utterly irrational, fleeting notions as the possibility of psychic clairvoyance and thought waves (across the Bronx?) and my unconscious "knowing." "I knew it," I say lamely. "I felt it."

"It was a bad mistake on that cute resident's part," she goes on. "Tillie had her first session with him today, as you know. Whatever the reason—maybe she resented Dr. Powers' having transferred her—she just sat there. Wouldn't even look at him. So he suggested that she lie down on the couch in his office, take her time, and just say whatever came to her mind. I suppose that's what his analyst had told *him*. Anyhow, Tillie just lay there for about ten minutes, and then she began the whole delusional business again. 'My barge,' she said. 'This is my barge. Fetch me my handmaidens.' And then some of the lines you'd tracked down in Shakespeare when she first came in here—you remember—'Horrible villain! Hast thou no care of me? Shall I abide in this dull world. . . .' The whole bit."

"That man is absolutely out of his mind!" I almost shrieked. "He doesn't know what he's doing! Of all the *insane* things to have done!"

"He's got a lot to learn," she says ruefully. And adds, "I can imagine how you feel—after all your good work. But then, as you know, it takes only a small turn of the screw. . . "

I think, bitterly, but do not say, "—of the *screwy.*"

Back at my own desk I face my dandelion-yellow legal pad, open, blank, waiting. I write: *People Are Crazy All Over*—".

"*Question:* Is it better—no, is it more tolerable—for her to return to the hell of her Egypt or to a purple purgatory?

"*Admonition to myself: Physician, heal thyself!*"

15

LINES WRITTEN AFTER PROLONGED IMMERSION IN FREUD, HARTMANN, PIAGET ET ALII

ID

I never saw a person's id,
I hope I never seen one.
But I can tell you if I did
I'd fashion me a heavy lid
To place on it to keep it hid,
Which is, I gather, what God did
When he first saw a free one.

SUPER-EGO

That part of ego we can call super
Is part policeman and part snooper,
It's super-cilious and haughty
And tries to catch you thinking naughty,
It warns you that you will get caught
For doing things you shouldn't ought.
Oh hell, if only Eve and Adam
Had left those apples where God had 'em!

EGO

As for that middle-man, the ego—
Ubiquitous, it goes where we go.
Derivative? autonomous?

A construct? or homunculus?
It tries to grapple, strives to see
The nature of re-al-ity,
Defending now, yet out to learn
It scarcely knows which way to turn,
It has so many functions, forms,
So many strategies and norms—
May heaven help us as we're groping
To grasp how ego copes with coping!

16

A NOTE ON SIBLING

'Twas sibling and the Freudian tomes—.

It's the jabberwocky sound of that word. I know that Lewis Carroll starts " 'Twas brillig—" and yet, for reasons that probably lie in my all too commonplace childhood, the word "sibling" stubbornly pushes "brillig" out of place. To me perhaps its a contrived sounding word, made up, to name a diffused happening or an unsatisfying activity ("I've been sibling here all day") or a subtle sensory impression ("They tip-toed through the silent sibling snow"). It simply refuses to spell brothers and sisters for me—at least not *my* brothers and sisters. So finally I lift myself up to go to Webster (Second Edition) and flap over its heavy sections to track the thing down.

Sibling. It's there all right. Freud didn't even make it up. It's pure Anglo-Saxon and then Middle-English, first "sibb" and "gesib," then "sib" and "sibling."

"Sibb" as noun meant related, akin, the offspring of the same parents; as adjective it meant intimate, inclined toward, congenial. "Gesib" says "see gossip." A gossip, Middle English type, was a related person, a kin, a friend, a comrade. It was someone, obviously, with whom one could cozy up and have head-to-head talk especially about those outside the gossip group. Later "to gossip" meant to "run about and tattle." That makes sense. These related, intimate, congenial sibbs, off-spring of the same parents, for all their kindred coffee klatching would sometimes go running and tattling to their parents. That's in the nature of sibbs, or even present-day sibs, and certainly of siblings, which I take to be a diminutive form of sibs—little ones.

Funny thing—it's this running and tattling part of sib life that's the connotation in our modern use of sibling. The word that always cozies up to sibling, links arms with it, and gives it a furtive kick in the shins, is "rivalry." "Sibling rivalry" is what makes psychoanalyzed parents lie awake nights anxiously figuring at what age it would be best to give their first child his first sibling. Later, whatever they settle on, they find out that while their first child's age will determine what weapons he will use—whether the milk bottle, the violent embrace or the poisoned word—his reaction is inevitably that three is company and four's a crowd.

Sibling rivalry is largely responsible for the screaming and scrapping and scolding that now and again whirls up like a small sandstorm in family life and that repeatedly gets coaxed and commandeered into an uneasy state of calm. The child guidance clinic, the family welfare agency, the psychoanalytic sanctum all echo with past or present problems of sibling rivalry.

But what about the other aspect of being—and having—a sibling? The part that's congenial and intimate and crony? Somehow parents and psychiatrists and social workers and sophisticated siblings haven't thought much about that.

The truth is that siblings can be—and are—playmates, not just pests. They can be companions, not only competitors. They can be partners in small crime or in small good works. Against parental anger or disapproval they serve as buffers and diluters, a company to retreat to for healing and secondary security. Against the gaping hole of parental absence they fill in by substitutions of homely familiar noises and acts. They're relatively safe as complaint departments, especially when the complaints are of the powers and peculiarities of jointly owned parents. Where better than among siblings can parents' meanness and cruelties be grumbled over, or later, parents' stupidities and lack of reason be righteously judged by a jury of peers, or, much later still, parental helplessness and sadnesses be shared and jointly borne? Somehow "sibling support" ought to take its rightful place for consideration along with sibling rivalry. Because along with rivalry and annoyance and downright hate among siblings there exists also the securing sense that those who are bound by blood and battle have close quick bonds, communication that is visceral as well as verbal, and, sometimes, downright love for one another.

Does this sound mimsy? Does it out-grabe? 'Twas—and is—in the meaning of sibling.

1989 Afterword

As I reread this, some twenty years later, I suddenly realize that it is one of the few of my published papers that never drew a comment, yea or nay. Maybe nobody read it. Or perhaps, if they did, they considered it a trivialization of an important subject. I note that within the past two years or so several full-scale books have come out, giving space and detail to the positive aspects of sib-ship, and I make a mental note to look into them one of these days to see what's new.

What's old is the rivalry—as ancient as Cain and Abel, or Joseph and his brethren. That rivalry, whether it is expressed in actual or fantasied murder or in the nursing of a feeling of envy or hurt, is as inevitable and normal as the human longing to be most loved, most admired, most paid attention to.

We are not born equal (except for identical twins). No two or more siblings are ever born into the *same* family: parental relationships to one another undergo changes; financial difficulties or advantages affect family life and mood; preferences for one or the other sex; rejection or pleasure in resemblances—these and other factors may call up feelings and behaviors in parents that make their marks. So each newborn baby, desired or barely tolerated, takes its chances at the moment of its entry into its family. Poor lamb! Or lucky dog! What parents must strive for is equality of opportunities for lovingness and recognition and reassuring individual attention.

Present day parents, certainly those who have been exposed to what has become popular psychology, are far more psychologically knowledgeable in many areas of child-life than those of even only a generation ago. The advent of a new baby is more freely shared with the sibling-to-be as "our" baby, and small tender gestures such as feeling the embryo kick in the mother's abdomen are encouraged. (Here I cannot resist recounting two incidents. With her three-year-old cuddled in her lap, a friend of mine told him that deep down in her a new baby was growing. He reached up, opened her mouth wide, and hollered into it, "Hello, you down in there!" And a five-year-old friend, standing by while his mother breast-fed the new baby, piteously whined that he too wanted to be nursed. "But that's only for little babies," said his mother, "not for big boys like you!" He persisted loudly, and finally she said he could have his turn when the baby had finished. He took one draught. "Yuck!" he yelled. That was the end of *that* aspect of rivalry.)

Much of open, conscious rivalry melts away as children begin to develop friendships of their own, attachments to other love- and attention-giving adults, such as teachers, favoring grandparents, aunts and uncles—in short, when young people find that all their eggs (or egos) are not in one parental basket. And that there are a number of ways by which to win love and confidence and absorbing interests. So the relationships between and among sibs may undergo many changes on the positive side.

In my long-ago experience of placing children away from their abusive, neglectful, often mentally ill or defective parents, I was repeatedly struck with the powerful bonds of attachment that seemed to remain in most of these children. Repeatedly hurt, physically or emotionally, by one or both parents, fearing them, suffering blind guilt or hate against them, they still yearned to go back to the crippling situations from which they had been rescued. Why? I've often wondered. Was it simply the preference for the known and familiar as against the uncertainty of the unknown? Or some mysterious sense of blood-bonding? Or was it a powerful, all but unconscious need for "belonging," for being at one with a person with whom daily transactions were charged with powerful emotion, ugly, searing, devastating though they might have been?

I think of this in connection with sibling relationships too. Rivalrous as they may be, there occurs even in early childhood a uniting and protectiveness, one of the other, against any incursions or threats from the outside. Particularly as they grow older, and assaults of illness, deaths or other misfortunes begin to debilitate the family structure, siblings often band together to give one another mutual support. At the very least there tends to be a sense among them that they have mutual obligations towards one another, and that they have at least a "right" to expect of one another.

Not only do the emotions of misery and sorrow bind them. Shared joy may also do so. Mixed with the murmurings of guilty envy that the triumph or happiness is *theirs*, not *mine*, there is often the accompanying sense that I may warm myself in their reflected effulgence, because I "belong" to them, and they to me. They are my other selves.

17

LOOKING TOWARD DECIDING:
BOOK DEPARTMENT

It cannot be avoided. There comes a time in the affairs of life when inventories must be taken—not just of the self but, especially in later years, of one's astonishing accumulation of *things*. Artifacts can easily be given away—to the thrift shoppe, to the nephew of your husband's sister-in-law, to the trash heap. Shall it be done in one swell foop, or—and here comes the trouble—bit by bit, by careful consideration, which inevitably involves you in memories, associations, weighing choices, postponements.

How, for example, can one throw away folders and files of one's own half-developed papers that have patiently awaited revisions, additions, completion? Or how throw away snapshots and photographs of real people? It's like throwing away a human being. ("Just look!" I cry to my husband, "at this adorable laughing child!" Trouble is, I don't know who it is.)

After spending about an hour over our late afternoon martini and circular discussion, my husband and I agree to start in the morning to look over our books. We must "get rid": choose, decide, be ruthless, act!

I recall a conversation game we used to play at college. Which ten books would you choose to take with you to a desert island? Not counting Shakespeare or the Old Testament, of course—they are basic equipment, like food and water. Back to mental paralysis.

Most books, potential victims and potential survivors alike, just stand there in infinite resignation, in tight rows, waiting, waiting—for what? For some human being's touch, for being opened to the fresh air, with pages flipped, or one page smoothed down by a human hand, scanned by a human eye, given a vacation from their confining tenements?

Given breathing space, some books flop down dispiritedly, wearied by age or years of neglect. A few books (I am convinced of this) have the capacity to propagate. Some reviewer must have persuaded them that they were "seminal" works. So they cozy up in the dark of night and then hide their progeny behind themselves. Else how account for the double-shelving you find now and then, or for the discovery of a book you never knew you owned? Here one stands: *Ten Days That Shook the World,* hidden behind a forbiddingly heavy (What, pregnant again!) *Das Kapital.* All right—that's a far-out fantasy—but it is true that in some as yet undiscovered way books conform to a version of Parkinson's Law: they will fill up any extra space you have.

I determine now to develop some criteria for selection, rejection, and organization. There are several categories that, for all their remarkable efficiency, the library sciences and the Library of Congress have quite overlooked, so I set them down here as my guides:

1. Books That Have Grown Old Along with You
2. Books That Left Their Mark
3. Books That You Can and Do Forget
4. Books You Always Meant to Read, But . . .

Among the first: their spines are cracked and wobbly, some with fairly frequent usage, but most simply by just existing, subject just as we humans are to vagaries of heat and cold, dryness and damp, sunshine and mold. They age, as we do, imperceptibly, until one day their pages have become fragile and crumbly, their connective ligaments and tissues have weakened, their once smooth and bright skin coverings are dulled. Some are not even recognizable any more because their once-bold titles, their proud identities, have faded into anonymity. Yet, open them carefully and you will find that their spirit, their essential substance is intact. What they have to say may be dated or may now be found trivial and naive in the light of the changes that have occurred in social and psychological thought, not to mention changes that have occurred in your own taste or knowledge or beliefs, but they are like the old human friends you've known. Some seem to have stopped in their development of mind and attitude at some point long ago. And others—probably those that were far ahead of what you were ready to perceive and understand when you first read them—are remarkably relevatory and vigorous in spirit, despite their shabby and dejected exteriors.

I draw our several of these old friends, and am struck all over again with the marvel of the invention of books—their having been conceived and written down, their having been printed, their powers to humanize and to bind people to one another. Even the least among them (excepting only those that are manifest trash, "books" in form only) stands as a testament to man's persistent urge to reach out to his fellows, to talk with them, to tell, to teach, persuade, explain, engage, amuse, elevate, to catch the interest of other human beings and bind them to himself and himself to them. Within this category of books you grew up with are those with whom you've kept in recurrent touch, that you've read and reread because, as with long-loved people, they continue to nourish and stimulate you.

Take *Alice* for instance, both *In Wonderland* and *Through the Looking Glass*. She is tattered and beat, poor dear, because I have carried her about as a constant companion for more than three-score years and ten. She has never failed me. The paradox, the pun, the pointing to the absurdity that lurks in people's literal-mindedness and pomposity, the wildly imaginative leaps away from what Schopenhauer called the "tyranny of reason"—all those forms of irreverence still can make some daily hum-drum circumstances sparkle for me.

One of the most enjoyable hours of my life occurred recently when our visiting son and daughter-in-law and four-year-old grandson were driving home with us from too late an evening visit with friends. To keep awake we began to sing, and then, to add variety I began to recite from *Alice*—the Jabberwocky, the Walrus and the Carpenter, the Lobster Quadrille. To my delight my son joined me, word-perfect, and we took turns declaiming the verses. Now our sleepy little one stood up, wide-awake, clapping his hands and crying, "Do it again!" Far-fetched as it may seem, I was gladdened by yet another uprush of bond-feeling with my son, by yet another invisible but vibrant link that attached us one to the other. Because, of course, all relationships of love and union begin and grow from even brief shared pleasures (or pain), shared feelings of likeness (or difference)—in short from shared emotional or attitudinal investments.

Honesty impels me to add that *Alice* was also responsible for a few of the uneasiest hours in my teaching life. One day I issued an ultimatum. I told a class of twenty-two graduate students not to return to the course (on treatment of psycho-social problems) until they had read *Alice In* and/or *Alice Through*. The look of incredulity on the faces of the students told me I had overstepped my professorial bounds. But a retreat would have been a betrayal, both of Alice and of my own convictions. Yet, in the middle of the night I wondered whether I'd be hearing about this caprice—from the dean? From the chancellor? From the A.C.L.U.? But really, I'd argue, they had it coming. I had been talking about the *centrality of purpose* as determinant in the choice of therapeutic method in working with troubled people. "Just remember what the Mock Turtle warned us long ago," I'd ended. "No wise fish goes anywhere without a porpoise." Nineteen out of twenty-two faces looked respectfully blank and/or puzzled. *"Alice,"* I explained. Two persons grinned in knowing recognition. One man wrote something— God knows what—into his notebook. So I delivered my ukase.

Actually everyone did return to the class, and I was so grateful that I did not follow through with an inquisition. I suspect they had diagnosed my behavior as incipient senility and were bent on clinically observing further evidences of a mind crumbling. But now I ask you, in the querulous tone of the old-old: "What *do* young people read nowadays?" I mean, after they have mastered reeling and writhing?

Category 2: Books That Left Their Mark—and therefore cannot possibly be abandoned, any more than you'd abandon the people who have been significant to you. Some of these books overlap with Books You Grew Up With because we are most open to the influence of others, books included, early in our lives. In childhood and youth we are most malleable, our appetites, emotional and intellectual, keen and at the ready. We are unarmored, relatively undefended, and what we take in from outside ourselves embeds itself deeply. Sometimes, indeed, so deeply that we cannot remember or put our finger on the source or influence, and we say, "I have *always* thought, or felt, or believed. . . ."

"I have always believed" that the best preparation for entry into any of the people-serving professions (or, for that matter into mature adult living), long before our immersion in sociological or psychological fact and theories, is immersion in those books that bring all sorts of human beings in all kinds of circumstances with all varieties of human dilemmas and their outcomes into our ken. Only so can most of us expand, diversify and enrich our understanding and experience of the human condition.

Each of us has only one earthly life to live. Full of advantage and adventure though it may be, it is still time-and-place limited, person-and-experience confined. To be drawn into knowing and feeling with the range of human life that books offer, whether they are wholly imaginative or are pointedly presented reality, is to live many lives, and to know (sometimes with joy, sometimes with anguish) one's kinship with a host of other human beings. That is the basic condition for caring about others, for understanding human frailities and foibles, for our belief in human potentials for change and progress.

Or so it seems to me. And I face again the question that has intrigued me for many years. Does reading widely when young create and deepen the capacity for empathy and compassionate identification with other human beings? Or is that capacity inborn, genetically at-the-ready to become spur to immediate responsiveness, to the swift at-oneness with another's experiences? And thence the eager reader?

One book in point: Here stands *The Man Without a Country*. It left its mark on me when I was ten ("Happy tenth birthday!" is written in browned ink on its flyleaf). And I see, as I turn its now fragile pages, that I left my mark on it too. There are dried blotches of a ten-year-old's tears on some pages. In a way it is a cruelly moralistic book. Written by Edward Everett Hale, a prominent minister and patriot (odd—no one is called a "patriot" anymore!) in an effort to inspire loyalty just prior to the Civil War, the book had its greatest readership during the Spanish-American War.

It is the brief story (part fact, part fiction) of one Philip Nolan, a young army officer who, in a moment of fury, cries, "D—n the United States! I wish I may never hear of the United States again!" At his court-martial the punishment decreed was that his wish should be fulfilled: that he must never set foot on his country's soil again nor hear of it. Put upon a Navy ship, he roamed the vast oceans perpetually, to the end of his life.

What an unlikely person and situation with whom a ten-year-old, midwestern little girl, happily cosseted within a large and loving family, should identify, should weep over! Somehow, however, whatever the book's merits or faults, I understood from it at once and painfully the emptiness and infinite loneliness, the bitter desolation that would lie like a stone upon your heart if you were cut off from your ties with family and friends, and from your own, your native, land. No one of the sociological or psychological tracts on anomie or social isolation that I studied years later conveyed to me more deeply the pathos, even tragedy, of a human being stripped of his place and purpose in life.

But, I grumble, this becomes a Sisyphean task. Select one book that left its mark upon you and another and yet another demands to be noticed and re-viewed. They differ in many ways from one another, and their import and impact are in part the product of the life stage at which you read them, your personal concerns, your developing critical standards, and so on. Again I plead guilty to pusillanimity—or is it loyalty? All right—stay right where you are, Jo March, and Huck Finn, and Robinson Crusoe, and Kristin Lavransdatter, and Jean Valjean, and Sidney Carton, and Orlando, and Willie Loman, and-and-and—I've taken some part of each of you into my being in one way or another. So I shan't put your bodies away. And I'll be back with some mending tape to bind up your infirmities.

The grown-up section of Books That Left Their Mark seems to consist mostly of those that are books of ideas, concepts, criticisms, expositions, and/or theories. They are all but endless testament to the fecundity of the human mind in its search to fathom being and nonbeing, aspects of life and death. Most of them speak mind-to-mind, but in the best of them the heart is also invaded and involved.

I inherited Michel Montaigne from an uncle of mine when I was in my twenties. "Dry" I thought as I flipped the small-print pages. Moreover I was turned off by underlinings and marginal comments that someone else, not Uncle David, must have done. Many marginal notes were not in either Uncle David's hand or style. His tended to be laconic, and ran from "Oh yeah?" to "Sic sempre"—while the other commentaries ran in fine-script pedantic para-graphs. My annoyance was increased by the fact that what was underlined was, to me, of no relevance. (Have you ever borrowed a book from a friend, or, worse, from a university library, where you'd expect the loftiest of ethical and intellectural standards, and found that some previous reader had underlined passages—what's worse, all the wrong ones? Had missed the point? Had been in some trancelike state as he read?)

I confess that of late I'd begun to notice that in my own books I had in the past underlined points that hold little present meaning for me. "For heaven's sake," I think, "why did I mark *this?* When *that* is the main idea! And then I remind myself that what we find important at any one time is affected by the special context of time and place of the reading as well as of our particular bent and pursuit as we read. So what is significant in one context may be found empty of meaning in another.

At any rate—between "dry" and defaced I had shelved Mon-sieur Montaigne.

Some thirty years later I drew him out again, and became his enchanted devotee. What a scholarly, literate, rational, tempered, unblinkingly honest man! What insightful awareness and amused tolerance of himself, and thence what insightful acceptance and compassion he had for others. What a range of interests in the common phenomena of cultivated human life! So fully have I found myself in accord with him over these many years that I sometimes am afraid I have plainly plagiarized him, quite unconsciously. Certainly I have paraphrased him, without proper attribution probably, since what he said on this and that so often found its immediate echo in my mind, an immediate embrace. It was he who provided *le mot juste* or *la pensée juste*. If I am guilty I am in the company (in the raggle-taggle rear) of Shakespeare, and Freud, and hundreds of other oft-quoted men and women who took intellectual nourishment from Montaigne.

Now, once again, I am absorbed in Montaigne's essays, but now in the context of his thought and reactions on living and dying. He was fifty-nine years old when he died—an old, old age for the sixteenth century. His "life-review" moves me deeply. Stay with me, *mon vieux*, my four-hundred-year-old immortal good companion!

Still on Books That Left Their Mark: Not long ago I reread Socrates' *Apology*. When I had read it years ago I knew it to be a masterpiece of eloquence and ethical principle. This time I found I was reading it not just with my eyes and mind but with my heart and soul (whatever that latter is), and with awe. Here, standing before those who are to condemn him to death is the quintessence, the all-but-perfect model of a civilized human being. How proud his gods should have been of him!

Here stands a whole, a fully put-together, integrated man. He has lived what he has taught: a self-examined, self-disciplined, inner-directed life. He has earned and found pleasure in the love and admiration and learning of those who were his acknowledged students and those many others (indeed, the "youth of Athens," his accusers said) who were influenced in their thought and behavior by his example and his teachings. So, himself fulfilled by the devotion and gratifying development of those he nourished and cultivated and civilized, he is able to face death with serenity and realism. Not without some natural reluctance, and not without some uncertainty about what awaits him after death, but true to the self he had been and the course he had held throughout his lifetime: the pursuit of virtue. (P.S.: One defect—he was mean to his wife. But he was "only human"!)

It's an easy decision. I will take the *Apology* with me to that desert island—or to whatever dwelling place I'm assigned to hereafter.

Now I can make short shrift of the category Books You Can and Do Forget. I glance across several shelves of modern novels. Friends send them to you when you have a cold, or are about to go off on an "escape" trip. They help to pass the time sleekly, and, with notable exceptions, meaninglessly. I mean, how vital and vicarious an experience can you draw from chapter after chapter, sketch after sketch of couples obsessed with the minutiae of sexual, domestic, parental, cocktail strategies, or from young women indulging in one long primal scream at not having been born men, or from cardboard people, featureless, fragmented, feckless, two-dimensional?

Do I sound like the last of the Edwardians? I am, I guess. Is modern-day life as splintered, discontinuous, trivial, rootless as the current literary genre makes out? Perhaps for some it is. Norman Cousins put it aptly, I think, when he said that the trouble with most modern fiction is that there's no one in it you would care to meet.

One thing I do admire about the new fiction. It is usually so attractively dressed. The jackets are striking, vivid, original in design. They seem to add the vibrant brashness of youth to the sober, serried ranks of old books. "Let's let them stay a while," I coax my husband. "They brighten things up. And maybe they'll grow out of it."

In a trivialized version of the "pursuit of virtue" I return to the business of weeding out. Category 4 embarrasses me: Books You Always Meant to Read, But. . . . The worst of it is, I myself bought most of them. There is something reassuring about paying for, owning, and finding shelf room for a book you know you "ought" to read "sometime." It's some compelling sense that by possessing and handling a book a kind of osmosis occurs, and its contents will somehow permeate the membranes of your skin and brain.

I flinch under the unforgiving and contemptuous stare of Tolstoy. I did begin *War and Peace*, Count Leo. In fact, I began it several times—but somehow I never got to finish it. (I *do* know how it came out though, because I saw the movie.) I avert my gaze and catch a side-glimpse of my elegant edition of *The Divine Comedy*. Honestly, I did read the whole of the *Inferno*, Signor Alighiere. That was when I took a wonderful course in college from a woman who, with her high, smooth forehead and thinly plucked brows and the heavy antique gold chains she wore, looked like the very incarnation of a Renaissance noblewoman. Once, Signor, I made a special trip to

Ravenna to pay homage to you at the commonplace iron-fenced crypt they put you in. But, purgatory and paradise, despite the presence of Beatrice and Virgil, were—well, something of a bore. Somehow, hell was full of far more interesting people. I'll find out, of course, in not too long!

Still on "meant to read"—I turn to a grouping of all-but-untouched volumes, unexplainably tired-looking. They are *Collected Works of . . ., Collected Stories of. . . .* Not only are they weary of their life of neglect, but they are too fat, and ought to be ashamed of themselves. I bought them many years ago, before I realized the truth that art is long and life is brief, and I had illusions about later-middle and old age as periods with free and open time, when one could immerse one's self in uninterrupted reading.

What I did not understand were several now obvious facts: one's tastes in literature change astonishingly. One's eyes change too (always for the worse) and collected works are almost invariably in such small print as to make reading difficult. Strength wanes, and books that are too fat (all right, too physically weighty) become burdensome. One's sense of time changes. (So many things yet to do and see and read about—and so little time!) Thus, without conflict I take a number of these volumes and put them tenderly into the hungry openmouthed giveaway carton. Which leads my husband to thank God, and to remind me that this was the purpose and point of this whole book inventory.

But it's a brutal business. It's like putting loyal old friends and enticing nodding acquaintances into boxes, and condemning them to oblivion. However—I brighten up at this—those books that are sound enough in mind and body to be given away will have an assured rebirth or afterlife. Other people may read them, or at least give them oxygen by flipping their pages. They may feel revived to be touched by new hands, scanned by new eyes, reacted to by new would-be communicants. Farewell—and hail!

18

JABBERPSYCHE

1989 Foreword

Riffling through the pages of the galaxy of journals of psychiatry-psychology, scholarly or popular, I come off with the impression that one is expected to be dead-serious about it all. There seems to be no room for laughing at ourselves, or even casting a compassionate smile in the direction of the misguided. So, I take my chances here.

I noted, in my comments on Freud (herein), that there has arisen within the past few decades a high tide of revisionism. Some of it was long overdue, especially when literal-mindedness made dogma of hypotheses. Much of what Freud put forward is, in my considered opinion, still productive to deeper exploration and understanding of the human condition. I have been struck by the vengefulness that has characterized some of the nay-sayers.

This doggerel made itself up after my reading some of those latter attacks. Therefore I take no responsibility for it, but pause only to apologize to Lewis Carroll for presuming to revise *him*.

'Twas scribbling, and the anxious tomes
Did psychiatric in the id,
All empathetic were the pomes
And the drab prose out-did.

"Beware the oedipus, my son,
The phallus as a source of sin
Is an idea whose time is done,
And upper level things are in."

He took his Macintosh in hand,
Long time the publisher he sought,
Then waited he by a trauma tree,
And stewed awhile in thought.

And as in retrospect he stood
The oedipus with lusts aflame
Came abreacting through the wood,
Ambivalent it came.

One-two-three-four—and more, and bore
His verbal blade went snicker-snack,
Up to the hilt—then with his guilt
He went regressing back.

"And hast thou slain the oedipus?
Come to the printed page, my boy!
Oh fey schizoid, oh de-frocked Freud!"
Cathartic was his joy.

'Twas scribbling, and the anxious tomes
Proliferated on the shelves
As newborn giants and elder gnomes
Revised themselves.

19

CHILDREN IN EXILE

Every now and then I see a child's face that pierces my heart, and my mind races back to those brief hours a half-century ago when I took three refugee children from New York City to Buffalo and Chicago. I never hear of children who, for whatever reasons, good or bad, are taken from their familiar places and people but that Werner and Erika and Liselotte present themselves before me. How are they now? And what? Grown middle-aged, with children of their own, perhaps? Beautiful or plain? Sleek with satisfaction or pinched with misery? Fulfilled or empty and searching? Did they ever find and see their parents again? Have they ever come to feel at home?

The last boat out of Italy had brought them to America. They had been hurried out of Berlin and Vienna, like hundreds of other Jewish children, sent off in their parents' final desperate decision that they must be saved. The intensive work of refugee agencies had yielded affidavits for them, guaranteed good homes where so-called uncles and aunts would take them in as if they were their own. They would care for them and educate them and nurture them with love too, but the latter was a delicate and complex business, it was made clear, and care must be taken because children carry their absent parents alive within them, and they may fiercely fight or stonily resist being loved too much too soon by strangers. Of this the prospective eager foster parents had rightly been forewarned.

I just happened to fall into those few hours with these three children. I was taking the night train from New York to Chicago, and my friend, a social worker from one of the committees for refugees, asked if I could shepherd them overnight, just to make

Copyright 1977, National Association of Social Workers, Inc. Reprinted with permission from *Social Work*, vol. 22, no. 2 (March 1977): 137–39.

things easier for them. I would see that Werner got off at Buffalo early in the morning and get the two girls onto their California-bound train from Chicago. Erika and Liselotte were steady, self-sufficient youngsters, my friend said. No trouble at all. Werner was an upset child, she thought. He had seen his father shot a few days before he left Vienna. It had something to do with his older brother's escape into Yugoslavia. When the police came to check on his whereabouts they said the father was responsible. But Werner was all bottled up—so he would be no trouble either.

They politely acknowledge my friend's introduction of them, the three, and they board the train with me, silently. Each clutches a bulging briefcase that holds nightshirts and a few clothes, passports, and (later I see) snapshots, writing paper, and the paperbound books and games and chocolate bars that my friend has stuffed in for their journey. Werner is going to a real uncle, an older brother of his father; the girls to "some people." Erika is the oldest, 12 or so, long blond braids, long black-stockinged legs, face flushed, eyes too bright. Liselotte, ten, sturdy in her prepubertal plumpness, is stuffed into a red velveteen dress, and a cocky plaid Scotch bonnet sits incongruously atop her solemn face. Werner, except for his dark dilated eyes, is the ghost of an eight-year-old, his face paper thin and white, his chin hunched into his woolen scarf.

The sleeping-car berths are already made up, and I show the children the washrooms and tell them in my awkward German how things work. Erika asks for the upper berth. Before I can ring for the ladder she has swung up, briefcase and all. "It's nothing," she says proudly. "I am an athlete." Then she pulls her curtains shut and goes to sleep. Liselotte undresses slowly, methodically, patting down her coat, her bonnet, the dress she struggles out of, her petticoat, one by one. Finally into her cotton nightdress, she says good night and carefully lies down. When I part the curtains to see if she is having trouble with the night-light I catch the gleam of a wet thumb being wiped on the sheet.

Werner sits on the edge of his berth. He is not sleepy. He will just sit up or walk up and down the aisle. I say he may do that. Or maybe he would undress in his berth and keep his lights on and look out of the window or read a book. He looks at me for the first time, darkly, incredulously, and then he begins to unbutton. I tell him I'll be right above him, and he can tap on his ceiling if he needs me. Just before I doze off, he taps. May he eat a piece of his chocolate?

Werner and I must be up early in the morning to get him off at Buffalo. I find him fast asleep with his berth lights on and a timetable clutched in one hand. I touch his blanket and he bolts up, breathlessly asks what time it is, begins to dress swiftly. He laces up his high boots with precision, he marches with his toothbrush and collapsible drinking cup into the washroom, and on his return he puts on his coat and beret and knots his crocheted scarf around his thin neck. "My mother made it for me," he says, glancing in my direction.

We sit together talking in whispers so as not to wake the other passengers. We are late into Buffalo, so there is nothing to do but look out the window. It is a bleak, sullen April morning. I feel apologetic for my country, as though I should explain that it will soon be green and welcoming. Werner keeps his pale nose flat against the windowpane. I venture that before spring comes the landscape looks sad. He smiles vaguely. It doesn't matter, he says. At home the mountains were still covered with snow. Maybe they still are. The train suddenly jolts to a stop, then begins a slow crawl. "*Gott sie dank,*" Werner sighs. "The train is going slowly." When we pick up speed he sighs again. "*Gott sie dank,*" he says, "it goes faster now." I say he hardly knows which he wants most—to get to his uncle quickly or to put it off as long as possible. Now he looks at me directly and long, and having assured himself that we understand each other he smiles and turns back to the window.

"What time is it now?" he asks. I tell him and he counts off on his fingers, puckering his mouth. "*Bei uns,* in Vienna," he says, "it's half-past one at night. Everyone is asleep. My mother is sleeping." I do not correct him. Let his mother sleep.

His uncle is pacing the platform at the station, a gray anxious-looking man in an old mackinaw and baggy pants. Werner has scarcely stepped down from the train with me when he is roughly swept into his uncle's arms. When I board the train again he seems to be struggling in that prolonged embrace, his beret and scarf are falling off, his small face looks agonized.

Erika is up, awaiting permission to come off her perch. Her yellow braids and pink face shine as she returns from the wash-room. Yes, she slept well. Washrooms in America are wonderful! So may towels and faucets! Yes, she would like breakfast. As soon as Lise is ready. She's hungry. She's always hungry. Her parents said she is growing so fast. "And so long," she says, ruefully showing how her wrists stick out of her dark serge sleeves. She leans towards me, confidingly. "Last night I ate a banana and a chocolate bar," she says. "I woke up and I felt so empty in my stomach. From my heart to my stomach—empty. You know? So when I ate the banana and the chocolate it felt better."

Liselotte is methodically folding her nightdress into her case. She curtsies gravely and says, *"Guten Morgen,"* and asks if Werner has gotten off the train. In the dining car she looks at the black waiters with the round gray eyes of a kitten. She is not hungry but, yes, thank you, she will eat. Erika is excited. May she have coffee? She has only tasted ersatz, but her father and mother have talked about how good real coffee is. I offer her a taste of mine before she decides. She takes a careful, listening sip. Wonderful! But she will have milk.

Liselotte looks through her glass of orange juice as she sips it. Yes, thank you, she likes orange juice. Erika fairly hugs her glass. Oranges are wonderful! Her father had told her that in California the oranges drop from the trees into your mouth. She laughs excitedly at this fancy. "Can't you see us, Lise, walking along with our mouths wide open!" Her father had told her too that there were beautiful mountains in California. That's what she will love—to go climbing in beautiful mountains!

The dun landscape flies by. Liselotte begins to look white. Does she want to leave the table? She says pardon, please, but she's afraid she has to vomit. In the washroom she leans heavily against me as I mop her sweating round face with a wet towel. She doesn't know why, she says plaintively. Ever since she left Vienna something is wrong with her stomach.

Back in our car the porter puts up a table for us, and we set out some puzzles and games. We play lotto, first calling numbers in German and then, slowly, in English. Erika chews the scraggly end of one braid intensely, but Liselotte sits quietly, saying *"Bitte?"* when she misses an English number. After a while I suggest I'll read my morning paper across the aisle, and they can continue to play. The game begins to run down. They become quiet, and then begin to dig into their briefcases.

"I have so many letters to write," says Erika, "to my mother and father. But maybe they've gone to Holland. I don't know where they are now. My best friend went to Holland—"

"Do your mother and father have affidavits to come to America?" Liselotte whispers.

"Not yet. But I'm going to work hard to get them. I'll ask the people who are taking me. I'll beg them. Do yours?"

"It's ridiculous!" Liselotte has raised her voice and she suddenly looks like a fat little woman. "For 38 years my mother has lived in

Vienna. But she was born in Rumania. She must wait on the Rumanian quota. Maybe for 17 years—

"Seventeen years!" Erika echoes. "you will be 27 years old then!" "Maybe," she adds mischievously, "you will be a mother yourself by that time!"

"Don't talk foolishness!" Liselotte is half angry. "Not until my mother comes I won't!"

Now Erika is compassionate again. "Is everything in order for your father to come? Papers? Passports?"

"Everything is in order," says Liselotte. "But the consul says maybe my father can't come. At all. Something is wrong with his heart."

Erika shrugs. "My best friend's father was arrested," she says, "and Werner's father—" She trails off, then leans fiercely towards Liselotte. "If I beg the people who are taking me, and if I am very, very good they surely will give me an affidavit for my parents. Don't you believe so?" Liselotte spits on a finger and wipes the tip of one shoe clean. "Who knows?" she says. They are silent together.

"Did your mother and father come to the station when you left?" asks Liselotte.

Erika dives into her briefcase and brings out a wrinkled letter. "This," she says, "is the letter my mother and father gave me on the train. I shall keep it all my life. No one shall ever see it but me!" She smacks three wild kisses onto the envelope and puts it back into her case.

"My mother and father couldn't come to the station," Liselotte says, dreamily. "It was after nine o'clock. The curfew for the Jews had rung."

I get up and suggest we play another game. "Anagrams? With German words?"

Erika sits upright. "Not German. American. It is our duty to learn American words." They set about turning over the letter tiles, but listlessly.

When we near Chicago I begin to prepare them for their continuing journey. I remind them of how to call the porter and the names of things to eat, and that there will be a Fraulein, a stewardess, on the California train who will watch over them. And that after three more nights and two more days they will be met by their new uncles and aunts, one in San Francisco and the other in Sacramento, and they will be glad to be there at last. They nod attentively and keep their eyes fastened to mine.

Liselotte pulls out a pen and postcard and says she must write to her mother and father. Erika reminds her she wrote only last night in New York, but Liselotte gives her a blank gray stare and repeats she must write to her mother and father. She fills the card with crooked German script and asks me if I will mail it. Then she solemnly places the ridiculous Scotch hat on her head and looks disapprovingly at Erika who is stuffing her beret into her coat pocket.

We board the waiting western train. I tell the stewardess a bit about the children and bring her over to meet them. "My gosh!" she says brightly. "Poor kids! I'd hate to be them!" Liselotte's hands are gripped across her red velveteen stomach. I ask if she thinks she needs the washroom, but Erika takes charge. "Children must not complain," she says severely, in clipped German. "My father says we must do our best."

I put an arm around each of them, and suddenly Erika pushes deep and hard into my shoulder and presses against me as I draw her in, but Liselotte draws away, her eyes like gray glass. She curtsies and thanks me, tonelessly, for my good care.

When their train pulls off I remember the postcard and I read it on the way to the mailbox. "Dearest Mother and Father," it reads (in German), "Now we are coming to Chicago and soon we will be on the train for California. America is a terribly big country. It takes many days to cross it. A thousand kisses to you both from your only little daughter, Liselotte, ten years old."

1989 AFTERWORD

My encounter with these children occurred fifty years ago. I wrote it up then. In 1977, when Vietnamese children were being shuttled to American shores by plane and boatload, I dug it out of my "file and forget" folders, and, with reference to the influx of a new group of refugee children, sent it to *Social Work*. (Here I have deleted the references to Vietnam.) Except for that, the sketch stands as it was a half-century ago, as sharp and poignant to me as it felt then.

Where are they now, I wonder? How are they? Oh, Erika and Liselotte and Werner—you live deep inside me! You are part of all that I have known of human hurt.

PART FOUR
A LONG LOOK BACK

20

LOOKING BACK TO SEE AHEAD

1989 FOREWORD

Within the past decade or so I have had many invitations to
lecture or present "plenary papers," and the most frequently suggested subject has been "the future of social work." This topic I
have respectfully but resolutely declined. I am increasingly certain
that foresight is not an inevitable attribute of the superannuated.
It is certain, too, that in today's world where time and events do
not simply "pass" or "occur," where change is often swift, un-
predictable and assaultive, the accretion of past knowledge is not
as reliable or transferable as it once was. So I have determined to
decline the role of seer.

I do believe, however, that some clearer perspective, some temper-
ing sense of the relative import of events and circumstances, some
greater capacity to separate the chaff from the wheat, to tolerate the
lapses and foibles of human behavior (including one's own)—that
these qualities of the "long view" may be found in such old hands
and old heads as have consistently sought to probe and understand
and in small ways to improve the human condition. I cannot be at
all confident that the perspectives I hold are clear-eyed and useful to
others, but on the chance that they may be I have been willing now
and then to speak of what my experience of our professional past
has been, and to such implications for the nearby future it may
hold. Thus the theme of this piece.

Until now I have withheld its publication, for several reasons.
As a lecture I have often revised it, sometimes substantially to
meet the time and place and circumstances under which it was
delivered. Further, as a lecture it had to be limited to at most an
hour, at which point the listener's flesh rather than his intellectual interest determines his intake. I had long held before myself
the prospect of bringing to it the elaboration and precision that a

responsible historical review owes its readers. But it began to grow into a formidable, full-fledged book. So, with what I choose to call "realism" (others may give it a less neutral name) I decided, torn between reluctance and relief, to leave that task to someone younger and stronger than I. (I confess, I have come to resemble one of my more unadmired characters in literature: the Red Queen. It was she, you recall, who kept running as fast as she could to stay in the same place.)

What, then, I ask myself (before you ask me!) is the justification for my placing one of the versions of this lecture into print? For whatever reasons, it has had highly interested responses from the many social workers who have given it their ears. It is my hope that perhaps it may serve further to stimulate, to evoke— perhaps even provoke—from those wiser than I some more thorough and scholarly account of our professional past-into-present becoming-and-being-and-doing that the subject surely deserves.

I leaped into social work bright-eyed and avid right out of a college major in English Literature and into a waiting caseload of forty-five cases in a private family agency. The person who was my supervisor introduced me to social casework practice by placing Mary Richmond's *Social Diagnosis* on my desk and suggesting that I read it before I made a "visit." I *did* know how to read a book; I did not know what a "visit" was, but I did as I was told. I had no idea then that what Mary Richmond was trying to do was to bring social work out of the haphazard "friendly" visiting practices into a semblance of "science," by using both medical and legal models of fact-finding and subsequent diagnosis to establish an orderly, systematic approach to problems of people's social malfunctioning.

At first I found myself somewhat mystified and even annoyed by Miss Richmond. She was utterly logical, systematic, reasonable. But the people who became my "clients" stubbornly resisted being logical and systematic or reasonable. Beset by all manner of difficulties, I found them behaving in all sorts of puzzling ways.

There was the woman who, to my utter astonishment, was having what we used to call an "affair," despite the fact that she was already in her *forties* and confined to a wheel chair; the man who persisted in believing his wife was unfaithful despite all the incontrovertible evidence I placed before him; the adolescent girl who was touchingly responsive to my counsel with her and then returned home to threaten her mother with an ice pick. And so on.

What I, along with my fellow caseworkers, attended to was the gathering of facts and information about the client's problem so that we could make what we thought was a "social diagnosis." Only thus, said Mary Richmond, could a "scientific" treatment plan be formulated, and we strove mightily to qualify as "scientific." There were many other things that Mary Richmond said that revealed her natural understanding of the interplay of psychological with social factors in human beings—but it took time and experience to fully grasp her wisdom and her depths.

"Get the factual data" was the guiding principle. And "data" were the stripped-down facts of the so-called *objective* reality. Only short shrift was given to the facts of the client's feelings, his hurts, his fears, his embarrassments, the facts, in short, of his *subjective* reality and its involvement as cause or effect, of the presented problem.

Help was to be given on the basis of verified need, based on verified misfortune and verified lack of other resources. If you were unfortunate enough to have brought the misfortune upon yourself by your poor judgment or irresponsible behavior, then the expectation was that your recognition of this fact would naturally be the start of your responsible reform, with the help, of course, of a truly concerned and sympathetic social worker. That worker, in some difference from today's social workers, was usually quite certain about what *ought* to happen, quite sure about what was *good* for people.

Our conception of the client was that he was a poor thing, heartbreakingly pitiful at times. But, by that very condition, he was less as a person than we were. By and large the client himself thought or felt that too. (The concept of psychological needfulness as "real" was not yet prevalent.) When he was asking for money, it was quite "conventional" (to use Mary Richmond's apparently accepting term) to conceal what the social worker might consider a resource. Some of us thought this was part of the faulty character of those who had not had a good upbringing, perhaps the very fault that made them poor and inadequate. Others of us thought that such concealments were only natural in the face of the pressing questioning-to-the-last penny attitude of the "haves." (But the latter were secret thoughts rarely expressed.)

Here and there among us were those who were "naturals" at understanding or at least glimpsing what social deprivation and disadvantage did to warp and distort the personality and behavior or, turned about, how problems of personality could create problems in social functioning. But by and large most of us were still carrying the long-held, hard-to-relinquish concepts that if there was a will there was a way. When people could not make it on their own, something was missing in them—some quality of get-up-and-go, or intelligence, or character—which made them more to be pitied than scorned, perhaps, but less to be respected.

The "visitor" or "investigator" or "caseworker," by whatever name, was their superior, their patron. A patron might be warm and kind, or cold and punitive, but a patron held the purse strings and the power. (In its Roman sources a "client" was one who "leaned upon," was dependent on a "patron.") Small wonder, then, at the paradox that while the client was always being urged to make changes in his behavior or circumstances, the *power* for change was held to lie in the hands of his social worker, not in him. How to connect with his motivation, his "willing," how to free him to know his own feelings and to think towards self-determined decisions—all this was yet to be discovered by us. No wonder the Milford Conference participants more than half a century ago wrote in honest regret, "the philosophy of participation is more easily understood than is the method of achieving it."

It may surprise you to hear, however, that despite all this we were often helpful to people. What we lacked in skill, we in part made up for by our concerns and commitments—by our moral zeal to make things better for people. Sometimes this took the form of bossiness and interference; sometimes it was received and responded to by helpless-feeling people as evidence of our true caring for them, as offering them the nurture of attention and compassion that they had found wanting in their daily lives. In many instances where people's own motivations or capacities were unequal to their tasks, we rolled up our sleeves and did *for* them. We cajoled their landlords, we explained to the gas company, we took their children to the clinic, we accompanied them and interpreted for them in courts—we did all those things that have recently been rediscovered under the names of "advocacy" and "active intervention."

The results? If the efforts "paid off," the client's emotional alliance with us was strengthened, their stress was lessened, their equilibrium at least temporarily restored. Sometimes, I suppose, dependency was deepened. Often, however, the client's energies were freed to reinvest in the tasks of his daily living. And there was often, too, the reality that he did not himself have the capacity or the nerve or the entree that we as agency representatives had, nor the language or coping skills to navigate such bureaucracies as existed even then—schools, hospitals, factories, and offices—that controlled so many aspects of his life.

Sometimes I think that we tend today to look down upon such vital services, relegating them to the side, or rationalizing our avoidance of them by pious formulations about client "self-determination" and his need to learn self-dependence. In doing so, we may overlook many of what are insuperable obstacles to a person's ability to connect with the available opportunities in his external reality. Such services lack glamor, but one cannot overestimate their powerful psychological impact on the person who needs them.

Such were the views and practices of most caseworkers in most "adequate" to "good" agencies around the country in the late twenties and early thirties. There was, however, a small, magic circle of psychiatrically oriented social workers in the fabled East—Boston, New York, Philadelphia. They presented and published occasional papers that reflected a growing awareness and understanding of the inner forces within all of us—including our clients—but their numbers were small and their actual incorporation into practice was delayed for many years. As recent dissemination theory reveals, there tends, in every profession, to be a considerable lag between what its theoreticians-researchers-advanced practitioners put forward and what is translated into practice. Social work is no exception to this. So, while there was a cadre of leader social workers who were oriented to the dynamics of human behavior, they constituted a small and encapsulated enclave.

Our views of man—of what people were "like," of what behaviors were "natural," "normal," "acceptable" were gradually penetrated by psychodynamic thought. But they were to be stirred up and radically changed by even more potent forces, by forces of social, economic, and political upheaval. The decade of the thirties was a revolutionary one for all of us. In it there was a shattering economic collapse. In it there grew the cancer of fascism. The floor boards of economic security were shaken for every one among us, and splintered for some. The optimistic taken-for-granted rights and freedoms of democracy seemed both more precious and more vulnerable as totalitarian tyrannies grew in power, and as the vast

Atlantic Ocean became very narrow indeed. It seemed not to separate us from the turmoils in Europe but rather to connect us with them.

Social work felt the impact of these changing conditions perhaps sooner than most other professions, surely harder than most. The clients of social work are often marginal people, and thus are often the first to be affected by social catastrophies. In the family agency in Chicago where I worked, we knew long before October 1929 that an economic landslide was occurring, simply by the steady increase of applications for relief by grey-faced men who had been laid off from long-held jobs. Later (1935), in a New York family agency, we knew long before the public gave it recognition what Hitler's ascendancy was to mean, simply by the swelling stream of stricken refugees who were presenting themselves for help. Both the Depression and the political-racist holocaust in Europe turned our long-held smug sentiments upside down and inside out.

At the doors of social agencies was a new kind of client: a middle-class unemployed man and a middle-class displaced person. He was often middle class not only in the economic level he had previously maintained but in his educational and cultural level as well. People were coming to ask for relief who had always before been self-reliant and self-sufficient; they were people like the caseworker's own parents, own friends, own self. "There but for the grace of God go I" lurked uneasily in every caseworker's mind every day.

Several radically new ideas began to permeate our thought. One was that the person who was a client was often not the cause of his problems, nor was he necessarily responsible for his need. Another, promoted and undergirded by public income maintenance and social security programs and fueled by some outstanding social workers, was that if society could not provide work, a man had a *right* to be helped. Subtly, but surely, caseworkers' attitudes and perceptions of their clients changed. Why, these were regular people, salt of the earth, but victims now of ruthless economic or political or racist deprivations. As manifest victims, they had the right to ask, to get, and still to be respected.

Now *empathy and compassion* began to take the place of pity. Pity moves from above, downward. It may be heartfelt, yet it is the feeling of the better for the lesser, of the winner for the loser. Compassion is, literally, "suffering *with*" the other; it is the feeling of at-one-ness. Empathy—what Freud called *ein-fuhling*, "feeling into" an other—is a subtle change but a powerful one. It makes a considerable difference in the relationship between a helper and the person who needs help.

It was in this period (articulated and eloquently defended by the social workers active in our national government's New Deal) that there came full-blown social work's affirmation of "the client's right to self-determination." It arose out of social caseworkers' fear that by accepting public monies, the relief client might be coerced to act in less than free ways, that he might be made to feel subject to political pressures, that the conduct of his life might be subject to the will of the purse string holders. So it was argued by social workers that by becoming a "beneficiary" a person did not lose his rights to self-governance. Perhaps the "right to self-determination" took on an especially sacred quality because it was also an assertion of the freedom of democratic man at a time when across the European continent individual rights were being obliterated. Thus, the right to self-determination, even for the least of men, became a battle cry among us, though we were not sure what responsibilities accompanied it.

It may fairly be said, I think, that the establishment of a public assistance system was one potent factor in the dissemination of psychodynamic knowledge in social work. For one thing, a number of psychiatrically oriented social workers moved into the public welfare agencies as supervisors and trainers of their heterogeneous and quickly assembled staffs. Some went out of high idealism, gratified that at long last the government was taking responsibility for meeting people's basic needs. Others were thrust into them because the Depression had cut down the operation of child guidance and adult outpatient clinics. But all went with the hope that mass services could be humanized.

There came a day in the private family agencies when all clients who needed chiefly money support or whose problems were held to be caused by economic insecurity, were transferred, wholesale, to the departments of public welfare. Remaining in our private agency caseloads now were people with problems relatively unrelated to economic need, people with problems of interpersonal malfunctioning or intrapersonal malaise—marital and parent-child conflicts, children's emotional or behavior difficulties, intergenerational stresses. In some combination of release and anxiousness, we swung, in what was almost a polar arc, from the too overwhelming problems of the outer society to what seemed to us to be the more manageable problems in that fascinating realm of man's inner world, from his socioeconomic to his inter- and intrapersonal problems.

This swing to psychodynamics was in part due to the caseworker's own need to find some escape, some surcease from a long involvement in battering socioeconomic conditions that keep us anxious, often despairing, continuously fatigued. To study one single person closely, to view him through the lenses of the now more readily available psychodynamic theory, to believe how inexorably his past determined his present, and to find, moreover, that *he* attested to feeling better for talking about himself and his feelings—all this was sweet and heady stuff. It was, moreover, relatively manageable. Beyond that, it carried prestige because psychodynamic theory was considered "high level," and growing in its popular appeal and interest.

But these personal gratifications were only part of what pushed us. The observant ones among us had long recognized, but had been unable to explain or deal with the gaps between a person's "wanting" and "willing," the swings of "yes-no" that kept some people in suspended inaction, the splits between feeling and thoughts, or thoughts and action, the impulsivities and conflicts and irrationalities that often overran the dictates of reason and conscious intent. And while we had known, we had not fully understood, the healing and motivational powers that caring relationships seemed to hold. So there had long stirred in many of us some eager hope that the keys by which to unlock the mysteries of human behavior were all but at hand.

It was (early) Freudian theory to which most of us were exposed, and which we viewed either with suspicion or with passionate espousal. It's an old story that disciples tend to be more doctrinaire than their teacher or guru; and as for disciples of disciples, in them it is not unusual to find rigid orthodoxy, extremism, and sometimes distortions of theory that would astonish its progenitor. So, it is no wonder that some follies and absurdities were advanced and perpetrated in Freud's name not only by social workers but by their psychiatric mentors too; and that sometimes, for want of a bit of common sense, the kingdom of Freud's imaginative and incisive thought was lost here and there. Beyond arguments about whether or not the oedipal conflict is inevitable and universal or whether there is or is not a "death instinct"—beyond these and other Freudian postulates that became dogma or anathema there are several contributions that Freud made to our view of man that I believe have been incontrovertibly generative. I can only touch on them here—and hope I will not do them too great injustice.

Freud did not invent the unconscious—it had been recognized by philosophers and thinkers for more than two thousand years. What Freud put forward were his explorations of and speculations on its contents and workings. There leaped from his illumination an understanding of many of the puzzling behaviors we saw in our everyday practice: the mother who indulged and then battered her baby, the chronically drunk and chronically remorseful father, the man and woman who seemed chained together by bonds of hate, not love, and that these and others were subject to drives of which their possessors had no conscious notion, and therefore over which they had no control. We saw, too, that these drives knew no class or cultural or educational or economic boundaries.

These understandings affected social work practitioners in many ways, some good, some specious. Among the "good" was our learning to shut off our own too-busy motors and to listen, attentively, sensitively, to the sounds below the surface of the client's motor. A whole new dimension of man opened to us, his layers of being and feeling under the skin.

Second, Freud illuminated childhood. In all the decades that social work had been involved in the protection of children, whether by parental guidance, by promotion of child welfare legislation, by provision of substitute parental care, the nature of the child's developmental needs, the kinds of psychological nurture he needed had been only minimally explored. Developmental stages, differentiated needs, tasks, opportunities—all these aspects of the child's being and becoming, with which today we are so engrossed, both in practice and in research, are outgrowths of Freud's explorations and propositions, seeded by his bold postulates about the inner life of the child.

Expectably, many of his postulates were limited by the time and place in which he lived; they were skewed, too, by his determination to find congruity between biological and psychological phenomena. The major point is, he pushed the Western world to look closely at childhood experience for its potency in the development of personhood.

Just this one more contribution of Freud upon our changing view of man will I touch on. It is not possible to study man's inner world without becoming acutely self-aware, without experiencing a humbling recognition of one's own vulnerabilities and irrationalities, without, in short, recognizing one's own kinship with every other human being. Caseworker or client, therapist or patient—we are all products of our yesterdays and today, all striving for the same nurture and gratifications, even though the forms in which we seek them will be different. Only from this deeply experienced self-understanding does an alliance between ourselves and others flow.

Yet this period of immersion in the inner man had its problems too. Many among us lost our perspective on man-in-society. The "social" drifted out of social work, not simply in our slackened concern about the reforms or reinforcements in the services and resources people needed but also in our view of the individual man. We lost sight of the powerful effects of his current everyday social transactions, which is to say, of the penetration into his psychic life of such social experiences as work and school and other relationships. We lost sight of the fact that any current social experience in some vital self-to-other or self-to-circumstance encounter will, if it is emotionally charged, become internalized, to color and shape his feelings *and* thought *and* behaviors. *Today's social wound becomes tomorrow's psychic scar.*

There was another serious pitfall in the narrowed, if deepened, pursuits of psychological understanding. It is expressed in the French saying that "to understand all is to forgive all." "To forgive all" is based upon an assumption that the person cannot help what he is or what he does because he is only the product of a fixed determinism. So, then, can he be held responsible for *being* and *doing* differently? Can he be expected, say, to manage his behavior if he is simply the creature or product of his past experience and his unconscious drives?

Some of us grew uncomfortably aware that a practice based predominantly upon a belief in psychic determinism and the iron hand of the past could only be a practice of despair. Bit by bit many caseworkers along with some psychologists and psychiatrists began to search for—and then to find—evidences of the will and push to health and survival and adaptation among human beings. Many of us reminded ourselves of the repeated clinical evidence we had seen of the remarkable thrust for health and survival in people. We had seen, for instance, thousands of refugees and displaced persons, who had been uprooted or dumped like carcasses out of concentration camps, rise up resolutely from the ashes of their former lives to try their wings again. We had seen thousands of "idlers" (a term common among "conservatives" at the time for the unemployed) flock back to work when the war boom made it available. We had seen, within our own communities, remarkable instances of cooperation and collaboration among diverse people, drawn together not only by their fear of a common enemy but also because of their gratification at being connected with other people in a common task or goal, of having found some recognized social place among their fellowmen.

So, a few among us began to wonder why it was that we knew more of man's sickness than of his health, whether we had been more understanding of his failures than of his persistent dogged coping, and what that coping consisted of; about whether his present-day experiences and the interchanges with potent and significant others might not hold potential influences as dynamic and certainly more subject to management than those of his past. Even when that past is active and alive in the present, there is evidence to suggest that a person's perception and "feel" of it may be strongly affected by his experiences of the present, and further by his anticipations of the nearby future. Thus among those of us who were searching to expand our understanding of the multidimensions of man, seeking to give new emphases and directions to our practice, a number of fresh perspectives emerged in the fifties.

Most vital, in my judgment, were these: The psychology of the "id" gave its central place to that of "ego." Our explorations began to include the study of man's consciousness, of his intentionality, of all those functions and strategies of his mental apparatus and his behaviors that he utilized in his daily efforts to cope, to adapt and to master. Spurred by creative and convincing psychological research and clinical observations, many of us sought to test out in practice the possibilities as well as the limitations inherent in people's conscious motivation, in their cognitive and interpersonal competencies, and in such external conditions and opportunities as offered means for the experience of the self as capable or improvable, and of the social environment as promising, not simply as punishing.

These perspectives and tryouts did not deny the existence of the unconscious nor of its powers to inhibit or distort conscious self-management. They suggested rather that there's more to man than we dreamed of when we dwelt chiefly upon his failures and sickness, or when our focus upon his incapacities and his victimization closed off our recognition of his potential coping powers.

Side by side with these developments there emerged perspectives usually credited to existential psychology. They were introduced into social casework by the Rankians, via the so-called functional school of casework. Some of you may have heard of the schism that split social casework apart in the forties and early fifties—the war between the so-called diagnostic and functional schools of thought. It took on an all-but-religious fervor, and as one of the heretics who barely escaped excommunication, I find it reassuring to look back at it today to remind myself, in the face of all our today's fragmentations and tangential activities, that many of those theses and antitheses of some years ago resolved themselves into some congruence, into some *synthesis* of ideas that hold central cores of agreement.

From the Rankian school several ideas were found to hold considerable consonance with neo-Freudian ego psychology. One was that of the conscious *will* and its bearing upon what the person will or will not mobilize himself to do. Another affirmed the power of the *present*, the *now*, as holding, in regard to many kinds of problems, more potency for change and for problem solving than the past. My problem-solving model of casework, published in 1957 but which had been developing in my practice for some years before that date, banked heavily upon this latter proposition. Indeed, all those partialized and time-limited forms of treatment today called "short-term" or "crisis" or "task-centered" rest upon belief in the dynamic potency of the white-hot present problem in its present-day manifestations, particularly when it is dealt with in a compassionate relationship by a caring and competent helper.

It was in the fifties, too, earlier than the War on Poverty, earlier than the Civil Rights Act, that social caseworkers began to turn their concerns once again to those people who needed but did not want to seek help, people variously called "hard to reach" or "multiproblem." It was a resurgence of our sense of social responsibility to those who, by their behaviors and needs, were hazards to their own, their children's, or often to their community's well-being. Our view of such persons was rather different from what it had been many years before when the bad and *un*beautiful people had been held to be needful, yes, but somehow deficient in character or capacity. Our position in the fifties was that such persons were victims of economic, racist, educational deprivations, and that their conditions were the fault of Society, spelled with a large, snakelike

S. Indeed they often were. Yet, such a stance can paralyze the social worker and his client both. It can lead to the same defeatism that occurred when the "fault" was held to be all but inexorably in the psychic determinism of the past. It said to the person in trouble, "You are only a victim, a helpless pawn of your Society." Helpless is hopeless; hopeless is apathetic.

The view of man that sustained those of us who immersed ourselves in trying to help those who needed but did not seek help was not a new one, but it was used in some new ways. It reaffirmed that all behavior has survival purposes. And that, thus, hostile, resistive, ungracious, suspicious behavior was both understandable and even acceptable when one took measure of chronic disadvantage and deprivation that had been experienced by the hard-to-reach or hard-to-hold client. There was no denying the need for many kinds of societal reforms and restructures. But there was no denying either that the more deprived and destructive the individual or family life the less able were they to "wait for the revolution," or even for the resolution of the "now problems" that beset them. Therefore they needed to be helped *now* to lessen their stress, to free their energies, to link them with the resources they needed. *The case could not wait till the cause was won.* Further we clearly saw that the "cause" needed more than case-by-case attention.

To deal with the non-voluntary client, the non-applicant (as with the abusive parent or spouse, the delinquent adolescent, etc.), often required of us some further changes in our own attitudes and practices. We recognized (swallowing hard) that it was only natural and expectable that such persons would be fearful and hostile to unasked-for interference. Thus we accepted the necessity to face out with such needful but "hard-to-reach" people our understanding of their feelings against us, and along with this to firmly but gently confront them with the actuality of their problems and of the potentially unhappy consequences for *them*. And that there must follow a search together for some common meeting ground, for what *they* wanted for themselves, their reasonable hopes, their idea of what would satisfy them, of what the caseworker could realistically do to help them and their problems change.

We began to see with renewed clarity the motivational powers in empathy, in short-term forms of help, in focussed, time-and-scope-limited forms of problem-solving, in providing material aids that not only relieved stress but aroused the belief that someone representing society was concerned to be helpful. It scarcely needs saying that these insights and accompanying skills added a long-needed dimension to our work with many people, not just the "hard-to-reach."

Stimulating to our thought, informative, supporting many of our half-formed theories came freshets of research findings and theoretical formulations from the (now interested) behavioral sciences. One was the tested and proven power of love and nurturant relationships. Another was the impelling proposition that the inborn "aggressive drive" was in essence a drive for mastery, for the pleasurable experiencing of the self as a cause, a "maker," a "doer." For some of us it underpinned the conviction on which some few of us had long operated: that insofar as feasible the client himself must be helped to be *active in coping*, active beyond "telling."

From psychoanalysis and dynamically oriented psychology came a reassessment of the powers of the conscious ego, of its conflict-free competences, of conscious motivation, of the effect of mental awareness and knowledge upon feelings, of the variety of coping mechanisms beyond defense; notions of the dynamics in social role demands and expectations; the implications inherent in the "psychology of the self"; a rediscovery of Dewey's action-oriented problem-solving—these and many other ideas, hypotheses, propositions began to rub shoulders, even to speak to one another. And we began to find that there were many compatibilities among them. In a tumbled, often circuitous way there began to be an expanded awareness of the connectedness between the heart and the mind, and between them and the psychodynamics of social life.

Of course, it is expectable that in a time of restiveness and change in the whole culture there will emerge a lot of tangential and even silly offshoots and specializations. Tinsel may glitter more enticingly than sterling, and there are those who will be lured by it. So I stop to remind us that however stylish or engaging a theory or belief, our rigorous criterion must be its usefulness in our work with *most* people *most* of the time.

All but overwhelmed, but at the same moment drawn forward by what there is yet to be grasped, explored, understood about the terrors and wonders of mankind, determined always to fling each newly minted coin upon the counter of experience and common sense to test its genuineness or counterfeit, I stop to take a deep breath and to ask, "Has there been progress?"

From the perspective of more than a half-century I believe that there has, in the main, been great forward movement in the quest to humanize our society and enrich its individual human lives, and that social work has taken its vital part in that quest.

When I entered social work there was *no* federal system of public assistance, *no* medicare or medicaid, *no* tax supported system of mental health services, *no* unemployment compensation, *no* social insurances, *no* social security, *no* public supports for special work-training or higher education. These and many other opportunities for raising the level of human life exist today. To be sure, they are full of faults; they need constant vigilance and even radical revisions. But no one has dared to say out loud that they should be abolished. Rather, the hue and cry for better social conditions, resources and opportunities have risen remarkably. What we tend to forget is that the rising level of expectations for what constitutes a "good life" also heightens the sense of need and sets higher standards of adequacy both in the individual's sense of well- or ill-being and in that of his society.

Once, not too long ago, the standard of a reasonably "good life" meant simply access to the basic means for economic and physical survival. Today, by widespread concensus, it seems to include the expectation that every person ought to strive for and to have within his reach such opportunities as will actualize his capacities to find reasonable harmony and even occasional joy in his daily person-to-person, person-to-tasks life, and thence to contribute to the common good. In brief, the quality of human life has become part of the widespread social concern, and from this a remarkable array of human welfare services have had public support.

Further, we are as a people concerned—perhaps because we are free enough and secure enough to be able to look out from ourselves—with many problems that seem to be "new." Most of them are as old as original sin. To touch on a few: Child neglect and child abuse—even infanticide—have been known all over the world, across the centuries, and now into this very day. It is only recently, and only in some parts of the world, that what a parent does to his/her child is considered to be a matter for public concern and intervention. Prior to this century a parent's treatment of his child might have been deplored and disapproved of, but it was done privately, eyes averted. Well into the eighteenth century, even in western countries illuminated by the Enlightenment, infanticide and child abandonment were high. (Rousseau himself—and I put this in parentheses because I say it in a whisper—he who in his *Emile* first explored the psychology of a child's learning, sired a number of unwanted babies, and took those little bundles to one of the first foundling hospices in France, pushing them through the revolving door, to become the wards of nuns, and went on his philosophic way.)

As for mental illness: any reading of the literature or history of the past reveals the age-long presence of mental-emotional disturbance in every time and place. The mentally sick person was hidden in the attic, barely fed or tended to, or thrown into filthy lunatic asylums, taunted in the streets as idiots, or flogged or burned as witches and devils. Few recognized the agonies and degradation of the patients' suffering.

It has long been held that in the past the aged were harbored and valued within their family circles. What we tend to forget is that until the marvelous medical advances of this twentieth century most of the so-called aged died before they were fifty years old. The truly old were a minuscule portion of the population. Moreover, if love and respect for the aged were more than half-true, why are there adjurations in the Old Testament about the necessity of the young to respect their elders? Or why does Plato deplore the instances of young Athenians insulting their old fathers? Or why does Shakespeare's King Lear clutch our hearts as the prototype of the aged parent who, having given away his property and thus his power, can no longer command his children's respect? The fact is that there has never before been a time when the body and soul needs of old people have been given such general and generous attention.

In short, few of our present-day problems are new. What *is* new is the heightened and community-wide awareness and concern about them. Our very recognition and distress about the existence of such problems, our cries of "havoc!" about these ancient forms of human evil and human hurt are themselves indicators, not necessarily of the greater incidence of their occurrence but of the heightened societal sense of caring and then of daring to try to cope with them.

There is yet another phenomenon we tend to overlook as we point the finger of alarm. We live in a time when oral and written reportage about people all over the world is immediate in its high-decibel impact on us. We live the best; but we are kept edgily aware of the worst. The push of a button on a box in our living room or the pickup of the newspaper at our door confronts us with immediate, sharp awareness of human conflict, evil, anguish. Our consciousness of the desperations and terrors of human life has been raised and intensified to what at times feels almost intolerable. If we are to keep our balance, we must remember always to distinguish between what *we are newly aware* of and what is truly a never-before-existent problem.

It is a heartening fact, I believe, that as our social *consciousness* of the problems in human living has risen, so has our social *conscience* expanded and public responsibility increased, in the effort to deal with them. What *is* new in this century is the astonishing development of the ways and means by which to heighten man's well-being. Full of faults and failures as they are, they bespeak our determination as a society to look out from our own little private lives in order to actualize the compassion and responsibility we have come to feel for the lives of others, strangers though they may be.

Allow me just one more look into the past. I came on a letter written over a hundred years ago from George Sand to her good friend, the novelist Gustav Flaubert. You remember George Sand— that flaunting French feminist, quasi-socialist, prolific novelist, challenger of social strictures. (I'd like to think she might have been a social worker had there been such creatures in France in her day—though I dare say she would have been a thorn in the flesh of her agency.) She was almost seventy years old when she wrote this letter, at a time when France was ravaged by political and social turbulence.

Flaubert had complained that he was feeling physically sick and spiritually despondent. Perhaps with some notion that his illness was psychosomatic (though that concept had not yet been formulated), George Sand wrote him sternly:

> This is no time to be sick . . . and certainly no time to grumble. What we must do is cough, wipe our noses, get well and declare aloud, very firmly, that [our country] is mad, humanity stupid, and we ourselves are no more than a breed of badly designed animals. . . . [But] there is more. We must go on being in love with ourselves [and] the species to which we belong. . . . I am prepared to submit to

conditions of absurdity reflecting . . . that I perhaps am no less absurd than anyone else. What matters is that I begin to think how to improve myself.[1]

The paraphrase for us today: This is no time to succumb to despair or "burnout." What we must do is wipe our noses, lift up our beds (and our heads) and walk, aware that as in all human life there will be new or recurrent problems-to-be worked, and that some of the solutions recently proposed are absurd or worse. But we must go on being in love with the imperfect species to which we belong, spurred by our humanist tradition. What matters is that we think on how to improve ourselves so that we can better carry out social work's particular mission in our society's goal: to improve the quality of the everyday life of the everyday man, woman, and child whose individual worth we all have consistently affirmed.

And so we dare to do what we must do—to turn our eyes to see ahead.

1. *George Sand: A Biography of the First Modern Woman,* by Samuel Edwards (New York: David McKay, 1972). Permission to quote granted by Random House, 1987.

BIBLIOGRAPHY OF PROFESSIONAL PUBLICATIONS BY HELEN HARRIS PERLMAN

Books

1. *Social Casework: A Problem-solving Process.* Chicago: University of Chicago Press, 1957. Translations in Dutch, Swedish, Spanish, Italian, Greek, German, Japanese, French, and, in part, in several Asian and African dialects.
2. *So You Want to Be a Social Worker.* New York: Harper & Row, 1962. Rev. ed., 1970. Translations in Spanish and Portuguese.
3. *Persona: Social Role and Personality.* Chicago: University of Chicago Press, 1968. Paper edition 1974. Translation in French.
4. *Helping: Charlotte Towle on Social Work and Social Casework.* Chicago: University of Chicago Press, 1969. Paper edition 1970.
5. *Perspectives in Social Casework.* Philadelphia: Temple University Press, 1971. Paper edition 1974.
6. *Relationship: The Heart of Helping People.* Chicago: University of Chicago Press, 1979. Translation in Dutch. Paper edition 1983.

Articles

7. "Casework and the Problem of Jewish Youth." *Jewish Social Service Quarterly,* September 1936.
8. "Professional Development on the Job." *The Family* 19 (April 1938): 42–45.
9. "Content in Basic Social Casework." *Social Service Review* 21 (March 1947): 76–84.
10. "Casework Services in Public Welfare." *Proceedings of the National Conference of Social Work.* New York: Columbia University Press, 1947. Pp. 261–69.
11. "Parable of the Workers of the Field." *Social Service Review* 23 (March 1949): 21–24. Reprinted in *Perspectives in Social Casework.* Philadelphia: Temple University Press, 1971. Paper edition 1974.
12. "Classroom Teaching of Psychiatric Social Work." *American Journal of Orthopsychiatry* 19 (April 1949): 306–16.

13. "Mental Health Planning for Children." *Child Welfare* 28 (June 1949): 8–9, 16–18.
14. "Generic Aspects of Specific Settings." *Social Service Review* 23 (September 1949): 293–301.
15. "Teaching Casework by the Discussion Method." *Social Service Review* 24 (September 1950): 334–46. Reprinted in *Education for Social Work,* edited by Eileen Younghusband. London: George Allen & Unwin, 1968.
16. "The Lecture as a Method in Teaching Casework." *Social Service Review* 25 (March 1951): 19–32. Reprinted in *Education for Social Work,* edited by Eileen Younghusband. London: George Allen & Unwin, 1968.
17. "Are We Creating Dependency?" *Minnesota Public Welfare* 6 (June 1951). Reprinted in more than fifteen state welfare journals and in *Social Service Review* 34 (September 1960): 323–33. Also in *Social Work and Social Values,* edited by Eileen Younghusband. London: George Allen & Unwin, 1967. Reprinted in *Perspectives in Social Casework.* Philadelphia: Temple University Press, 1971. Paper edition 1974.
18. "The Caseworker's Use of Collateral Information." *Social Casework* 32 (October 1951): 325–33; *Social Welfare Forum.* New York: Columbia University Press, 1951.
19. "Putting the 'Social' Back in Social Casework." *Child Welfare* 31 (July 1952):8–9, 14. Reprinted in *Perspectives in Social Casework.* Philadelphia: Temple University Press, 1971. Paper edition 1974.
20. "Social Components of Casework Practice." *Social Welfare Forum,* National Conference of Social Work, New York: Columbia University Press, 1953. Reprinted in *Perspectives in Social Casework.* Philadelphia: Temple University Press, 1971. Paper edition 1974.
21. "The Basic Structure of the Casework Process." *Social Service Review* 27 (September 1953): 308–15. Reprinted in *Perspectives in Social Casework.* Philadelphia: Temple University Press, 1971. Paper edition 1974.
22. Essay Review of *The Nature of Choice in the Casework Process,* by Anita Faatz. *Social Service Review* 27 (December 1953): 431–33.
23. "Of Records and Supervision." *Social Service Review* 28 (March 1954): 83–85.
24. "The Casework Seminar in the Advanced Curriculum." *Social Work Education in the Post-Master's Program,* No. 2. Council on Social Work Education, New York, 1954.
25. "Ballad for Old Age Assistance, 1954" (verse). *Social Service Review* 28 (March 1954):90.
26. "Brainwashing: A Social Phenomenon of Our Time." *Human Organization* 14 (Fall 1955): 2.
27. "Social Casework Counseling." *Psychotherapy and Counseling. Annals of the New York Academy of Sciences* 63 (1955): 386–93.

28. "The Client's Treatability." *Social Work* 1 (October 1956): 32–40.
29. "Freud's Contribution to Social Welfare." *Social Service Review* 31 (June 1957): 192–202. Reprinted in *Perspectives in Social Casework*. Philadelphia: Temple University Press, 1971. Paper edition 1974.
30. "Family Diagnosis: Some Problems." *Social Welfare Forum* and *Casework Papers*, 1958. Pp. 5–17. National Conference on Social Work, New York: Columbia University Press, 1958. Pp. 122–34.
31. "Where Can They Go for Guidance?" *Guiding Children as They Grow*, edited by Eva H. Grant. National Congress of Parents and Teachers, 1959.
32. "Social Casework Today." *Public Welfare* 17 (April 1959): 51–54, 88–89. Under new title, "Casework in Development." Reprinted in *Perspectives in Social Casework*. Philadelphia: Temple University Press, 1971. Paper edition 1974.
33. "Intake and Some Role Considerations." *Social Casework* 41 (April 1960): 171–77. Reprinted in *Social Casework in the Fifties*, edited by Cora Kasius. New York: Family Service Association of America, 1962. Also expanded and revised in *Persona: Social Role and Personality*. Chicago: University of Chicago Press, 1968.
34. "Family Diagnosis in Cases of Illness and Disability." *Family Centered Social Work in Illness and Disability*. Monograph VI. New York: National Association of Social Workers, 1961.
35. "The Role Concept and Social Casework: Some Explorations." *Social Service Review* 35 (December 1961): 370–81. Reprinted in *New Developments in Casework*, edited by Eileen Younghusband. London: George Allen & Unwin, 1965.
36. "The Role Concept and Social Casework: What Is Social Diagnosis?" *Social Service Review* 36 (March 1962): 17–31.
37. "Some Notes on the Waiting List." *Social Casework* 4 (April 1963): 200–205. Reprinted in *Crisis Intervention*, edited by Howard Parad. New York: Family Service Association of America, 1963.
38. "Unmarried Mothers, Immorality and the A.D.C." (mimeographed). Florence Crittenton Association of Chicago, Chicago, July 1963.
39. "Identity Problems, Role, and Casework Treatment." *Social Work Practice,* 1963. National Conference on Social Work, Columbia University Press. Also, *Social Service Review* 37 (September 1963): 307–18. Reprinted in *New Developments in Casework*, edited by Eileen Younghusband. London: George Allen & Unwin, 1965, and (revised) in *Persona: Social Role and Personality*. Chicago: University of Chicago Press, 1968.
40. "Unmarried Mothers in a Social and Social Work Problem." In *Social Work and Social Problems*, edited by Nathan E. Cohen. New York: National Association of Social Workers, 1964. Pp. 270–320.

41. "The Charge to the Casework Sequence." *Social Work* 9 (July 1964): 47–55.
42. "Help to Parents of Retarded Children." Canadian Association for Retarded Children, Toronto, Ontario, October 1964. Reprinted in *Social Work and Mental Retardation,* edited by Meyer Schreiber. New York: John Day & Co., 1970.
43. "Teaching Social Policy." *International Journal of Social Work* 8, no. 1 (January 1965): 22–25.
44. "An Approach to Social Work Problems: Perspectives on the Unmarried Mother on A.D.C." *Program Development for Social Services in Public Assistance.* Washington, D.C.: U.S. Department of Health, Education, and Welfare, Bureau of Family Services, 1965.
45. "Social Work Method: A Review of the Past Decade." *Social Work* 10 (October 1965): 166–79. Reprinted in *Social Work Practice and Knowledge.* New York: National Association of Social Workers, 1966. Reprinted in *Perspectives in Social Casework.* Philadelphia: Temple University Press, 1971. Paper edition, 1974.
46. "Self-Determination: Reality or Illusion?" *Social Service Review* 39 (December 1965): 410–21. Reprinted in *Values in Social Work.* Monograph IX. New York: National Association of Social Workers, 1967; in *Self Determination in Social Work,* edited by F. E. McDermott. London and Boston: Routedge & Kegan Paul, 1975; also in *Perspectives in Social Casework.* Philadelphia: Temple University Press, 1971. Paper edition, 1974.
47. "Social Diagnosis Leading to Social Treatment." *Social Work in Child Health Projects for Mentally Retarded Children.* Washington, D.C.: Department of Public Health, Government Printing Office, 1965.
48. Preface to *Common Human Needs,* by Charlotte Towle (revised edition). New York: National Association of Social Workers, 1965.
49. "Social Casework." *Encyclopedia of Social Work.* New York: National Association of Social Workers, 1965. Pp. 704–14.
50. "Casework Is Dead." *Social Casework* 48 (January 1967): 22–25. Reprinted in *Perspectives in Social Casework.* Philadelphia: Temple University Press, 1971. Paper edition, 1974.
51. "A Note on Sibling." *American Journal of Orthopsychiatry* 37 (January 1967): 148–49.
52. "—And Gladly Teach." *Journal of Education for Social Work* 3 (Spring 1967): 41–50. Reprinted in *The Social Work Educator,* edited by Joseph Soffen. Council on Social Work Education, 1969; and (abridged) as "Great Teachers." *University of Chicago Magazine,* November–December 1968.
53. "Observations on Services and Research." *Unmarried Parenthood.* New York: National Council on Illegitimacy, 1967.
54. "The Neighborhood Sub-professional Worker-Comments." *Children* 15 (January–February 1968): 12–13.

55. "Casework and the Case of Chemung County." In *The Multi-Problem Dilemma,* edited by Gordon E. Brown. Metuchen, N.J.: Scarecrow Press, 1968. Pp. 47–71.
56. "Can Casework Work?" *Social Service Review* 42 (December 1968): 435–37. Reprinted in *Perspectives in Social Casework.* Philadelphia: Temple University Press, 1971. Paper edition, 1974.
57. Preface to *Brief and Extended Casework,* by William Reid and Anne Shyne. New York: Columbia University Press, 1969.
58. "Crisis and the Unmarried Mother." *The New Face of Social Work.* Proceedings of Spence-Chapin Adoption Service, 25th Anniversary. New York, 1969.
59. "Diagnosis Anyone?" Essay review of *Differential Diagnosis and Treatment in Social Work,* by Francis Turner. *Psychiatry and Social Science Review* 3 (August 1969).
60. "Casework and 'The Diminished Man.' " *Social Casework* 51 (April 1970): 216–24. Reprinted in *Perspectives in Social Casework.* Philadelphia: Temple University Press, 1971. Paper edition 1974
61. "The Problem-Solving Model in Casework." In *Theories of Social Casework,* edited by Robert W. Roberts and Robert Nee. Chicago: University of Chicago Press, 1970. Pp. 129–79.
62. "The Problem-Solving Model in Casework." *Encyclopedia of Social Work.* New York: National Association of Social Workers, 1971. Pp. 1206–17.
63. "Women in a University." An Address to the Trustees and Faculty of the University of Chicago. Reprinted (condensed) in *School Review* 79 (November 1970):1; and in *Education Digest* (February 1971) as "The Case Against Unisex."
64. "Social Casework in Social Work: Its Place and Purpose." In *Casework within Social Work,* edited by Graham Parker. University of Newcastle Upon Tyne, England, 1972.
65. Essay Review on *Freud: Living and Dying,* by Max Schur, M.D. New York: International Universities Press, 1972. *Social Service Review* 47, no.1 (March 1973): 109–13.
66. "Confessions, Concerns, and Commitments of an Ex-Clinical Social Worker." *Clinical Social Work Journal* 2, no. 3 (Fall 1974). Also published as Occasional Paper no. 5. S.S.A., University of Chicago, March 1974, pp. 221–29.
67. "Once More with Feeling." In *Evaluation of Social Intervention,* edited by E. J. Mullen and J. Dumpson. San Francisco: Jossey-Bass, 1974. Pp. 191–209.
68. "Lines Written after Prolonged Immersion in Freud, Piaget, Hartman, et alii" (verse). *Social Work* 19, no. 6 (November 1974): 698.
69. "In Quest of Coping." *Social Casework* 56, no. 4 (April 1975): 213–25.
70. "Social Work in Psychiatric Settings." Chapter 35, in *American Handbook of Psychiatry,* 2d ed., edited by Daniel X. Freedman and Jarl E. Dyrud. New York: Basic Books, 1975. Pp. 669–82.

71. "Believing and Doing: Values in Social Work Education." *Social Casework* 57, no. 6 (June 1976): 381–92.
72. "Interview with Helen Harris Perlman." In *Profiles in Social Work,* edited by Mary Gottesfield and Mary Pharis. New York: Human Sciences Press, 1977. Pre-published in *Clinical Social Work Journal* 5, no. 3 (Fall 1977): 229–38.
73. "Children in Exile." *Social Work* 22, no. 2 (March 1977).
74. "Social Casework." In *Handbook of the Social Services,* edited by Neil Gilbert and Harry Specht. Englewood Cliffs, N.J.: Prentice-Hall, 1981. Pp. 434–51.
75. "Foreword." In *Passing through Transitions,* by Naomi Golan. New York: Free Press, 1981.
76. "The Client as Worker: A Look at an Overlooked Role." In *Work, Workers, and Work Organizations,* edited by Sheila Akabas and Paul Kurzman. Englewood Cliffs, N.J.: Prentice-Hall, 1982. Pp. 90–116.
77. "Mrs. Smith Goes to the Poorhouse." *Social Work* 28, no. 4 (July–August, 1983): 323–24.
78. "On the Art of Caring." *Child Welfare* 64, no. 1 (January–February, 1985): 3–11.
79. "The Problem-Solving Model." Chapter 10 in *Social Work Treatment,* edited by Francis Turner. New York: Free Press, 1986. Pp. 245–65.
80. "Making Ourselves Up," essay review of *Who Am I This Time: Uncovering the Fictive Personality,* by Jay Martin. *Readings: A Journal of Reviews and Commentary in Mental Health* 3, no. 4 (December 1988): 8–10.

Autobiographical Material and Miscellany

Under the auspices of the National Association of Social Workers the transcribed tapes of an extensive interview on personal and professional aspects of Helen Harris Perlman's life history are on file at the following places:

Social Welfare History Center
David Klaussen, Curator
University Libraries
University of Minnesota
Minneapolis, Minn. 55455

Special Collections Department
Regenstein Library
University of Chicago
Chicago, Ill. 60637-1496

Library of Congress
Exchange and Gift Division
Washington, D.C. 20540

University of Washington Libraries
Curator of Manuscripts
Seattle, Wash. 98195